Crisis and change in
European Union foreign policy

Manchester University Press

European Politics

Series Editors: Professor Dimitris Papadimitriou (University of Manchester), Dr Kathryn Simpson (Manchester Metropolitan University) and Dr Paul Tobin (University of Manchester).

The *European Politics* series seeks to tackle the biggest issues facing Europe in the twenty-first century.

Previously published under the *European Policy Research Unit (EPRU)* name, this long-established and highly respected series combines an important scholarly legacy with an ambitious outlook on European Studies at a time of rapid change for the discipline. Its geographical coverage encompasses the European Union, its existing and aspiring members, and 'wider Europe', including Russia and Turkey, and the series actively promotes disciplinary, theoretical and methodological diversity.

The editors particularly welcome critical scholarship on the politics and policy making of the European Union, on comparative European politics, and on contemporary issues and debates affecting the future of Europe's socio-political and security outlook. Key areas of interest include Brexit, the environment, migration, identity politics and the ever-changing face of European integration.

Previously published:

Regulating lobbying: A global comparison, 2nd edition
Raj Chari, John Hogan, Gary Murphy and Michele Crepaz

Towards a just Europe: A theory of distributive justice for the European Union
João Labareda

Made in France: Societal structures and political work
Andy Smith

Crisis and change in European Union foreign policy

A framework of EU foreign policy change

Nikki Ikani

MANCHESTER UNIVERSITY PRESS

Published by Manchester University Press
Oxford Road, Manchester M13 9PL

www.manchesteruniversitypress.co.uk

British Library Cataloguing-in-Publication Data
A catalogue record for this book is available from the British Library

ISBN   978 1 5261 5564 1   hardback
ISBN   978 1 5261 8258 6   paperback

First published 2021
Paperback published 2025

Typeset
by New Best-set Typesetters Ltd

To my father, my inspiration

Men do change, and change comes like a little wind that ruffles the curtains at dawn, and it comes like the stealthy perfume of wildflowers hidden in the grass.

John Steinbeck, *Sweet Thursday*

Contents

List of tables

List of figures

Acknowledgements

Many people have supported me during the years it took to write this book. In particular I would like to thank professor Christoph Meyer for his invaluable insights during the various stages of the writing process. I would also like to thank professor Anand Menon for his assistance with the research. I am equally indebted to King's College London, the department of European and International Studies in particular, for providing an excellent research environment for me during these past seven years.

I am grateful to the UK Economic and Social Research Council, which has funded the research project on Learning and Intelligence Use in European Foreign Policy (INTEL), supporting the case study work and empirical research for this book. I would also like to express my gratitude to the many interviewees at the various institutions of the European Union who were willing to give up their time to share their insights with me. I would like to express special gratitude to Manchester University Press and the series editors for *European Politics* for their enthusiasm for this project and for their helpful support throughout. I am also indebted to the reviewers who have made many helpful suggestions for revisions and improvements to the book.

I extend special thanks to my friends for their patience, friendship and support throughout these years. These include Saad S. Cheema, Gabriel Orazi, Igor Reyner, Thomas Gould, Benjamin Dalton, Katherine Brook, Virginia Lanas Rodriguez, Trineke Palm and Eva Michaels. I would not have been able to write this book without the continuous support and confidence from my loving parents, Cyrus and Sholeh, and my sister Nessa. I am also grateful to and thankful for Eloise for being the light in my eyes. Finally, I am forever grateful to Ivan, for his support, advice and encouragement throughout.

List of abbreviations

AA	Association Agreement
ACF	advocacy coalition framework
CEAS	Common European Asylum System
CEPS	Centre for European Policy Studies
CFSP	Common Foreign and Security Policy
CJEU	Court of Justice of the European Union
CSDP	Common Security and Defence Policy
DCFTA	Deep and Comprehensive Free Trade Agreement
DG DEVCO	Directorate-General for International Cooperation and Development
DG HOME	DG for Migration and Home Affairs
DG NEAR	Directorate-General for Neighbourhood and Enlargement Negotiations
DG RELEX	Directorate-General for External Relations
DG ECHO	DG for European Civil Protection and Humanitarian Aid Operations
EaP	Eastern Partnership
EASO	European Asylum Support Office
EBRD	European Bank for Reconstruction and Development
ECEAP	Estonian Center of Eastern Partnership
ECFR	European Council on Foreign Relations
EDF	European Defence Fund
EEAS	European External Action Service
EIB	European Investment Bank
EMP	Euro-Mediterranean Partnership
ENI	European Neighbourhood Instrument
ENP	European Neighbourhood Policy
EP	European Parliament
EPC	European Political Co-operation
ESDP	European Security and Defence Policy
EU	European Union

EUGS	European Union Global Strategy
EUISS	European Union Institute for Security Studies
EUSR	EU Special Representative
FPA	foreign policy analysis
GDP	gross domestic product
HI	historical institutionalism
HR/VP	High Representative of the Union for Foreign Affairs and Security Policy/ Vice-president of the European Commission
IOM	International Organization for Migration
IR	international relations
IS	Islamic State
JHA	Justice and Home Affairs
MENA	Middle East and North Africa
MEP	Member of the European Parliament
MPCC	Military Planning and Conduct Capability
MSF	multiple streams framework
NATO	North Atlantic Treaty Organization
NGO	non-governmental organisation
PBK	Pervõi Baltiiski Kanal (tv channel)
PCA	Partnership and Cooperation Agreement
PESCO	Permanent European Structured Cooperation
QMV	qualified majority voting
SCAF	Supreme Council of the Armed Forces of Egypt
SPRING	Support to Partnership, Reforms and Inclusive Growth
SWP	Stiftung Wissenschaft und Politik
TEU	Treaty on European Union
UfM	Union for the Mediterranean
UN	United Nations
UNHCR	United Nations High Commissioner for Refugees

Introduction

Imagine it is the spring of 2010. You are sipping a tea in a Tunis café. Looking out over the Medina, you hear cars whistling below on the cobblestoned streets, carrying their owners back home after a day of work. You are pondering the year ahead. Could you imagine that within a year, on the Avenue Bourguiba, just a short walk from where you are sitting now, thousands of protestors would march against Ben Ali, the authoritarian ruler of Tunisia, and would succeed in toppling his regime after twenty-five years? And if so, could you imagine this uprising would trigger protests in neighbouring Egypt, the most populous country of the Arab world, where protestors would overthrow Hosni Mubarak after a thirty-year rule, within a fortnight? Sitting here, watching the sun set over the city, could you imagine how tidal waves of revolution would sweep the region? That out of these protests would emerge a conflict which would escalate into a decade-long civil war in Syria?

Fast-forward three years. Your travels have brought you to the pebbly beaches of Yalta, on the south coast of the Crimea. You watch the Black Sea, along which mountains rise, covered in vineyards and orchards. You think of how surprised the world was by the Arab uprisings and set out to imagine another year ahead. Would you guess that, within a year, President Putin of Russia would sign a treaty to annex the very peninsula on which you are sitting right now, breaking several international treaties and flouting international law to do so? Could you imagine the next President of the United States would be Donald Trump, who would praise Putin – and along with him many dictatorial leaders worldwide – for his leadership skills, and who would say of this annexation of territory that 'the people of Crimea, from what I've heard, would rather be with Russia' and, more confusingly, that the Crimea was 'taken away from President Obama'?

The world is in flux and change appears to be everywhere. It is this ubiquity of change that is a key theme in this book. Over the past decade news headlines, think tank reports and scholarly works and students have come to investigate the changing international system, the way it developed into a multi-polar or multi-order world, and how these transformations are impacting how we conduct and study international relations. New powers are said to be on the rise and the arrival of new, transboundary actors is upending post-war international affairs.

If we zoom in on the European Union, we find that the plethora of crises has spawned a rich literature keen to investigate how these affect the European project. Research programmes have emerged which look at the impact of the multitude of crises, and of the transformations that have taken place in global affairs in recent years, on the EU's position and stability, but equally at their potential to affect European integration (Börzel and Risse 2018; Jones, Kelemen and Meunier 2015; De Wilde and Zürn 2012; Rhinard 2019). Other analyses focus on the challenges the many crises pose to the European Union, its identity or its strategic calculations, which necessitate change (e.g. King and Le Galès 2017; Youngs 2018; Dinan, Nugent and Paterson 2017; Degner 2019).

This book takes a decidedly different approach. Instead of probing how global change is spurring a qualitative transformation of the European Union, it provides a pragmatic and specific framework to unpack the process by which the decision to change foreign policy is made during specific crisis episodes. How do crises in EU foreign policy produce policy changes, and why?

The key goal of this book is to improve our understanding of EU foreign policy change, how it happens and what it looks like. To achieve this, this book will develop an analytical framework and a typology of change suitable for this task. First it takes an inductive approach, assessing two recent episodes in which EU foreign policy changed. What can an in-depth investigation of these episodes tell us about EU foreign policy change? Subsequently, I set out a typology of EU foreign policy change most appropriate for categorising and studying foreign policy change at the EU level.

The analytical framework and the typology I develop for understanding EU foreign policy change is subsequently 'test-driven' in three recent cases of EU foreign policy change after crisis. In doing this, this book adapts published theorising on foreign policy change (which has mainly centred on the USA) in a way that is applicable to the EU context.

This book thus serves a dual purpose. Empirically, it offers a comprehensive account of how the EU has changed its foreign policy in response to five foreign policy crises over the past ten years: the Arab uprisings, the Ukraine conflict, the subsequent crisis of Russian disinformation, the migration crisis and a wider crisis of European security and defence that followed the Crimea annexation. The empirical chapters thus offer those wishing to investigate and understand the policy changes which followed these crises a rich reconstruction of the reform episodes, drawing on a variety of primary and secondary sources as well as sixty-four in-depth interviews with policy officials.

Theoretically, this book contributes to the existing literature by improving both our understanding of the process of EU foreign policy change and our conceptualisation of the different forms of policy change that may follow this process. It provides for students wishing to study the way the EU responds to foreign policy crises a single analytical framework with which to do so, as well as a series of case studies which demonstrate the workings of the analytical framework.

Studying the processes and outputs of EU foreign policy change is more than a theoretical endeavour. The way the EU responds to foreign policy crises has direct implications for the lives of people within and outside the Union. When a crisis hits, we expect decision-makers to respond. The EU's response to the challenges in its European neighbourhood arising from a more assertive Russia, as well as its engagements with the autocratic regimes surrounding the Union, have for example had major ramifications for both the stability of these countries and for the security of the EU. The EU's response to unrest in its neighbourhood may affect the EU's energy supplies, whilst its inability to pursue Union-wide policy changes in for example Libya or in the Syrian conflict continues to put the lives of the citizens of those countries in danger. It may equally result in a further rise in refugee flows, which is in turn fuelling the rise of populism and increasing Europe's internal political volatility.

Crises thus reinforce the need for change. Developing a more precise way of assessing attempts at foreign policy change intended to respond to these challenges therefore allows us to assess these responses critically. Equally, paying special attention to the process of policy change may improve our understanding of the greatest obstacles to change, which may serve to avoid unrealistic expectations of how quickly and how profoundly EU policy can change.

In this book I thus develop an analytical framework which explains the process by which EU foreign policy changes and the results of that change. To do this, I use the theoretical lenses of historical institutionalism (HI).

Historical institutionalism is an approach to studying politics that suggests that in order to understand politics, we should see it as a continuous process that is embedded in institutions. Institutions are the organisations, rules, routines, policy structures or social norms which guide our societies. They may be tangible organisations such as a parliament, or intangible institutions such as the institution of marriage. They may be formal and codified, or informal.

Generally, historical institutionalists study formal institutional arrangements, written rules, policies and frameworks. Likewise, they share the assumption that historical context impacts on political life, and that institutions are a legacy of this context. Using a historical institutionalist lens thus stipulates that to understand European politics today, both the EU's internal and foreign policies, one must look at how institutions and historical context affect the political decisions made and those not made. I use a historical institutionalist lens for several reasons. Most importantly, the historical institutionalist literature, particularly its 'second wave' which emerged in the last five years, offers a developed conceptual toolbox for studying change, as will be detailed in chapter one, 'Historical institutionalism and change'.

Next to its theoretical usefulness in explaining the process of policy change, historical institutionalism is very well suited for studying the particularities of European Union decision-making. As explained in 'Puzzle and aims' below, existing accounts and typologies of foreign policy change tend to fall short in important respects when we want to study foreign policy change at the EU level. They tend to study states and governments as the primary actor. Often, their focus predominantly is on US foreign policy.

The EU context is distinctly different. European institutions bring together and constrain the multiple state and non-state actors in the process of EU foreign policymaking. The behaviour and strategic choices of these actors are embedded in a particular social, political, economic and cultural context (Steinmo 2008). European foreign policymaking is thus a multi-layered process, with a wide range of actors deciding on and operating policies at varying levels. The policy areas studied in this book form no exception. Historical institutionalism offers a conceptual toolbox suited for the analysis of policy change in such a fragmented and multi-faceted polity.

Theories of foreign policy change

Those wanting to investigate why and how policy change can be witnessed in particular areas of EU foreign policy as a result of crisis have hitherto been forced to confront the issue by combining a variety of theoretical lenses. The question of when and how policy changes has indeed been discussed in the fields of international relations, foreign policy analysis (FPA), European studies and public policy studies.

In the next section of this introduction I discuss the most important theorising within these fields. I will show the different angles from which the issue of foreign policy change has been studied. Then, based on a gap

I identify in this literature, I shall sketch out why a dedicated analytical framework for studying EU foreign policy change is useful, and what it should look like. The framework builds upon this existing theorising, but aims to consider the specificities of the process between a critical juncture and foreign policy in the European context.

International relations

Global transformations are for obvious reasons of great importance in the field of international relations (IR). A problem that arises for students of EU foreign policy change is, first, that many of the seminal IR studies on foreign policy change originate in the United States and thus focus on the USA as a primary actor, or on other nation states. Their units of analysis are national governments and the foreign policy apparatus surrounding these. More problematically, in IR policy change is generally evaluated at the riskiest level, pertaining to issues of war or peace. Scholars have focused on sudden dramatic events or turning points, such as war, which are directly related to major changes in the political system (Gilpin 1981; Ikenberry 2001; Krasner 1984). Ikenberry (2001: 3) for example studied historical junctures as 'dramatic moments of upheaval and change within the international system, when the old order has been destroyed by war and newly powerful states try to re-establish basic organising rules and arrangements'.

A problem with this approach, as has been established in the literature, is that such dramatic foreign policy changes are rare. Much more frequent are instances when policy is changed as a result of critical junctures that are less major or pervasive in scope than war, that may still propagate transformative changes in certain policy areas (Hall 2016: 41). These are left ill-explained in the field of IR.

Moreover these approaches pay scant attention how and why we can expect change to follow. As Goldmann (1988: 4) argued, 'it is uncommon among foreign policy theorists even to make a strict distinction between pressures for, or motivators of, change and pressures for, or motivators of, lack of change'. What is more, the emphasis on bureaucratic inertia and path dependency which can only be broken by major upheaval, common in many of these accounts of foreign policy change (Krasner 1984; Pierson 2004) has underplayed the role of agency in the processes of change. In the case of changes to the foreign policy of the EU – a composite, multi-actor and multi-level policy – the impact of agency is not easily ignored.

More useful to the present endeavour are explanations in the field of IR which centralise narratives and 'analogical reasoning'. This refers to instances when decision-makers try to make sense of new situations by drawing upon historical analogies. Narratives are social constructs, frames which actors activate and deactivate strategically and purposefully (Saunders 2011; Krebs 2015). Memories and narratives created during past events that decision-makers think were similar affect evaluations of current issues. Prior to the US-led NATO intervention in Kosovo in 1999, for example, US President Clinton drew heavily on the lessons from Bosnia a few years previously stating '[w]e learned that in the Balkans, inaction in the face of brutality simply invites more brutality. But firmness can stop armies and save lives. We must apply that lesson in Kosovo before what happened in Bosnia happens there, too' (The White House – Office of the Press Secretary 1999). The analytical framework presented in chapter one, 'Analytical framework: the building blocks', shares some of its assumptions with this strand in the literature as it considers how actors justify policy shifts, or policy continuity, by using such narratives. Actors interpret crises. This interpretation often include allusions to what kind of policy change is necessary.

Foreign policy analysis

Whilst both deal with the most pressing questions emerging from the realm of international affairs, the main difference between FPA and other IR approaches are FPA's focus on the actor and on the decision-making process, involving problem recognition, framing, perception, goal prioritisation, option assessment and final decision-making (Hudson 2005: 2).

FPA scholars have argued since the 1980s that students of international relations need to engage better with how and why foreign policy may change. Buzan and Jones (1981) argued 'that established theoretical approaches to the field had over-emphasised continuity at the expense of change'. As a response, there have been important works examining foreign policy change within FPA literature which focus on providing a conceptualisation of various levels of change. An important strand are the 'input-output models' of foreign policy change, such as those by Hermann (1990) and Holsti (2016). These typically follow three steps: in the first step they identify important background factors and sources as the input for change. These inputs then move on to the decision-making process, which is influenced by cognitive and bureaucratic factors, and finally they may result in an output of foreign policy change.

In order for the sources of foreign policy change to actually result in a redirection of foreign policy, they thus need to overcome an intervening process of transition towards potential policy change. Researchers studying policy change using such a model thus aim to determine how information about potential failures or problems enters the system, and under what conditions those potential failures or problems trigger major change (Hermann 1990: 13).

An important notion in this strand of the FPA literature is that the foreign policy change following this process is categorised by Hermann and others in an incremental and cumulative way, along what is called the 'Guttman scale'. This scale implies that each level of change is progressively significant. The most limited form of change is an adjustment, an adaptation to the level of effort required to implement, or the range of actors or institutions affected by, a policy. One step further are programme changes that involve a different method or means to address the goal or problems; followed by problem or goal changes that replace or drop the goals originally identified and, finally, changes of international orientation, which are the most major foreign policy changes that concern a strategic shift (Hermann 1990: 5).

Gustavsson (1999) developed a similar, three-step model of policy change in which domestic and international sources of policy change are mediated by individual decision-makers who act to bring about change, bounded by the decision-making process. He pays attention to cognitive factors related to the decision maker, but equally examines the procedures and processes of making decisions, both formal and informal, that affect how individuals behave. His subsequent typology of foreign policy change is similar to that of Hermann.

Other FPA models of foreign policy change share the three steps (input, processing, output) but focus on 'stabilisers' in the policy process, such as bureaucratic inertia (*cf*. Goldmann 1988; Skidmore 1994). Yet other FPA scholars, such as Carlsnaes (1993: 8–9) and Rosati (1994), prefer a cyclical model of change, approaching it over longer time frames in order to detect recurrent patterns in the processes of foreign policy change.

Both the topic under study and the methods adopted in this book share features with FPA, most notably the notion that the process of decision-making, and the considerations of actors in this process, are the main source and determinants of behaviour and change in international politics. This approach opens up the study of European foreign policy towards studying not just policy outcomes, but the decision-making process and context preceding it, as argued by Brian White (1999, 2001).

The FPA approaches to foreign policy change have prompted criticism since they provide solid explanations of stability. Indeed, there generally exist strong biases towards studying policy continuity (G. T. Allison and Zelikow 1999; Goldmann 1988; Welch 2005). The dependent variable, change, has received much less attention (Kleistra and Mayer 2001: 387; Ashbee and Hurst 2020).

As it developed, FPA came to encompass a wide range of methodologies and approaches. The psychological and government-oriented perspectives that dominated FPA during the 1970s and 1980s were complemented by second and third waves of institutionalist and constructivist adaptations (for an overview, see Hudson and Vore 1995; Kaarbo 2003). Equally, FPA has been applied to EU foreign policy over recent decades (Carlsnaes 2004; K. E. Smith 2014; White 2001; M. E. Smith 2004).

Although the FPA analyses above yield very valuable insights for students of foreign policy change, especially on the sources of change, a complementary theoretical perspective is helpful to consider the variable impact of institutions and EU member states in this process of change, and how we might explain and categorise the various forms of policy change that may follow.

European studies

The crisis-ridden 2010s generated a vast realm of scholarship on 'crises and the European Union' (e.g. King and Le Galès 2017; K. E. Smith 2014; Youngs 2018; Dinan, Nugent and Paterson 2017; Degner 2019). Richard Youngs recently focused on how the many crises with which the EU is faced may constitute a single 'poly-crisis' which necessitates a different form of EU integration, which he argues should be citizen-led. He makes the case that qualitatively different forms of European cooperation are both possible and necessary (Youngs 2018: 6).

Like many of the other analyses, Youngs takes a macro-level vantage point that looks at the European Union in crisis writ large, and at reform. The analytical framework proposed in this book, as I shall outline below, is different. I do not probe a qualitative transformation of European cooperation or integration, nor do I aim to explain why this is or is not attainable. I do not advocate a new model or approach to European integration to better deal with crisis. This book rather provides an analytical framework to unpack the process of making decisions to change foreign policy during specific crisis episodes. It focuses on the decision-making process and how this produces particular policy outputs.

There have been many focused and specific accounts of the EU foreign policy response to the many exogenous crises it has been faced with over the past decade, among them studies on how the EU responded to the refugee crisis, the Arab uprisings, the Syrian civil war and the Ukraine crisis. Several strands are identifiable across this literature. Some studies tend to focus on policy evaluation. They asses the actions taken or not taken by the European Union in response to crises, provide a normative appreciation of their effectiveness and tend to be characterised by 'strong sense of policy orientation and prescription' (Schumacher 2015a: 381). On the EU's response to the refugee crisis but equally in the literature on EU crisis management, such studies are dominant (Trauner 2016; Barbulescu 2016).

After the Arab uprisings, authors described the EU's immediate responses as well as its hesitation (Schumacher 2011; Teti 2012), suggested ways in which the European Neighbourhood Policy (ENP) should change (Tocci and Cassarino 2011) and assessed the extent to which the policy changes were appropriate and sufficient to meet the challenges in the region (Behr 2012a; Börzel, Risse and Dandashly 2015; Börzel and Lebanidze 2015; Dennison 2013).

In contrast to this book, this literature mainly focuses on evaluating the EU's performance in these foreign policy crises. The studies of EU foreign policy responses after the various crises encountered in the 'neighbourhood', for example, tend to underline the continuity in the EU's approach to this region and its inability to adequately adapt its tools and instruments to changing circumstances. After the various recent reforms, the main European policy to deal with the countries neighbouring the Union to the east and south, the ENP, has been accused of being 'old wine in new wineskins' (Tömmel 2013: 19) and marked by 'conceptual continuity' (Korosteleva 2011: 249), whereas the EU's policy response to the various crises has been called 'much ado about (almost) nothing' (Börzel, Risse and Dandashly 2015), the EU being a 'leopard' that cannot 'change its spots' (Behr 2012b).

Admittedly, an early lesson for every student of change is that, while everything changes constantly, it can appear as if everything always stays the same. The EU, more even than individual nation states, is a slow-moving supertanker, which complicates swift and major policy changes. Inertia, not change, abounds. Yet the old and often quoted truism – *plus ça change, plus c'est la même chose* – obscures the point that both change and continuity can be extremely varied. The prevalent focus on the obstacles or impediments to policy change does not accurately capture the fact that both policy change and policy continuity can take many forms. Moreover, one of the limitations of these analyses, according to Noutcheva (2015: 21) was that they tend to assume there is a cohesive unity of action to the EU, thereby disregarding the institutional pluralism that marks EU foreign policymaking.

The Ukraine crisis generated a variety of assessments of the EU's behaviour. There was a strand of neo-realist writing in which authors expounded the crisis in Ukraine as part of an 'inevitable' clash between Russia and the West (Mearsheimer 2014; Haukkala 2015). Others focused on how the Ukraine crisis was rooted in structural flaws in the EU's approach to its shared neighbourhood with Russia (Cadier 2014; MacFarlane and Menon 2014; Sakwa 2017). Conversely, other scholars explained how decision-making processes in the European Union during the Ukraine crisis led to its particular policy response (Natorski and Pomorska 2017; Noutcheva 2015).

Thus, the literature on EU foreign policy responses can be roughly divided between approaches which centralise policy evaluation and approaches that focus on policy explanation. In the latter group, explanations of the response to crisis are either sought in structural aspects – the EU's relationship with Russia for example – or in institutional features – the particularities of EU decision-making. It is this last strand that this book adheres to, although I do so with the explicit aim of subsequently conceptualising the various policy changes made by the EU. I argue that appraisals of the responsiveness, appropriateness, adaptability and especially the lack of change in the EU foreign policy will benefit from a better theoretical and analytical understanding of policy change, which across these studies is often not conceptualised or even defined.

Public policy studies

Outside the realm of IR and foreign policy, theoretical approaches in the field of public policy studies have scrutinised the problem of policy change, policy learning and policy diffusion at length, in institutional, rational choice, network, socio-economic and ideational approaches.

There is a relevant body of research which explains how policy change happens at the national level when the appearance of compelling problems or political events opens a 'policy window' for change (Kingdon 1995; Zahariadis 2017; Herweg, Zahariadis and Zohlnhöfer 2017). This window can be exploited by policy entrepreneurs or opponents of current policies, who attach solutions to problems (or the other way around) while trying to build political support for these solutions. Policy agenda attainment thus produces change. This approach is called the multiple streams framework, where the streams are flows of problems, policies and politics which act as constraints on policymakers. When these streams align, a window of opportunity may open to pursue policy change. Kingdon (1984: 174) drew on the analogy of 'space windows', which represent that moment in time when the stars align in the optimal position for a rocket launch to occur.

The approach I take in this book shares features of the multiple streams framework, particularly the explanatory influence of context. Yet where the multiple streams framework centralises individuals as policy entrepreneurs, my analytical framework assesses the influence of institutional arrangements, which as explained above I consider more appropriate when studying the European foreign policy context. This assertion that institutions exert strong pulls on the process of change is a key part of the historical institutionalist approach taken in this book.

The advocacy coalition framework, abbreviated to ACF (Sabatier 1988; Jenkins-Smith et al. 2014; Sabatier and Jenkins-Smith 1993) focuses on how coalitions around core policy beliefs emerge and create stability. Policy change occurs when these ideas adapt and new coalitions form in response to social economic changes or to political events. It sees policy learning as a source of mainly minor policy change. Major change, ACF scholars argue, is instigated by external system events which may shift or upset coalitions.

Punctuated equilibrium approaches, finally, focus on explaining long periods of policy continuity. Powerful 'policy images', which tend to be connected to core political values and which have well-defined public articulations, offer robust resistance to change. According to these approaches policy change may happen when crises or political events create shifts in the public agenda which give rise to new policy images and which thus 'puncture' the policy equilibrium (Pralle 2003; Baumgartner, Jones and Mortensen 2017).

Neither the multiple streams framework, nor ACF, nor the punctuated equilibrium approach, are able to predict whether or not issues which have emerged on the policy agenda will lead to policy change, as the same dynamics that may cause an issue to emerge on the policy agenda determine whether change will occur (Boin, McConnell and t'Hart 2008: 195). Moreover, the logic, especially in the multiple streams framework literature, is that what characterises windows of opportunity is the occurrence of policy change.

As I argue in this book, windows of opportunity may also lead to *no change*, or change that is not substantive but symbolic and ambiguous in nature. There is theoretical and empirical value in analysing reform windows which did not lead to traditional, substantive policy reforms. Moreover, the focus is often on what conditions open a policy window for change, whether material or ideational changes in the environment. Yet the change process does not operate in a vacuum but in a European institutional context, which impacts on it dramatically.

The multiple streams framework has been tweaked and applied to EU decision-making processes (Zahariadis 2017), although a key challenge in applying the framework remains understanding how the individual preferences and behaviour of the policy entrepreneur relate to their broader institutional context.

The seminal work of Peter Hall (1993), 'Paradigms, social learning, and the state', was a major contribution to the literature on policy change, not just in public policy studies but well beyond. Hall identified three forms of policy change which are each associated with a higher level of change. First-order changes are incremental adjustments made to the settings of existing policy instruments, such as adjusting the budget to a novel development. Second-order changes involve a first step in the direction of strategic action, as they involve changes to the policy method, or procedural changes in response to past experiences. Third-order change, according to Hall, entails a change to 'instrument settings, the instruments themselves and the hierarchy of goals behind policy', which he calls paradigm change. Such paradigm change is expected to be extremely rare, as it requires both that new ideas to guide policy revisions are available and adopted, and that first- and second-order change are completed (Hall 1993: 293). Hall's typology is thus cumulative and incremental along the Guttman scale, and in that respect is similar to the FPA typologies suggested by Hermann (1990), Holsti (2016) or Gustavsson (1999) that I discussed in 'Foreign policy analysis' above. In it each order of policy change he describes is progressively significant.

The addition of paradigm change by Hall changed the scholarly discussion of policy change, hitherto dominated by a focus on incrementalism and the way in which governments 'muddle through', making marginal adjustments to the status quo (Lindblom 1959: 79). In the period that followed, which Howlett and Cashore (2009: 34) call the 'post-incremental' orthodoxy, scholars took to juxtaposing incremental and paradigmatic change, linking them as periods of continuity and marginal adaptation that were 'punctuated' by periods of paradigmatic changes (Baumgartner and Jones 2002; Baumgartner et al. 2009). Others focused on how institutions structure these policy dynamics (Thelen and Steinmo 1992) or how the path-dependent effects of institutions mean that moments of policy stability are likely only to be altered through 'shocks' (Mahoney 2000; Pierson 2000b).

Hall's three-level typology and its cumulative logic came to be widely used in analyses of policy change and policy learning across disciplines, as discussed in chapter one, by scholars assessing foreign policy change among others. Although the drivers of policy change differ across accounts, the argument that one can expect the policy instruments or method to change and to be calibrated as the context changes, while the general abstract policy aims and macro-level ambitions in a specific policy area are overwhelmingly stable, is widely adopted.

Puzzle and aims

A review of the literature exposes that there currently exists no dedicated framework designed for studying foreign policy change at the EU level. This is an issue because the predominant cumulative typology of policy change commonly used in FPA and public policy studies has some limitations for students of EU foreign policy change. Most importantly, the clear-cut division between first-, second- and third-order change is not always obvious in actual policy, particularly not in the case of European foreign policy. Policy dynamics that fall outside this categorisation, or which in some way cut across categories, are not well described.

From the financial crash to the Eurozone crisis, from the spiralling EU–Russia relations to the rise of disinformation or the Syrian war, the EU's policy responses in recent years have shown that the various external pressures impinging on the Union have had a variable impact on its foreign policy. Sometimes, swift policy responses are announced in the wake of crisis. In 2011, the EU launched a naval border patrol to deal with rising refugee flows in the Mediterranean within mere days. At other times, the response is sluggish or seemingly inadequate, as in the early days of the European response to the spread of the coronavirus. Then there are policy changes that seem much ado about nothing. They often start with grand rhetorical gestures, such as when EU foreign policy chief Catherine Ashton promised to 'revamp and renew' the EU's policy towards the countries bordering the EU to the east and south, 'in light of the new challenges' after the Arab uprisings in 2011 (Ashton 2011d). Such promises, as will be demonstrated later in this book, are frequently followed up with vague or limited actual changes in policy.

This study proposes, based upon an in-depth investigation of recent foreign policy change episodes, changes to EU foreign policy may cut across the categories proposed by Hall, containing elements of more than one order, as well as elements that fit none. The problem is not just that policy changes might be mislabelled in this three-order typology, but that the conceptualisation of three-level policy change following a cumulative Guttman scale – which implies that each level of change is progressively significant – offers an inaccurate description of the policy process leading towards the particular policy outputs we observed. It insufficiently accounts for the process and the outcomes of policy change in the European 'neighbourhood'. In so failing, it risks feeding unrealistic expectations regarding how rapidly and how profoundly EU foreign policy may change. I argue that not all policy continuity is an exact repetition of past policy and practices, just as not all policy change can be categorised as ranging between minor and major change. This leaves us with the question how to conceptualise foreign policy changes that differ so widely in scope and ambition?

Schumacher and Bouris (2017) very recently aimed to tackle the question of EU foreign policy change by transposing the typology of Holsti (2016) to previous years' reforms of the European Neighbourhood Policy. Criticising the lack of IR studies into what has changed in the international system, or into how minor change might be distinguished from fundamental change,

Holsti had presented four 'markers' that usher in change: trends, 'great events', 'great achievements' and significant innovations. These markers, in his view, define when change occurs. The outcome of change can be divided into

1) *change as replacement*, when patterns and structures are replaced;
2) *change as addition*, when new forms of change are layered on old ones, leading to increasing complexity;
3) *dialectic change*, when new forms are built upon the old, and both co-exist; and finally
4) *change as transformation*, when cumulative changes over time 'bring new forms to life' (Holsti 2016: 40–45).

Schumacher and Bouris (2017: 14) transposed Holsti's typology to cover various changes made to the European Neighbourhood Policy. 'The key rationale of the volume', Schumacher and Bouris state at the beginning of their book, 'is that the revised ENP is confronted with multi-faceted and highly volatile dynamics of internal and external change, and that these changes need to be understood holistically and *contrasted with* elements representing continuity' (Schumacher and Bouris 2017: 5, emphasis mine). Studies of EU foreign policy change are rare and it is thus welcome that the authors pay attention to the various policy changes made to the ENP over the years surveyed. Yet by contrasting 'policy continuity' with 'policy change' it remains unclear how the policy in question has changed (through what processes, facing which impediments), or why it has changed this way.

The transposition of Holsti's approach – which was never intended to focus on the particularities of policy change or institutional change but on change in the international system more broadly – does not specify how the four markers actually lead to policy change, nor does it offer an explanation regarding the mechanisms and decision-making process through which policy change may occur. Put simply, by categorising causes or 'markers of change', and policy outputs, we may know *that* change occurred, but we do not know why *these particular* policy changes followed.

Here thus emerges one of the most important challenges this book contends with. Whereas a range of studies dedicated uniquely to foreign policy stability and foreign policy change exist for the US context such a clearly delineated field of study is absent for the analysis of EU foreign policy change. This book provides a single, dedicated, analytical framework that serves to investigate the way the EU adapts its foreign policy in the wake of crisis.

My key argument is that in order to understand EU foreign policy change in the wake of critical junctures, one needs to understand the decision-making process following those critical junctures in order to shed light on what kinds of policy change – however minor or unsubstantiated – we *did* see, at what level they took place, what their actual substance was and why this particular output came out of the decision-making process. To understand the outcome, I argue, we should consider how institutions and temporal context affected this process. Such a holistic, decision-making-focused account of EU foreign policy change is, I argue, currently under-represented in the literature on EU foreign policy.

A historical institutionalist approach to EU foreign policy change

The analytical framework for studying EU foreign policy change developed here draws on historical institutionalism. Two key hypothesised explanations of EU foreign policy change derived from historical institutionalism are put forward in chapter one.

First, in short, it is assumed that institutions allocate power and political authority in the change process, and determine how this power can be exercised. For example, the French constitution determines that only the parliament can declare war. At the same time, powerful actors can attempt to sway institutions to their preferences continuously, making use of the features of the institution in question to do so. An example is the Supreme Court of the United States, where the incumbent president has the power to nominate justices, which can greatly impact on the institution's course.

Institutions thus are 'plastic': they give form and they take form. Although they have an important impact on politics, they remain malleable and can be changed. The concept of plasticity, I argue, is an interesting one when studying European politics and policy, especially in EU external policies. In many of these policy areas, there exist a multiplicity of institutions, often layered on top of one another. These conditions, as I shall explain, are conducive to the existence of plastic institutions.

The second hypothesised explanation for foreign policy change concerns the impact of time and context. Decisions are not made in a vacuum but in a temporal context during which many developments, not all of them foreseen, may affect decision-making or policy preferences. This holds particularly true when studying policy change after a time of crisis. Both historical context and sudden events can generate and reinforce actor preferences, power relations and patterns of resource allocation (Fioretos, Falleti and Sheingate 2016: 6). Events such as accidents or disasters quickly find their way to the policy agenda. Decision-makers may perceive these events as 'decision points', amplifying the salience of an issue or policy area, making them more eager and willing to propose policy changes. Context can thus influence the emergence and transformation of institutions.

Accordingly, we need to embed our analysis of the process by which EU foreign policy changes into its particular time, both assessing the historical development of the policy area, which greatly impacts the process of change, and looking at events or occurrences that may have suddenly created an additional urgency for rapid change.

After sketching out the key tenets of historical institutionalism and the analytical framework for change used in this book in chapter one, chapters two and three provide two in-depth case studies of EU foreign policy change, namely the reforms made to the ENP in 2011 after the Arab uprisings, and those to the same policy after the Ukraine crisis in 2015.

The EU set up the ENP in 2004 to govern its relations with sixteen states neighbouring the union to the east and the south. These were states that in all likelihood would not accede the EU as member states, and the EU wanted to build a policy framework for such countries. It also wished to create a 'buffer zone' of prosperity and security around the Union. From the outset, the ENP was a technical and bureaucratic policy instrument, rather than a political project. It consisted of various specific policy dialogues and 'road-maps', financial envelopes and packages on issues like market access, green growth and political and economic reforms.

The ENP almost immediately became the subject of debate. First, because the EU's approach – making its benefits conditional upon the country complying with EU rules and standards – did not work as well as it had in the 'enlargement' process, where the 'carrot' of membership had a great impact on the willingness of countries to pursue real reform. Later, as crisis upon crisis hit the European 'ring of friends', the ENP was considered an inadequate tool in a multi-polar world in which the eastern and southern 'neighbourhood' had become *loci* of geopolitical competition. The ENP has been declared dead so often, by scholars and the media, that it has become a true Lazarus of European policies.

Despite the criticism of the policy itself, the ENP is an excellent place to start theorising the issue of EU foreign policy change; firstly, because it provides us with a clearly delineated area of EU foreign policy in action. For nearly a quarter of a century the ENP, unlike for example the Common Foreign and Security Policy where member states retain a crucial role in both the policy's conception and operation, has been a policy framework executed on a daily basis by the European Commission and the European External Action Service (EEAS). Studying change in the ENP implies investigating EU foreign policy in action.

There are likewise methodological advantages to developing a framework for EU foreign policy change by studying two similar change episodes in the ENP. Although sparked by very different crises, the 2011 and 2015 ENP reforms share features that are crucial in the analytical framework used here: the occurrence of a critical juncture, a subsequent reform window during which the EU formally revised the policy as a direct response to the events that had occurred and finally the presentation of a revised European Neighbourhood Policy. This allows for a systematic exploration of the process of EU foreign policy change.

In order to improve our conceptualisation of foreign policy change at the European level, I adopt a measurement of change from the realm of public policy studies. Howlett and Cashore (2009; also Cashore and Howlett 2007) proposed to measure change by disaggregating the *level* at which the change is directed; the *substance* of the policy change; and, following from this, the *directionality* of policy change. By directionality is meant the extent to which policy reflects a shift towards a new paradigm. Change that pursues the same sets of objectives as the status quo follows the same 'direction'. At the other end of the spectrum there is change that is nonlinear, representing a break with the past.

Such a disaggregation of policy change is useful, as the case studies show, because it allows me to add nuance to the conclusion that there has either been 'a little' or 'a lot' of change, or that major changes are necessarily preceded by a wholesale revision of policy. It renders the assessment of policy change more precise in indicating what type of change we observed.

After the empirical chapters in chapter four I assess how these findings concerning the ENP contribute to a conceptualisation of foreign policy change at the EU level. Here I draw on the theorising on policy change from the field of public policy studies, particularly on the typology of change provided by Peter Hall (1993) mentioned in 'Puzzle and aims' above, as well as on HI studies of policy change. I suggest two complementary analytical categories which elucidate under-studied ways in which the EU evolves its policy in the wake of challenges: symbolic change and constructive ambiguity.

Symbolic changes, as I shall explain, are rhetorical allusions to change, or 'accommodating gestures' which indicate a willingness by decision-makers to take action, to demonstrate they are willing and able to take immediate steps to deal with the crisis at hand and to avoid future, similar occurrences. Their primary audience is usually the greater public, although symbolic steps may likewise be taken to accommodate political opposition. Yet despite the grandiloquence of symbolic changes, upon scrutiny we find that the policy itself remains unchanged. Symbolic policy change is an important product of the temporal context, as the public pressure which decision-makers face in the wake of these crises motivates them to meet the moment by taking steps which are visible. Yet symbolic changes are generally entirely rhetorical in nature. Symbolic change is not a wholly new concept. Some authors have called this type of change '*faux*-paradigmatic', policy changes which appear to be significant yet which end up being reversed soon after (Cashore and Howlett 2007).

This book, however, adds two important findings regarding symbolic change. First, it finds that symbolic changes are a frequent and important outcome in EU foreign policy change. Second and more importantly, I found that they are more than '*faux*-paradigmatic'. Rather, symbolic changes have the potential to foster long-term, incremental change because they often promote knowledge and capacity building at the European level. Because the first steps are primarily rhetorical and made in response to intense public pressure, the key actors are more likely to agree on symbolic changes. But, as the case studies show, they may promote and foster further integration in that particular policy area, especially in EU foreign policy, which is frequently built on fragile and tentative compromise between different member states.

Constructive ambiguity describes policy changes which are viable because, being formulated in vague terms, they mean different things to different key actors, leaving significant room for interpretation, and thus garner support from diverging interests. They may be a strategy which political entrepreneurs use to push for a policy initiative, while at the same time not offending those with the power to support or block those initiatives. Like symbolic change, constructive ambiguity is not a new concept and has been used in the field of public policy studies, but often to describe vaguely worded international agreements (Palier 2005; Jegen and Mérand 2014; Dingley 2005).

However, constructive ambiguity has generally been conceptualised as a strategy of 'incomplete contracting', where the shortcomings of these agreements or the political conflicts are obscured and concealed by using vague terminology (Farrell and Héritier 2005; Edelman 2001). Moreover, scholars have argued that political entrepreneurs rarely employ constructive ambiguity because of the risk that the coalitions around vagueness and ambiguity are hard to sustain (Jegen and Mérand 2014; Hoffmann 1995).

Instead, this study finds that constructive ambiguity, like symbolic change, may be a frequent outcome of the policy change process at the European level, especially in the wake of critical junctures. The following chapters show that this is not always the postponement of decisions, nor an intentional concealment of conflict. Rather, they are politically functional outcomes of policy change: the way in which EU foreign policy is governed exacerbates the consequences of diverging member state preferences, because policy change hinges on actor agreement. Radical and substantive policy adjustments would have to be approved by all member states. Ambiguous policy changes allow decision-makers to move forward despite disagreement.

Institutions: historical development, plasticity

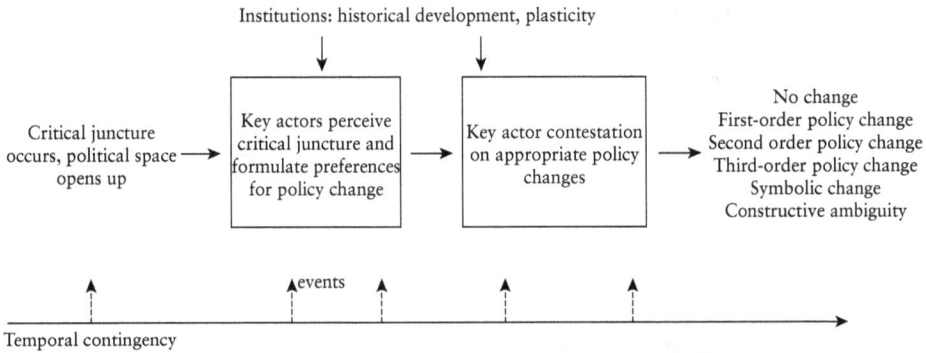

Figure 0.1 Analytical framework EU foreign policy change

Figure 0.1 displays the analytical framework for EU foreign policy change proposed in this book. Symbolic change and constructive ambiguity do not merely measure or categorise the degree or kind of policy change that follows from the decision-making process. Their purpose instead is to underline that not all policy change is substantive in nature the way first-, second- and third-order policy change are. But the lack of immediate and substantive policy change does not mean the process of policy change has failed or that symbolic or ambiguous policy changes are 'defaults' in the process of policy change, or represent postponed decisions. Rather, I argue, they represent distinct options or strategies in the policy change process, a different way of responding to crises, especially under certain conditions, and so deserve further attention. They thus offer an additional analytical layer for understanding how EU foreign policy change may occur and what specific forms it may take, complementing the traditional three orders, since this book establishes the three orders do not capture the full story when we think about EU foreign policy change.

Chapter five takes this framework on three 'test-drives' by looking at three recent critical junctures for EU foreign policy which triggered policy change episodes: the EU policy changes developed in response to rising disinformation coming from Russia in 2014–15, the policy changes resulting from the migration and asylum crisis of 2015 and, finally, the EU's policy response to the greater critical juncture in European security which came to the fore in 2014. Test-driving my theory in these cases of policy change allows me to put to the test the assumptions and analytical steps developed in the earlier chapters, about how the process of EU policy change works, assessing the design and handling of the analytical framework. Taking the analytical framework on a series of test-drives also allows me to demonstrate how it can be applied to varying practical instances of EU foreign policy change.

These five empirical studies, as will be detailed in chapter six, draw on a wide range of policy documents, non-papers,[1] white papers and speeches, complemented with a review of the secondary literature and sixty-four semi-structured interviews.

Strengths, limitations, scope conditions

A particular strength of the analytical framework proposed in this book is its applicability to the case studies examined here. Moreover, the combination of two in-depth case studies and three shorter test-drives of the theory in this book is helpful in fleshing out the class of situations which form appropriate testing grounds for my analytical framework.

The first of such scope conditions concerns time frame. Chapters two and three discuss two cases of ENP reform, whilst chapter five test-drives the theoretical findings that follow from these case studies on three recent and relevant policy responses to crisis. Whereas ENP reform in 2011 and 2015, as well as the first two test-drives, involved critical junctures lasting no more than two years, the final test-drive – on EU security and defence – concerns a crisis of a slower-burning nature, and a much longer critical juncture. What emerges is that, although the analytical framework proposed here is best suited to analyse critical junctures lasting up to two years, a longer critical juncture does not pose a methodological problem to the application of my framework, although in-depth process tracing becomes much more resource-intensive in longer cases.

A second scope condition which emerges is that the analytical framework is most useful for assessing change to a delimited policy. Although the test-drives show that the framework can be applied to wide policy areas, such as migration, which encompass a variety of policies, what emerges is that the more delimited the policy framework – for example the ENP or strategic communication – the easier it is to assess changes to the policy in the wake of a crisis.

The analytical framework proposed in this book contributes to the existing literature on foreign policy change by focusing on these processes at the European level in particular, in an arena which is inherently multi-actor and multi-layered. Given its toolbox for understanding the way complex and multi-layered institutions may be disrupted by dramatic moments of change, historical institutionalism provides a valuable lens through which to view the EU policymaking process when it comes to change.

Moreover, the analytical framework proposed here considers not just the structural or institutional factors which influenced the process of policy change, but also the impact of temporal contingencies: short-term and medium-term events or trends that affected the decision-making process. Theory development benefits from such a simultaneous attention to structural factors and the decision-making process (Mckeown 1986). It allows the researcher to search for consistencies in policy processes and preferences across time, whilst at the same time allowing for the explanatory influence of temporal contingencies on the policy change process. By explicitly taking into account the 'timescape' of a reform process, historical institutionalism has much to offer the analysis of EU policymaking, especially against a backdrop of increasing 'strategic surprises' stemming from the European vicinity.

By looking at specific, brief, reform episodes, I studied shorter time frames than most HI analyses, which usually look at institutional change taking place over periods of years or decades. My analysis, however, did not discount the broader structural-historical trends that may have affected the reform process. Rather, I prioritised the reform episode itself, preceded by an analysis of the structural and conjunctural features of the temporal context that may have impacted the reform episode. I thus divide the temporal context into three registers: 1) the structural impact of time; 2) the conjunctural impact of time and 3) the liminal impact of time, as I shall explain further in chapter one, 'Temporal contingency'. This approach is less deterministic than path dependency approaches that focus on how earlier choices and trajectories are difficult to reverse owing to strong mechanisms of positive feedback and increasing returns. By allowing both structural explanations and temporal contingencies as important explanatory factors, this analytical framework aims to produce more accurate explanations of why change did or did not occur, and why these particular changes emerged from the policymaking process.

There are limitations and drawbacks inherent to any research design and theoretical approach. A first limitation is practical in nature. At the core of this HI explanation is the question of how specific sources of change are mediated by the institutional context, preferences and contestation among actors in the EU decision-making process following a critical juncture, as well as by temporal contingencies. The 'input' of EU foreign policy change in the case studies are critical junctures which emerged from outside the Union. A limitation of this study is that the EU's overall foreign policy portfolio and its strategic direction are affected by a great many factors, which are not neatly distinguishable into exogenous and endogenous, or categorisable as specific crises. They may emerge from a complex interplay of global developments and domestic perceptions. They may also be transboundary crises or political events that tie into a variety of issues. The Libyan conflict illustrates this complex multi-causality. The Arab uprisings brought the fall of dictator Muammar Ghadafi, spurred by a bombing campaign led by NATO. But the violence and conflict that followed goes way beyond the Arab uprisings, and ties into the rise of ISIS/Da'esh, internal fractions and militia warring over control of Libya, and outside powers pursuing variable interests.

Breaking down the European response to this multi-faceted crisis using the analytical framework proposed here would require detailed process tracing covering how various actors in the EU perceived these various interrelated causes. Although the outcome of such a close reading of the case would allow the researcher to deal with the complexities and the variabilities of the case, it makes this approach very time-consuming and thus less apt for larger comparative studies.

A second limitation concerns levels of analysis, a drawback that applies to most scholarly work in foreign policy analysis or other areas where the decision-making is the object of study. Continuous choices need to be made with regard to what are considered the most important facilitators of and constraints on policy change. What, for example, is the impact of individual decision-makers, their personality and their personal agenda, on the process of policy change? And to what extent do domestic politics within EU member states, and their electoral cycles, need to be taken into account in analysing the process of change? The response to this problem in this book has been to investigate the policy preferences of the key institutional and member state actors as they were put forward in the decision-making process following the critical juncture, such as through non-papers and speeches. The ideas reflected in these types of evidence are themselves a product of decision-makers 'evaluating their environment' (Welch 2005: 23), yet such evaluations and processes by which preferences are formed are not the object of study here. In other words, exactly how key actors arrived at their preferences is not my focus.

Note

1 Non-papers are documents written by ministers/governments of usually a few countries before negotiations in which they align positions, which are made public before those negotiations.

1

An analytical framework for studying EU foreign policy change

This chapter proposes an analytical framework for studying changes to EU foreign policy. The Introduction explained how the ambition to draw up such a framework for the EU level is founded on a theoretical dialogue between historical institutionalism (HI), foreign policy analysis (FPA) and public policy studies.

The key argument of this study is that to understand changes of EU foreign policy in the wake of critical junctures we need to understand the *decision-making process* following those critical junctures, in order to shed light on what kinds of policy change it produced, at what level they took place, what their actual substance was and why this particular output came out of the decision-making process. To understand the outcome, I argue, we should consider how institutions and temporal context affected this process. Figure 1.1 summarises the analytical framework for EU policy change in this book, focusing on this decision-making process.

After first discussing how HI contributes to its foundations, this chapter sets out each of the building blocks of the framework. It explains what is meant by 'critical junctures' and how they may open up the political space for foreign policy to change. It explains how institutions shape the process of such change in the EU, not just because the institutional landscape is the setting in which the decision-making process takes place, but also because institutions determine who the key actors are and what their power is to pursue policy change. Actors with the opportunity and power to influence institutions may act as powerful agents of policy change. This chapter will explain how such key actors may reframe the debate, generate new ideas and shed new perspectives on policy issues, and can attempt to rally support for their perception of the critical juncture at hand, as well as of the best course of action to pursue (Bicchi, 2002; Kingdon, 1995). The first guiding question for students of EU foreign policy change is thus: how did institutions impact on the decision-making process that led to policy change following the critical juncture?

This process of contestation over the course of EU foreign policy, this chapter subsequently argues, is shaped (secondly) by the temporal contingency. This implies that the world as we know it did not have to be the way it is – it was not logically necessary – but has come to be this way owing to various events, not all of them foreseen or expected. Following this logic, outcomes in politics could have been different if the temporal context had been different. They are a product of the interaction of institutions, actors *and* events, and historical processes. In order to explain the process of foreign policy change, we thus need to know what was the historical context of the policy change process in which the critical juncture took place, and whether there have been events or occurrences which changed the perceptions of the key actors during the process of policy change, increased the urgency of change or otherwise shaped the decision-making process. The second guiding question in the framework, thus, is how did this temporal context impact on the decision-making process?

After these parts of the framework have been addressed, this chapter explains how to measure the output – the policy change which follows from this process. Building forward on insights from public policy studies, it proposes to assess EU foreign policy change through mapping three constitutive elements:

1) the level of change;
2) the substance of change and
3) the direction of change.

The chapter ends with a section on research design, which will expound the method of historical process tracing and the forms of evidence used. I end the chapter with a summary of the framework, which could serve as a guide for students applying the framework to their own case studies.

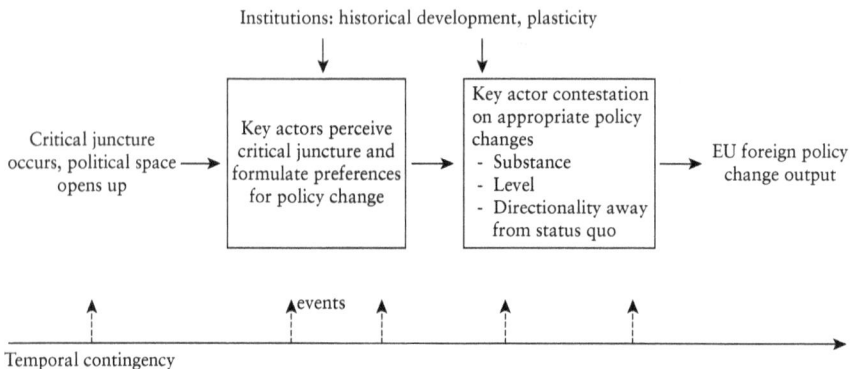

Figure 1.1 The decision-making process of EU foreign policy change

Historical institutionalism and change

The institutionalist school of political science emerged in the 1960s and 1970s as a criticism of dominant models of politics which assumed that political institutions are efficient reflections of underlying societal forces. At the time, the difficulty experienced by new social movements fighting for social justice in getting their grievances on the political agenda undermined such claims of institutional efficiency (Immergut 2006). Authors such as Skocpol (1979) centralised the political role of institutions and their effect on the state. They underlined that institutions are not efficient reflections of societal demands, but rather political arenas fraught with conflict. Institutionalism got its name from the 1984 article 'The new institutionalism: organizational factors in political life' by March and Olsen. Although they still spoke of 'one' institutionalism, the field quickly branched out and has become divided into various groupings, of which rational choice institutionalism, sociological institutionalism and historical institutionalism are the most common (for assessments of each, see Hall and Taylor 1996; Schmidt 2014; March and Olsen 1984; Katznelson and Weingast 2005).

Historical institutionalism is a research tradition with a rich internal debate that will not be redrawn here. Generally, historical institutionalists tend to share two essential assumptions. The first is that institutional configurations are 'humanly devised constraints that shape human interaction' (North 1990: 3). Institutions are not neutral or static, but rather dynamic arenas of conflict and contestation in which political power balances may be reproduced and magnified (Thelen and Steinmo 1992; Fioretos, Falleti and Sheingate 2016; Thelen 1999). The second assumption is that historical context impacts on political life, and that institutions are a legacy of this context. HI therefore posits that social and political dynamics should be understood by situating them in a temporal sequence of events and historical processes (Pierson 2000c). HI scholars thus study political life diachronically, 'as life is lived' (Sanders 2009: 39). This stands in contrast with the 'synchronic causality' common in the natural sciences, which spilled over to the social sciences and stipulates that patterns and developments are similar across systems and across time. These studies take 'snapshot' views of political life in one institutional setting at a time, in order to find systematic patterns. To explain the outcome of the US presidential election of 2016, for example, historical institutionalists would urge us to look beyond the individual voter preferences of that day in November, assessing how a variety of mechanisms may have converged to lead to the election of Donald Trump, such as the political development of the electoral system, the hyperpolarisation of the country, its cultural cleavages, its historical inequalities (racial and economic), the election campaigns of both Hillary Clinton and Donald

Trump and unforeseen occurrences during the election race (see Lieberman et al. 2019). Likewise, the rapid advances of the German army in the early months of the Second World War cannot be explained without acknowledging the interwar advances in technology which made these *Blitzkrieg* tactics possible.

Historical institutionalists have studied change in many ways. Two important concepts in their explanations are the notions of path dependency and 'punctuated equilibria'. Path dependency refers to the difficulty of changing earlier choices and trajectories owing to strong mechanisms of positive feedback and increasing returns. Institutional arrangements get locked in and become difficult to change (Pierson, 1996, 2000a; Sorensen, 2015; Mahoney, 2000). A classic example is the QWERTY-keyboard. Designed in the mid-nineteenth century to minimise susceptibility to typewriter jams, it remains the norm for most computer keyboards worldwide.

Path dependency has been the subject of debate within the HI tradition, however, for several reasons (for a discussion, see Immergut 2006). In the explanation of policy change put forward here, the concept is a useful way to explain why, generally, institutions remain stable. But too close focus on such institutional inertia ignores the potential impact of both agency and events. The analytical framework used here therefore takes a less deterministic approach to history, as I centralise the notion of temporal contingency: that context, including unexpected events, may alter previously stable sequences and thus impact on political outcomes.

The concept of punctuated equilibria is related to path dependence. It stipulates that institutions remain stable until they are confronted with an external or exogenous shock (Steinmo 2008: 129). Scholars have conceptualised such equilibria as periods of continuity and incremental adaptation, 'punctuated' by periods of paradigmatic change (Baumgartner et al. 2009; Baumgartner and Jones 2002, 1993; Gourevitch 1996; Krasner 1984). Some scholars have focused on how the path-dependent effects of institutions meant that moments of policy stability were likely only to be altered through 'shocks' (Mahoney 2000; Pierson 2000a).

A more recent 'second wave' in HI scholarship complemented the initial conceptions of institutional inertia and 'stickiness' by focusing not just on how institutions constrain agents, but also on how institutions can be transformed by agency, in a more 'plastic' conception of institutions, emphasising the role of agency and power in institutions (Capoccia 2016b; Hall 2016; Thelen and Conran 2016). Similarly, the impact of time and contextual causality has gained more importance. This contextual causality implies that it is the interaction of institutions, actors and historical processes that defines the outcome. In order to understand policy change, the researcher therefore has to engage in historical research, including a focus on the micro-political events that occur in the time frame under scrutiny (Immergut 2006).

Historical institutionalism has also made it to the field of European studies. Bulmer (2009: 307, 311) argued a decade ago that HI has 'untapped potential' to shed new light on EU integration. While HI has been used for the study of European integration processes (Pierson 1996; Aspinwall and Schneider 2000; Schneider and Aspinwall 2001) and, more recently, to study the EU's response to the financial crisis (Verdun 2015; Mourlon-Druol 2020), it is virtually absent from studies of the EU's foreign policy. Explaining EU foreign policy has been left to the other new institutionalist approaches (Peterson and Sjursen 1998; Regelsberger, de Schoutheete and Wessels 1997; M. E. Smith 2004), which have a limited focus on policymaking within the institutional scope of the Common Foreign and Security Policy or the Common Defence and Security Policy. Although insightful in understanding how institutions might develop a power and legitimacy of their own, the focus on European foreign policy cooperation in these intergovernmental arenas which characterises these approaches can lead to a limited account of EU foreign policy (Carlsnaes 2004: 502). Moreover, it reduces the assessment of changes in the EU's foreign policy to the causes and consequences of changes within the Union's institutional set-up (Koenig-Archibugi 2004). It is rather the interplay of 'plastic' institutions and temporal developments, which second-wave historical institutionalism put forward, that this book considers crucial in understanding EU foreign policy change, as will be explained below.

Analytical framework: the building blocks

Three HI concepts stand at the core of my analytical framework for studying EU foreign policy change after crisis:

1) critical junctures;
2) the effects of the institutions governing European foreign policy and their plasticity; and
3) the impact of the temporal context on the decision-making process.

Critical junctures

Critical junctures form a central concept in the analytical framework proposed in this book. Critical junctures, based on the literature, are characterised by three parts: a temporary loosening of the constraints of structure; a moment of heightened contingency; and a temporarily increased role of agency (Capoccia and Kelemen 2007; Katznelson 2003; Soifer 2012; Sorensen 2015; Capoccia 2016a). In this subsection these parts will be discussed in turn.

Pursuing meaningful policy change is always difficult. This is perhaps especially the case with European integration in policy areas of critical (symbolic) importance to European member states, such as defence. Member states are reluctant to give up powers in support of the EU in these areas. The institutional structure, in other words, is generally quite solid and difficult to change. This means 'agents' – decision-makers such as the High Representative of the Union for Foreign Affairs and Security Policy/Vice-president of the European Commission (HR/VP) – have little power to pursue reforms. Existing institutional frameworks have a great say in determining the future, and in the way new challenges are interpreted and dealt with. If new challenges arise, these are generally tackled using the same existing institutional framework.

Sometimes, however, crises or shocks occur that change this institutional stability. Crises or 'new' events may occur which expose for existing institutional structures an insufficiency to address the issues at hand. For example, the election of Donald Trump made European political leaders worry that European defence integration needed to be strengthened, if the USA was really to retreat further from its role in protecting Europe; while the Arab uprisings led some to say that the EU's approach to its Southern 'neighbourhood' needed to change.

During a critical juncture, a crisis thus occurs which may cause institutional structures to suddenly lose their legitimacy. They are not well equipped to deal with the situation at hand. What happens is that they thereby lose their ability to determine future action, or may even receive blame for having enabled or failed to prevent the crisis. The institutional structure, which as mentioned is usually tight and stable, temporarily loosens. This increases the odds of agents (member states, the Commission President, the HR/VP, etc.) playing an important role in pursuing policy changes. A window of opportunity emerges.

During this time, various policy innovations and reforms may be proposed as a result of the events, and coalitions may be built around exceptional circumstances. Oftentimes, we see a purposeful utilisation of crisis rhetoric stressing the urgency of the events and the extent to which they have disrupted the existing institutional framework. An example was the Brussels terrorist attacks of 2016, which brought the limits of European counter-terrorism policies to the top of the agenda. Turkish and Dutch authorities claimed they had passed on intelligence on some of the attackers to their Belgian counterparts. Blame games ensued, and it was argued that intelligence sharing in the European Union had to be improved drastically (Bigo et al. 2016).

When this happens, we say the events heighten contingency: there is a greater chance that decisions occur which are 'out of the ordinary'. Because routines are disrupted, the political space opens to actors to redefine issues, and policy changes and reforms. A broader range of policy options is on the table than was there before and after the juncture. After the Brussels terrorist attacks, to return to this example, policy initiatives were launched rapidly to improve the collection and connection of information in counter-terrorism. The Council also reiterated that the EU Passenger Name Record Directive needed to be adopted urgently (Bigo et al. 2016; Council of the European Union 2016).

After a critical juncture, the path of policy stability is interrupted. Multiple future outcomes are possible as policy changes are up in the air. The determination of which of these outcomes will eventually emerge depends on the dynamics in the period that follows (Capoccia and Kelemen 2007; Boin, t'Hart and McConnell 2009).

These three features, the loosening of the structure, a heightened contingency during the early stages after such an event and the increased causal importance of agency compared to the relatively closed nature of later stages, are generally acknowledged as core features of a critical juncture.

As Capoccia and Kelemen (2007: 350–51) point out, it is useful to consider the duration of critical junctures as relative to the outcome observed. This depends on the historical context and the critical juncture in question. The temporary loosening of the usual constraints of structure is temporally bounded. Episodes of reform usually take place 'in concentrated bursts at particular conjunctures' (Hall 2016: 41). Although some scholars include policy change in their definition of a critical juncture (Collier and Collier 1991; Hogan 2006), it is explicitly not included in my definition. Quite to the contrary, the notion that critical junctures heighten contingency and broaden the scope of available policy options means that one cannot exclude inertia or little to no change as possible outcomes. Critical junctures may (and indeed often do) result in a re-equilibration of policy rather than in change (Capoccia 2016a: 95). Finally, critical junctures need not necessarily be caused by exogenous shocks. Fundamental change might also be the result of endogenous circumstances which upset the status quo (Howlett 2009). This research, however, focuses on two critical junctures that started with shocks: the Arab uprisings and the Ukraine crisis.

To summarise, in this book I approach EU foreign policy change as a process that may be kickstarted by critical junctures which create '"openings" when the range of possible future outcomes available to actors is large' (Capoccia 2016a: 77). International or transboundary crises may be critical junctures for EU foreign policy if they produce a heightened contingency and increase the importance of agency, compared to before the crisis emerges or after it is resolved. They are critical in the sense that they are necessary for these policy changes to occur, although there may exist important antecedent conditions. They form a potential starting point for change. Although crises do not always produce critical junctures, many crises do, thereby generating moments of opportunity for policy change (Kingdon 1984). Researchers aspiring to investigate how other crises may lead to foreign policy change may wish to use the analytical framework proposed in this book.

Institutional plasticity

Although historical institutionalist approaches vary in the kinds of institutional change analysed, they share the understanding that institutions are the legacy of concrete historical processes, and that they are the object of ongoing contestation (Thelen and Conran 2016: 60–61). Institutions are created for a particular purpose at a particular time by those in power. Institutions thus reflect the context in which they were made, and the power dynamics of that particular context. As mentioned in 'Critical junctures', above, these institutions are dynamic arenas of conflict. Powerful actors can attempt to modify them to their preferences, making use of the features of the institution in question to do so. This makes institutions, as well as the product of strategic action, the 'object' of strategic action (Hall 2010: 204). They are not intermediaries between powerful actors and outcomes, but 'plastic': they are able to give form and take form, being both constraining and malleable in the hands of powerful actors (Capoccia 2016b; Notteboom, De Langen and Jacobs 2013).

Understanding the institutional arrangements of a foreign policy area under examination and their consequences for decision-making is thus crucial to our analysis of policy change. Institutions define how power is allocated (who the key actors are) and exercised (what they want and what their means/options to achieve these aims are). Actors with the opportunity and power to influence institutions may act as powerful agents of policy change. They may reframe the debate, generate new ideas and shed new perspectives on policy issues, and may attempt to rally support for their perception of the critical juncture at hand, as well as the best course of action to pursue (Bicchi 2002; Kingdon 1995). The European Neighbourhood Policy, for example, its legal basis and the rules that guide its decision-making have historically been determined by the European member states and the European institutions. They are thus a product of a political process. When we try to understand how the ENP or EU security and defence policies may change, however, we need to determine how the rules and regulations guiding those policy areas in turn constrain the process of change.

An example of institutional plasticity is the Court of Justice of the European Union (CJEU). Although the CJEU was not expected to be an active political actor when it was established in 1952, over the years and through a variety of decisions it has become a formidable engine behind European integration (Kelemen and Schmidt 2012; Stone Sweet 2004). This role of the CJEU has sometimes led to fierce resistance from national courts, and was one of the issues Brexiteers mobilised against remaining in the EU (Blauberger and Martinsen 2020). The CJEU thus demonstrates how institutions remain arenas of political struggle long after they are formed.

The CJEU also illustrates the malleability of institutions. In a series of landmark decisions in the early 1960s, the Court decided that EU law has direct effect in member states, and that European law takes precedence over all norms of national law within the EU (Rasmussen 2014; Weiler 1991). This was a clear instance of an institution giving form to member states. Although its powers remain limited, since its creation the CJEU has expanded their scope and transferred significant sovereignty from the member states to the Union, showing that institutions can both give form and take form.

The first question chapters two and three aim to answer is how the institutions impacted on the decision-making process following a critical juncture. Since historical institutionalism underlines the importance of the institutions that govern the foreign policy under examination, and how they allocate political authority, this question seeks to identify who the key actors were. In chapters two and three, I specifically ask: who are the key actors in the European Neighbourhood Policy and what is their power to shape it? After mapping these power relations, I zoom in on the crisis I am examining: how did these key actors perceive the critical juncture? Did they think change was necessary, and if so, what kind of change did they aim for?

Temporal contingency

Timing and context matter. The world as we know it did not *have* to be the way it is – this was not logically necessary – but has come to be this way owing to various events, not all of them foreseen or expected. This absence of certainty and necessity is also referred to as contingency.

Contingency is a concept that is much easier to deal with empirically than theoretically. For example, we easily accept that our personal existence is contingent from the very beginning, that we are the product of a series of events that might have turned out very differently in slightly different circumstances. Similarly, it seems logical that dinosaurs would not necessarily have become extinct roughly 65 million years ago had asteroid PIA03379 *not* hit the Earth, abruptly stopping photosynthesis worldwide and making the survival of certain forms of life impossible. Likewise, every modern organisation is obliged by law to make 'contingency plans', without anybody questioning the logic that a fire or electricity failure *might* happen but does not *need* to happen.

Although we thus are willing to accept the impact of chance and context in everyday life, in the social sciences (where universal laws and necessities reign) the concept has always been difficult. Theories such as rational choice or behaviourism – which relegate contingency to background noise – continue to hold appeal. This may be because necessity and impossibility are much more straightforward to generalise and to incorporate in a theory than uncertainty and possibility (Luhmann 1998: 46).

Yet, as has been argued persuasively by Ned Lebow (Lebow 2000) precisely in the social sciences, the need to factor contingency into a causal explanation should be great. Unforeseen events are common and may have great impact, and even the presence of deep-seated underlying causes does not make any event inevitable (2000: 591). A pressing question since the 2016 US election, for example, is whether Hillary Clinton could have become president of the United States if FBI director James Comey had not sent a letter to Congress on 28 October 2016 in which he announced that the FBI would review additional emails from Clinton's private email server, after which her lead dropped significantly (Silver 2017). This impact of timing on decision-making and on foreign policy behaviour has recently resurfaced in the work of Hom and Beasley (Hom and Beasley 2020).

As mentioned, in HI theory this impact of timing and events, and how both may generate actor preferences and power relations, and reinforce them, has an important place. Rather than universal causality, HI assumes causality is contextual, contingent upon the temporal context. Scholars 'want to know not just *what*, but *when*' (Pierson 2004: 54).

The second question which guides our analysis of EU foreign policy change is thus how the temporal context impacted the decision-making process leading to policy change. As mentioned in 'Institutional plasticity' above, in HI analyses it is the interaction of institutions, actors and historical processes that defines political outcomes. In order to take this impact into account, I aim to reconstruct both change episodes. I create what Capoccia and Ziblatt (2010: 934) call a 'structured episode', which involves the reconstruction and analysis of a historical episode by adopting an *ex ante* view (rather than hindsight) to reconstruct 'what actors were actually fighting about' (Capoccia and Ziblatt 2010: 943). This reconstruction in turn allows me to identify which events, political developments or other features of the temporal context have impacted on the decision-making process through shaping the perceptions of the key actors regarding whether policy should be changed and if so how.

A difficulty with factoring in time is that it may lead to drawn-out historical descriptions, which are hard to connect to social science theory. This book instead takes a pragmatic approach, 'taking time into account' in a way that makes it possible to theorise the impact of the historical context. It divides time into three registers: the structural register, referring to long-term historical processes (decades, centuries), the conjunctural register, which deals with the medium-term historical context (a few years), and finally the 'liminal', which centralises particular events and occurrences (days, weeks, months), as shown in Figure 1.2. The structural register concerns historically formed structural, social and economic conditions, the rules and trends created in the past that impact our present lives. For the case studies in chapters two and three, this structural context is formed by the historical development of the ENP, and of European relations with its neighbourhood more broadly. For students of other policy areas, as well as for the test-drives in chapter five, the focus will be different but the goal of mapping the most important, historically formed features of the policy area remains the same.

The conjunctural impact of time concerns the medium term, spanning a few years. In economics, a conjuncture refers to the cyclical recurrence of economic circumstances that occur within the structural trends. Conjunctural theories offer explanations based on circumstances and conditions in particular episodes in history. For example, when we study the EU response to the Arab uprisings, we must consider that at the time Europe was in the midst of the Eurozone crisis: a sovereign debt crisis that broke out in May 2010 and left European financial and economic governance in disarray.

Finally, the liminal context concerns sudden events of importance that serve as turning points for decision-makers. The term comes from the Latin word *limen* which means threshold. Although used in history and sociology, as a concept liminality receives little attention in political science or in HI research, despite the fact that political actors tend to view events and political developments in terms of discrete eras and liminal transitions, as Welch (2005: 56). argued. This means that decision-makers perceive certain events, developments or dates as 'decision points', amplifying the salience of an

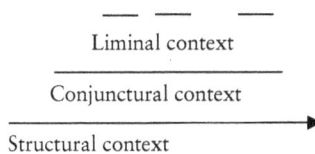

Liminal context

Conjunctural context

Structural context

Figure 1.2 The impact of time

issue or policy area, making leaders more strident in their willingness to propose policy changes. Events such as accidents or disasters, argued Birkland (2006), quickly find their way to the policy agenda. Following Cappoccia and Ziblatt's (2010) strategy, the criterion for these liminal moments, features of the temporal context or triggering events is whether they are deemed crucial by the key actors during the episode leading to reform. What events did the key actors perceive as crucial during this episode?

Policy change does not happen in a vacuum, but is embedded in a particular temporal context and shaped by the structural, conjunctural and liminal features of this temporal context. While, individually, these structural and conjunctural features of the temporal context may not be sufficient for this particular policy outcome to occur, they may amplify the impact on the decision-makers of liminal events taking place during the critical juncture. The reconstruction of a historical episode is important in HI approaches, as the researcher is encouraged to 'read history forward', to identify 'what actors were actually fighting about', and to 'assess the respective causal force of structural and conjunctural factors' in creating or adapting the institutions (Capoccia and Ziblatt 2010: 943).

In chapters two and three, therefore, I shall first sketch the historical context and then the medium-term conjuncture during which the process of change took place, after which the focus turns specifically to the particular events that occurred during the policy window which are most likely to affect the policy process – the liminal impact of the temporal context.

Assessing policy change

After the first two questions are answered, the book turns to a third, important question: how should we conceptualise the different kinds of policy change observed? In order to answer this, I consider the shortcomings of traditional (cumulative) conceptualisations of policy change in assessing developments in EU foreign policy. I build forward upon the broadly shared Hall typology, asking more open questions about the nature of policy change we can identify in the 2011 and 2015 reform rounds. I take an in-depth look at the lessons from chapters two and three, particularly at how both the constellation of actor preferences and the temporal context make certain types of policy change more likely. I will also argue why two analytical categories of policy change, which I label 'symbolic change' and 'constructive ambiguity', might provide a complementary perspective on the various forms that EU foreign policy change can take.

The reason why I use the Hall typology of policy change as a baseline is twofold. First, it is widely used in a large body of research that addresses policy change, which shares goals similar to that of this book (Baumgartner and Jones 2002; Cashore and Howlett 2007; Howlett and Cashore 2009; Jenkins-Smith et al. 2014; Sabatier and Jenkins-Smith 1993; Sabatier and Weible 2007). The typology Hall created served as a baseline for adaptations in many of these studies, as scholars have complemented and adapted it (Cashore and Howlett 2007; Howlett and Cashore 2009) or have developed categorisations that are similar in the sense that they propose progressive levels of policy change (Gustavsson 1999, 1998; Hermann 1990; Larsen 2005; Welch 2005). Since I aim to connect analyses of EU foreign policy to these debates on the nature of foreign policy change, using the traditional three-level approach to change as a starting point both serves as a useful theoretical positioning, and provides clues as to what would be better and more accurate descriptions of the policy change we are witnessing.

The measurement of change, as Bauer and Knill have argued (2014), has not always received due attention in the scholarship on policy change. What are students of policy change actually measuring?

A lack of clarity regarding measurement concepts leads to problems. First, it complicates comparisons between the results of different studies. Many analyses of policy change that followed in the wake of Hall's publication (1993) focus on a variety of elements and components of policy (instruments, goals, objectives, tools, calibrations), and thereby make a comparison of causes or dynamics of policy change across cases difficult (Howlett and Cashore 2009; Howlett 2009: 243; Bauer and Knill 2014). Differing approaches to measurement may have theoretical consequences. Bauer and Knill warn us, for instance, that a similar change phenomenon may be classified as either radical or incremental, based on the measurement scale (2014: 29). To avoid such confusion, I adopt an approach from the field of public policy studies proposed by Howlett and Cashore (2009). They suggest that scholars measuring policy change must first specify the *substance* of the changes: what was the qualitative content of the proposed changes?

The word 'policy' here may mean a variety of things. It is often used as an umbrella for a broad system of courses or principles of action in particular areas, e.g. defence policy, agricultural policy or indeed the neighbourhood policy. In other words, policies are regimes of ends and means-related goals (Howlett and Cashore 2009: 38). When our goal is to assess policy change, we need to clarify whether we are referring to the goals or the means to achieve them. And should we refer to goals, we must specify whether we refer to the macro-level ambitions of the policy, e.g. 'a secure United Kingdom'; more specific goals, e.g. 'protecting the skies above the United Kingdom'; or very specific goals and targets, such as 'gather minute-to-minute information on air activity above the North Sea'. Similarly, if we refer to policy means, we must specify whether we refer to general preferences for implementation, such as 'using coercive instruments'; more specific tools or methods, e.g. 'tax incentives for employers'; or very specific approaches, for example 'mandatory guidelines to create diversity and inclusivity in the workforce'.

Second and relatedly, students of change must specify at what *level* the policy changes occurred: did the policy goals change or were different means adopted to achieve them? Did changes occur at an abstract level or at a specific level?

Finally, we must specify the *direction* of the proposed policy changes. The notion of 'directionality' originates in the work of Nisbet (1972) who argues that policy changes need to be put on a spectrum. At one end there is linear change, which despite tweaks or increased investments remains within the status quo and follows the same 'direction'. At the other end of the spectrum there is change that is nonlinear, representing a break with the past. Analyses of policy change, starting with Hall and followed by others (Baumgartner and Jones 2002; Cashore and Howlett 2007; Howlett and Cashore 2009; Jenkins-Smith et al. 2014; Sabatier and Jenkins-Smith 1993; Sabatier and Weible 2007; Sabatier 1988), took over the notion of direction to distinguish policies that are cumulative and linear – that develop but remain within the same paradigm, pursuing similar goals – from policies which in substance move away from the previous policies, and thus constitute a break with the past. 'What is most important', state Howlett and Cashore (2009: 41) 'is not simply the number of moves away from the status quo which occur over time, but whether these changes [lead] away from an existing equilibrium toward another, or whether they represent a fluctuation consistent with an existing policy equilibrium.' When studying policy changes, we must therefore ask: to what extent do the proposed policy changes actually depart from the old policy? Do the revised policies tend to strengthen existing policies, or do their propositions deviate substantially from the status quo?

Chapters two and three, and the empirical case studies in chapter five, will assess changes in EU foreign policy by dividing them into constitutive elements: the level of change, the substance of change and the direction of change. Table 1.1 provides an example of how policy changes disaggregated along these lines will be shown in the following chapters.

Method: historical process tracing

The key method I use is historical process tracing. According to George and McKeown (1985: 35) process tracing means the researcher 'investigate[s] and explain[s] the decision process by which various initial conditions are

Table 1.1 How to disaggregate policy changes

	Macro-level	Meso-level	Micro-level
Policy goals	*Abstract policy aims* - Stabilisation (economic and political) (0/+) - ...	*Policy objectives* - inclusive socio-economic development (0) - ...	*Policy targets* - combatting "irregular" migration, human trafficking and smuggling (0/+) - ...
Policy means	*Implementation preferences* - step away from Enlargement methodology (+) - ...	*Policy mechanisms* - flexible deployment of ENI (+) - ...	*Policy tools* - ENI stable at €15.4 billion (0) - ...

0= no deviation from status quo, 0/+= very little deviation from status quo, += deviation from status quo
Source: Howlett and Cashore 2009

translated into outcomes'. One can use process tracing to uncover the decision-making process and the behaviour of actors in these processes, as well as the effects of institutional arrangements on these behaviours. Techniques of process tracing have since been defined and refined (Beach and Pedersen 2013, 2012; D. Collier 2011; Hall 2003). Historical process tracing combines 'regular' process tracing with a case-oriented historical method that is primarily aimed at providing a rich account of single case studies or studies which examine a small number of cases in depth ('small-*n*').

A core feature of the HI ontology is that it considers it impossible to explain political development by simply applying methods and epistemologies using variables that have fixed relationships over time. HI asserts that causal relationships are firmly embedded in their historical context, and are much more diverse than comparative, positivist methods of enquiry would posit. This contextual causality implies that it is the interaction of institutions, actors and historical processes that defines the outcome. In order to understand policy change, a historical institutionalist method thus requires 'genuinely historical research', as Pierson (2000b: 494) argued, by which is meant research that carefully investigates processes unfolding over time.

Yet the historical method is not merely a description of events – it draws on theory in order to explain how the steps contribute to the outcome. Therefore in this chapter I have made explicit the hypothesised explanations of change, in order to assess these (Bennett and Checkel 2015). It is argued that critical junctures do not automatically imply policy change. They are connected to eventual policy change through processes, or 'causal filters'. In this study these are institutional plasticity and the impact of the temporal context. In order to answer my research questions and thereby explore the value of the hypothesised explanations, I engage in historical research, including a focus on the micro-political events that occur in the time frame under scrutiny.

The case studies and test-drives in this book thus engage in historical process tracing in order to reconstruct and analyse the historical episode in question. What happened, when did it happen and why did it happen then are important questions that will be answered. Capoccia and Ziblatt (2010: 934) call such reconstructions 'structured episodes': a reconstruction and analysis of a historical episode. The reconstruction involves identifying the *key* political actors fighting over institutional change, the terms of the debate and the full range of options that they perceived, reconstructing the support these options had and analysing 'as much as possible with the eyes of the contemporaries', the interactions that led to the institutional outcome (Capoccia and Ziblatt 2010: 943).

Rather than focusing on all twenty-seven member states and all the European institutions to explain the process of EU foreign policy change, the framework proposed here focuses on the role and impact of key actors. Who the key actors are follows from the institutional effects I have discussed. The formal and legal features of the ENP determine the distribution of power and of decision-making authority: they determine who the key actors are in the policy area in general, but also in the specific decision-making process by which policy changed. As discussed in more detail below, the EU has historically governed and managed its relations with the 'neighbourhood' in a technocratic and trade-oriented way, and the ENP consists of various institutions with blurred lines of accountability. This has made the ENP quite plastic: as opposed to formal regulative institutions with very little room for deviation such as the Common Foreign and Security Policy (CFSP), the ENP is an institutional arrangement that leaves room for interpretative flexibility. It is built on a very limited legal structure that was explicitly designed to reinforce *existing* policies and instruments in place and therefore overlaps with many institutional arrangements. The ensuing institutional chaos within the EU's neighbourhood relations has historically left important leeway to member states to engage in policy entrepreneurship, either by taking the lead in the European Council, forging a coalition or by pursuing bilateral or parallel institutional initiatives. Examples of such entrepreneurship are the Swedish and Polish involvement in the Eastern Partnership (EaP) – the Eastern dimension of the ENP – and the French lobbying for the Union for the Mediterranean (UfM).

At the member state level, I selected France, Germany, Spain and Italy as key actors in the 2011 reform episode, and Germany, France and Poland in the 2015 reform episode. Both chapters two and three provide a detailed justification for selecting these actors in particular.

This focus on key actors also has a pragmatic aspect. The method employed here, historical process tracing, is a meticulous and detail-oriented process of small-*n* cases, which entails prioritising rigour and depth over breadth. More importantly, however, a focus on key actors is a theoretical decision in line with the HI research programme (Capoccia and Ziblatt 2010: 943).

Ontologically, historical institutionalism posits that crises are not mere 'objective facts', but rather are perceived and processed by the actors involved. The behaviour of decision-makers is thus thought to be informed by the way in which they perceive and understand their interests in particular situations, rather than by their 'objective' interests as such (Hay 2011: 70). After a crisis, decision-makers try to make sense of the events and of what the crisis means for their particular interests.

When studying the EU, the added difficulty is that such 'perceptions of interest' emerge in twenty-seven member states. Dramatic upheavals are very unlikely to be perceived uniformly by all involved, since their impact on different actors will vary (Boin, t'Hart and McConnell 2009: 84; Baumgartner 2013). After a crisis, therefore, we often see processes of interpretation and contestation, in which actors try to formulate their own interpretation of the crisis and the policy changes and reforms necessary to tackle it. This way in which critical junctures are perceived and defined by key actors as 'problems' for a certain policy area has an impact on the 'solution' – i.e. policy change – that will follow from the policy process (Daviter 2011).

To organise the key actors and their preferences, I use a helpful categorisation put forward by Boin, t'Hart and McConnell (2009), who divide the key actors after a critical juncture into groups: first, actors who argue there is no crisis or critical juncture, and that the events in question are, rather, an unfortunate incident; second, actors who deem the events to be a critical threat to the *status quo ante*, and therefore defend it against criticism; and third, actors who see the events as a critical opportunity to expose shortcomings of the *status quo ante*, and who are predisposed to blame and potentially

Table 1.2 Example summarised perceptions of the critical juncture

	Crisis as	Stance regarding ENP reform
Germany	Threat to status quo	Moved from status quo player to moderate change player
France	Opportunity to modify ENP	Moderate change player
Poland	Opportunity to strengthen ENP	Change player
European Commission and EEAS	Threat to status quo	Moved from status quo player to moderate change player

upend the status quo. Table 1.2 provides an example of how chapters two and three will display these findings.

The time frame for my analysis is guided by my conceptualisation of critical junctures. Since I characterise these as a temporary loosening of the structure, combined with a heightened contingency during the early stages after such an event and greater causal importance being given to agency compared to the relatively closed nature of earlier stages, it is the period between the critical juncture and presentation of the final reform document that qualifies. Chapters two and three therefore reconstruct both reform episodes chronologically, from the start of the critical juncture until policy redesign and reformulation had been completed with the presentation of the 'revised ENP' documents of 2011 and 2015. In the case of the Arab uprisings, this means the period between 17 December 2010 (the day Bouazizi immolated himself in Tunisia) and 25 May 2011, when the revised ENP was presented. In the case of the Ukraine crisis, the reform episode started ten days before the Vilnius Summit on 21 November 2013, when Yanukovych announced he would not sign the Association Agreement with the EU, and ended on 18 November 2015, when the revised ENP was presented. In these case studies, the revised policies were 'A new response to a changing neighbourhood' (2011) and 'Review of the European Neighbourhood Policy (ENP): stronger partnerships for a stronger neighbourhood' (2015) (Commission and High Representative for Foreign Affairs and Security Policy, 2015a; European External Action Service, 2015). The three test-drives in chapter five are also reconstructions of specific critical junctures. For the first, on the EU's response to rising disinformation, I assess a period from the start of the critical juncture in 2014 until the East StratCom Task Force was presented in 2015. For the crisis in migration and asylum, I assess 2015 – the year in which the number of asylum seekers entering the EU rose exponentially, and 2016, when the most important policy responses were presented. The last test-drive covers a longer critical juncture, lasting from 2014 until 2018, with the main policy changes presented in 2017.

Evidence

Historical process tracing builds upon both account evidence – the content of empirical material, such as meeting minutes, reports, official declarations, policy documents or speeches – and sequence evidence, the temporal and spatial chronology of events. It provides insight into the decisions that were made, when these decisions were made and how the temporal context translated onto the decision-making agenda.

Interviews can be part of historical process tracing, but form only an element of this, as the overarching goal is to provide a detailed reconstruction of the historical episode relying on a wide variety of evidence and material sources that are left behind in the policy process. As Skocpol argued in 'Why I am an historical institutionalist', 'it is not enough just to explore how people talk or think. We must also find patterns in what they do' (Skocpol 1995: 105).

The main evidence used to trace the historical processes in this research consists of official documents, non-papers and statements. These 'paper traces' of the decision-making process provided ample information, allowing me to answer the first two research questions, especially concerning the member state preferences in the process of ENP reforms. Member states proved to be eager to present their reform proposals and input for the ENP reform round in the form of declarations and statements. Unlike the member states, however, the European institutional actors did not provide a separate input in the consultation process on ENP reform, because they were in charge of coordinating the consultation process.

Therefore, in order to ascertain the position of the European institutions, I conducted sixty-four semi-structured interviews with EU officials working within the Directorates-General for Neighbourhood and Enlargement Negotiations (DG NEAR), for Migration and Home Affairs (DG HOME), the EEAS, the EU Military Staff, the European Defence Agency and the EU delegations in Algeria, Morocco, Tunisia, Egypt, Libya, Ukraine and Russia, as well as the East StratCom Task Force. These were undertaken in two waves in 2015–17 and 2019–20, as well as six exploratory interviews.[1] Seventeen of these sixty-four interviews were used for the test-drives in chapter five. These interviews were an important source of data to study next to official statements and declarations. They were particularly used in order to identify: 1) the perception of the critical juncture by the Commission and EEAS; and 2) what the European institutional actors considered the appropriate course for reforming the ENP. The interviews contributed to establishing the thoughts and attitudes of EU representatives and the reconstruction of events.

Initial questions regarding the policy process behind reform of the ENP were asked, but the intention was to allow the interviewee to elaborate on the policy process as much as possible. The answers and claims of the interviewees were weighed through corroboration with other interviewees' statements and an assessment of whether written documents supported their assertions. To that end, I spoke to at least two officials in every department/institution whenever possible (there are three exceptions), and presented the interviewees with statements derived from policy documents or responses from other interviewees.

Whilst they build on an important amount of empirical data, including interviews, these test-drives do not aspire to attain the same depth as chapters two and three. Those chapters are in-depth reconstructions of policy change episodes and contain a high degree of empirical detail. The three test-drives are much shorter, build on fewer interviews, and probe the institutional landscapes of the policy areas in less depth. Their purpose is to demonstrate the use of the analytical framework in quite different settings, to see EU foreign policy change at work.

Summarising the analytical framework

Nearly two decades ago, HI scholars suggested that the existing approaches to policy change, incremental and episodic, may not exhaust the possibilities and ways in which policy may change, 'nor even that [the bifurcation] captures the most important ways in which institutions evolve over time' (Streeck and Thelen 2005: 8). In this chapter I outlined why this still is the case in studies analysing EU foreign policy. The framework presented here should contribute to bridging the gap between the two approaches, explaining how critical junctures may translate into lasting policy change.

In the Introduction I argued that in order to understand EU foreign policy change in the wake of critical junctures, one needs to understand the decision-making process following those critical junctures, in order to shed light on what kinds of policy changes – however minor or unsubstantiated – we *did* see, at what level they took place, what their actual substance was and why this particular output came out of the decision-making process. This chapter has laid out the analytical framework that I will use to assess EU foreign policy change in such a holistic way. The guiding questions are how institutions impacted on the decision-making process following the critical juncture, how the temporal context impacted on this process and how we should conceptualise the different kinds of policy change observed.

This chapter has presented a theoretical framework to assess EU foreign policy change that builds forward on what is dubbed the 'second wave' in HI theorising which introduced novel concepts such as institutional plasticity. Based on the theory set out here, this book proposes the following steps for analysing EU foreign policy change in the wake of a critical juncture. In the first instance, the researcher must specify the institutional set-up of the policy area and how its historical development has produced this particular set-up. This means looking for the potential legacy of historically created institutions, institutional overlap or turf wars. Based on this analysis, one can assess the apparent plasticity of those institutions. As stated before, institutions are also arenas of conflict. Actors may attempt to modify the ways institutions are arranged to suit their political preferences by making strategic use of features of the institution. If an institution and the rules that bind it are rigid, this leaves actors with little power to modify them. But the more plastic institutions are, the more they may be malleable to the preferences of powerful actors. Researchers thus need to map how institutions allocate power and how power and decision-making is exercised within them.

After having assessed institutions as such, the attention focuses on the critical juncture under study and the question of who the key actors were during this critical juncture. Although, especially in a European Union of twenty-seven states, many actors may play some role in the process by which a policy is changed, it is possible to identify a smaller group of up to four actors as playing a dominant role in shaping the policy outcome, based on historical commitment to the policy under question and their behaviour during the critical juncture. It is important to select only the most important actors in this process. This is because once these are identified, the researcher must investigate their preferences in this critical juncture, considering both their historical preferences and the stance they adopted at the moment under study towards the policy or region in question. These policy preferences should be specified along with their substance, level and direction, as discussed in this chapter.

Subsequently, the researcher needs to reconstruct the critical juncture. The goal is to identify the key turning points or main events which changed the perceptions of the key actors. Here, as mentioned in 'Evidence' above, the researcher tries to 'read history forward' when creating such a reconstruction of the critical juncture and the way it was perceived by the key actors (Capoccia and Ziblatt 2010: 943). There may have been events which brought the key actors together or aligned their preferences, which greatly increased the urgency of policy reform or otherwise shaped the decision-making process. An example was the tragic downing of the MH17 plane in 2014, which as I will discuss in chapter three, created a temporary convergence among the key actors on the necessity of sanctions against Russia.

Hereafter, the focus turns on mapping the final output of the policy changes. Here again it is crucial to provide clear measurement by specifying clearly the substance, the level and the direction of the final policy changes. Once these are mapped, the researcher can assess how this output may be categorised and subsequently explained. Has there been no change; first-, second- or third-order change; symbolic change; or did the changes come down to constructive ambiguity? And, drawing on the reconstruction of the critical juncture, what would be the most likely explanation for that? Table 1.3 summarises the steps in this analytical framework.

Table 1.3 Summarising the analytical framework

Key questions
Step 1 What is the institutional set-up of the policy area under study and how has this been shaped historically? How plastic are the institutions?
Step 2 Who are the key actors in this particular critical juncture?
Step 3 What were their preferences regarding policy change? - Substance, level, directionality
Step 4 Reconstructing the temporal context: were there events, turning points or features of the temporal context that changed the perceptions of the key actors by either: - Bringing them together - Increasing the urgency of reform - By otherwise shaping the decision-making process
Step 5 What was the final output of policy change?
Step 6 How might we categorise and explain this output? - No change - First and second order change - Third order/paradigm change - Symbolic change - Constructive ambiguity

Note

1 The research for the case study of the Arab uprisings and that of the Ukraine crisis, as well as twenty of the interviews used in this book, were conducted as part of the INTEL research project, which investigates knowledge production and use in the foreign policies of the UK, Germany and the European Union during the Arab uprisings, the rise of ISIS and the Russia/Ukraine crisis.

2

Foreign policy change after the Arab uprisings
The Neighbourhood Policy revised

In 2010, the 26-year-old Mohamed Bouazizi was living in a village not far from Sidi Bouzid, Tunisia. Unable to secure a better job, he had become a street vendor, selling produce in the centre of a town plagued by corruption and a high unemployment rate. With the money he made selling fruit and vegetables, he supported his siblings and his mother.

On 17 December 2010, Bouazizi set himself on fire after having been humiliated by local law enforcement for not having the required permit to sell fruit and vegetables on the street. His act quickly incited outrage. It was not seen as an attempt at suicide, but as a political assassination, as per the words of a trade union member from the city of Sidi Bouzid, making Bouazizi a victim of the oppressive and authoritarian regime of President Ben Ali of Tunisia (Yousfi 2015: 324). Spread through social media, protests sprang up in the town of Sidi Bouzid.

None of the various smaller-scale uprisings during the early 2000s (such as the 2008 Gafsa revolts in Tunisia) escalated as did the events of 2010–11. From the summer of 2010 until mid-December, a series of existing stress factors throughout the region – among them the growing dissatisfaction with nepotism, patronage and favouritism, and insufficient economic growth – started to converge, catalysed by increasing oppression of the media and rising food prices. This translated into increased socio-economic rights activism.

Bouazizi's act of despair triggered a revolutionary movement. Protests began in Sidi Bouzid on the day of his self-immolation and grew day by day. On 24 December, the first Tunisian protestor was shot and killed by the police, while hundreds rallied in front of the Tunisian labour union headquarters, clashing with Tunisian security forces. Demonstrations escalated, as did the response of the Ben Ali regime. In early 2011, more casualties occurred. Ben Ali announced his resignation on 14 January 2011.

A page was turned as the mass protests in Tunisia triggered demonstrations in neighbouring countries, and across the region. In Egypt, after the brutal death of Khaled Said, beaten and tortured while in police custody in 2010, half a million social media users joined a Facebook page called 'We are all

Khaled Said'. A call to demonstrate on 25 January 2011 – Police Day in Egypt – was issued via this Facebook page, triggering a rally that was much more impressive than expected. The loosely organised opposition managed to mobilise thousands of people in downtown Cairo. Demonstrations spread to other parts of the country over the following days. The brutal repression the regime demonstrated and the arrest of thousands of marchers propelled the activism, calling for the resignation of President Mubarak.

After a 'Day of Rage' on 28 January several police cohorts pulled back, leaving the streets open for the demonstrators to move to Tahrir Square. Days of bloody demonstrations followed and, on 31 January, Mubarak made a speech in which he promised to let his son run in the coming elections in his place. When Mubarak resisted leaving office, the Supreme Council of the Armed Forces of Egypt (SCAF) threatened that, if he continued to refuse, he would face charges of high treason. On 11 February 2011 Mubarak surrendered authority to the SCAF. After eighteen days of uprisings, this marked the beginning of a period of transition in Egypt (Rutherford 2012: 35–63; Lynch 2013; Kandil 2012: 222–8).

This chapter focuses on changes the EU made to its foreign policy in the wake of the Arab uprisings, in particular on the way the EU reformed the ENP after the uprisings. The EU's policies *vis-à-vis* its neighbours, hitherto featuring a high degree of inertia, were suddenly presented with a major juncture when the mass protests erupted in January 2011, first in Tunisia, then spreading to Yemen, Sudan, Egypt, Bahrein, Libya and Syria. The revolutions that swept the Arab world thus constituted a critical juncture for the ENP, culminating in 'A new response to a changing neighbourhood'. This revised policy, presented in May, was the EU's strategic response to the Arab 2011 uprisings (Commission and HR/VP 2011a).

The first part of this chapter describes the structural context and outlines the various political institutional initiatives guiding EU relations with the Middle East and North Africa. Subsequently it details how the European Union was struggling on many fronts on the eve of the Arab uprisings. In the conjunctural context – the wider, medium-term political conjuncture in which the policy reform took place – Europe was already in the midst of the Eurozone crisis. This chapter subsequently argues that the way in which the EU policies towards its southern neighbours are organised bears testimony to the 'plastic' nature of institutions, which constrain key actors and their policies yet at the same time allow actors to mould them to the actors' purposes.

In turn, it identifies France, Germany, Spain and Italy as key member state actors in the 2011 ENP reform round, with the EEAS and the Commission as the most important actors at the European level in the process of reforming the ENP. The following section describes how this immediate temporal context influenced the process of policy change. It shows that the outcome – the different forms of change to the ENP – would have been different if the temporal context had been different; that this particular outcome was not necessary but at least in part the product of the particular temporal context. It provides various snapshots of the decision-making process, particularly between mid-January 2011 and late-February 2011 (when the ENP reform was announced). I conclude that over these six weeks there were several political developments which led to policy change. The rapid spread of the Arab uprisings; their evolution in Egypt, considered a crucial country for Europe and in the region; and the influx of large numbers of refugees fleeing the Arab uprisings greatly and quickly increased both the salience of the ENP and of the region, and the urgency of ENP reform.

Institutional set-up and historically created arrangements

Relations between the European Union and the countries in the Middle East and North Africa date back decades. In 1995 the member states of the EU and twelve Mediterranean partners met for a conference in Barcelona to set up the Euro-Mediterranean Partnership (EMP), an ambitious political initiative consisting of political, economic, social and cultural partnerships. The context was one of cautious optimism in the region, fuelled by the 1993 Oslo Accords. The EMP, more commonly known as the Barcelona Process, was the first partnership between the EU and the region to include an important element of region-building, aiming to recognise the 'Euro-Mediterranean space' politically as a region (Barbé 1996: 27).

The Association Agreements concluded as part of the Barcelona Process resembled those concluded as part of the process of EU enlargement, in which benefits were made conditional upon reforms. Crucial was the economic pillar, which had the goal of setting up a free trade area aimed at facilitating trade within the region and with the EU (European Commission 2020a). The focus on economic development was underpinned by the view held at the Commission that economic liberalisation is inherently linked to political liberalisation. As the Barcelona Declaration affirms, 'social development … must go hand in hand with economic development' (European Commission 1995).

The EMP was perceived to be largely unsuccessful. The structural problems in the region and the absence of cooperation or of a sense of regional union among the partner states led to a fragmented system of states pursuing relations with the EU. Political liberalisation did not emerge through the focus on economic development, as rent-seeking behaviour and authoritarianism continued. The faltering Middle East Peace Process and the paralysing politicisation of its forums undermined the EMP by the late 1990s (Youngs 2015).

The institutional development of relations with the region continued as, in 2004, the Commission's role evolved from preparing aspiring members towards managing neighbourhood relations, as it was given the lead in the European Neighbourhood Policy. Agreed upon in December 2004, the aim of the ENP was to 'develop a zone of prosperity and a friendly neighbourhood – a "ring of friends" with whom the EU enjoys close, peaceful and co-operative relations' (European Commission 2003: 4). The ENP integrated and expanded existing instruments already deployed by the Commission in the process of enlargement (Interview PO9):

> Our strategy is the same recipe we have used forever, in other regions of our neighbourhood. It is a 'try to make them like us and they will behave' kind of strategy. That is the approach we choose. Let them transform to our way of business. Let them plug into the internal market. It's the same kind of recipe which in the end comes from the enlargement processes, which has been the medicine for all [ills] in the neighbourhood.

The core element of the ENP is the formulation of bilateral Action Plans, in some cases called Association Agreements, agreed between the EU and its respective partners. These Action Plans map country-specific agendas and priorities for political and economic reform. And although the goals of the ENP are distinctively political, the process of achieving them is based on a piecemeal, bilateral and technical approach.

In the scholarship on the ENP, it is broadly accepted that the Policy reflects the technocratic and trade-oriented logic the Commission pursued in its enlargement policy (Gebhard 2010; Kelley 2006). A consequence of this stickiness is that the Commission has tackled its role in the 'neighbourhood' using the same approach and policy instruments it had deployed in the pre-accession process, aiming for 'regulatory approximation' in a dense structure of functionally oriented institutions, programmes and Action Plans, but without offering these partners the prospect of joining the European Union. Moreover, this trade-oriented approach is quite technocratic and process-focused in nature, as confirmed by all interviewees working for European institutions. As one senior EU official argued, the EU and its delegations are 'focused too much on process, rather than substance. Signing an Action Plan, signing a memorandum of agreement, signing an Association Agreement … It is what we do' (Interview PO14). Or, in the words of another EU official I interviewed (Interview PO4):

> The biggest problem of the EU is [that] the leadership only focuses on financial and economic aspects. The EU leadership totally ignores the strategic and geopolitical element.

The political context of the Mediterranean has changed substantially since the turn of the millennium. The post-9/11 landscape saw an increased focus on security and anti-terrorism, strengthened after the terrorist attacks in

Madrid and London in 2004 and 2005. As internal security considerations and the urge to fight Islamic terrorism increased, stability trumped democracy on many occasions, which was reflected in the ENP. While the ambition of the ENP had been for ENP countries to share 'everything but institutions' – everything except membership (Prodi 2002), in practice relations were dominated by issues such as migration, the fight against terrorism and access to energy supplies (Balfour 2012: 17). This securitisation of relations with the Southern neighbours likewise meant that EU member states were increasingly willing to continue their covert support of authoritarian regimes in North Africa, seen as partners in the fight against Islamist extremism.

To summarise, the historical development of the institutional set-up in the region created a dense framework of overlapping policy frames (Cardwell 2011). It mirrored the ambivalent objectives among EU member states, as well as the continuing dilemma between fostering stability and promoting democracy.

Within this structural context, the Arab uprisings transpired at an economically strenuous time for the Union. Europe was in the midst of the Eurozone crisis, a sovereign debt crisis that broke out in May 2010 and left European financial and economic governance in disarray. Neither the Eurozone infrastructure nor the EU infrastructure was prepared for a crisis of such a magnitude. It was a period of ceaseless high-level summits, often without satisfying results, and of political fragmentation across Europe (Baldwin and Giavazzi 2015). The problems of the Eurozone overshadowed European Council agendas and those of the national governments more intimately affected by it.

For southern European countries especially, the economic downturn impacted on their foreign policy capabilities by putting them under acute budget pressures. The crisis also affected the ENP partner countries which, although initially less affected owing to their relatively low exposure to the global financial system, saw their real economies shrink, their exports decline, inflows of foreign direct investment, remittances and tourism income drop and unemployment rates rise substantially (Cristina Paciello 2010). Within the EU, the Eurozone crisis exacerbated the already existing 'enlargement fatigue' and, more importantly, risked eroding the power of conditionality under the ENP, calling both the success of the European model and its attractiveness to partner countries into question (Whitman and Juncos 2012).

How plastic is the policy area?

As mentioned in Chapter 1, by 'institutional plasticity' I mean that institutions are not simply intermediary between actors and political outcomes. Institutions such as the ENP constrain agents, and at the same time are constrained by agency. They both structure and shape political decision-making *and* are shaped and re-designed and re-moulded by actors. In this section I shall set out how plastic the ENP was during the critical juncture.

The judicial basis of the ENP in the European treaties is weak. Article 8 of the Treaty on European Union (TEU) formally instructs the Union to 'develop a special relationship with neighbouring countries, aiming to establish an area of prosperity and good neighbourliness, founded on the values of the Union and characterised by close and peaceful relations based on cooperation'. The Treaty does not mention the ENP explicitly, but writes about good neighbourliness and neighbouring countries in vague and fuzzy ways (Hillion 2013).

Neighbourhood relations are included in the common provisions in Title 1 of the treaty, where the objectives and values of the Union are laid out. This is significant. It means that the neighbourhood policy can tap into the principal instruments at the disposal of the EU. It also means, however, that the policy stands completely apart from the procedures and instruments the EU has at its disposal under the CFSP. Crucially, the TEU created the European External Action Service, which was to assist the newly created High Representative for Foreign Affairs and Security Policy.

These innovations have had disruptive effects on the management of the ENP, which previously was fully in the hands of the Commission. The Commission department previously managing external relations (Directorate-General for External Relations, DG RELEX) became part of the EEAS which, according to a senior EU official I interviewed who had moved from DG RELEX to the EEAS, had left the institution 'scattered in terrible turf wars' (Interview PO18). Formally, the European Council provides the overall policy guidance for the ENP, while the European Commission and the EEAS conduct its everyday operation. ENP Action Plans or Association Agreements, which guide political relations with partners, are negotiated by the EEAS, while the Commission leads negotiations on trade agreements with the same partners. EEAS thus cooperates with the presidency of the European Commission, DG NEAR (Neighbourhood and Enlargement) and DG DEVCO (Development and Cooperation), a wide range of sectoral Directorate-Generals (depending on the issue area) and the EU's High Representative for Foreign Affairs and Security Policy, the HR/VP. Meanwhile the European Council, and thus all EU member states, hold final decision-making powers over the policy, under the Lisbon Treaty. The European Parliament (EP) does not hold decision-making powers over the ENP.[1]

This implies there has to be a tight coordination between these actors, but the Treaty does not indicate the terms of their interaction, leaving a blurry line of accountability and command between the HR/VP and the president of the Council (Hillion 2013: 5–6). To further complicate things, different member states in the rotating presidency of the Council all employ different strategies when dealing with the EEAS, some explicitly incorporating the Service in the process while others are inclined to exclude it (Vanhoonacker and Pomorska 2013).

Why is all of this relevant for assessing the plasticity of the ENP? The formal and legal features of the ENP determine the distribution of power and of decision-making authority: who the key actors are in the policy area in general, but also in the specific process of making a decision to change policy. The co-existence of overlapping institutions, the limited legal weight given to the ENP, the Commission's historic lack of autonomy in the 'neighbourhood' until 2004 followed by its later technocratic and trade-oriented approach, and the variety of bilateral partnerships the member states pursue with neighbouring countries together have made the ENP quite plastic: the ENP is an institutional arrangement that leaves room for interpretative flexibility. It is built on a very limited legal structure that was explicitly designed to reinforce *existing* policies and instruments in place and therefore overlaps with many institutional arrangements. The ensuing institutional chaos within the EU's neighbourhood relations has historically left important leeway for member state actors to take the initiative in those relations (Böttger 2008; Bicchi 2002). The simultaneous existence of the EMP for the southern Mediterranean countries, where the Union for the Mediterranean (UfM) also plays a role, and the Eastern Partnership (EaP) for the eastern neighbours, which in turn is part of the ENP, bears testimony to the room for policy entrepreneurship in the 'neighbourhood'. This makes the ENP a 'plastic' institution, constraining yet malleable in the hands of powerful actors.

On one hand, the scattered institutional arrangements around the ENP are regularly underfunded and, because of institutional outgrowth, often lack focus. On the other hand, the disorderly co-existence of various institutions combined with the ENP's distribution of political authority leaves room for manoeuvre to member state actors, who often pursue their own, often more comprehensive, bilateral policies in the region; and take the initiative in developing the eastern and southern dimensions of the ENP. They can take the lead within the Council or use 'minilateral' fora to form coalitions with other member states around their own policy preferences.

We have seen this with Sweden and Poland spearheading the EaP agreed upon at the 2009 Prague Summit (Copsey and Pomorska 2014), or with France in its quest to establish a UfM (Bicchi 2011) and its history of developing European integration with the southern Mediterranean (Bicchi 2002). Other, less successful recent examples are Italy's suggestion of a

'Marshall Plan for the Arab World' (Frattini 2011) or the short-lived German attempt to establish an 'ENP Plus' strategy during its presidency to reiterate the importance of the eastern dimension of the ENP, separating the 'European neighbours' – i.e. those in the eastern 'neighbourhood' – from 'the neighbours of the EU', referring to the southern Mediterranean (Copsey 2008; Emerson, Noutcheva and Popescu 2007; Kempe 2015).

The critical juncture

The mass protests in Egypt, Yemen, Sudan, Bahrein, Libya and Syria that followed the uprisings in Tunisia resulted in divergent trajectories in the region, although they share an essence as a rupture in which a long period of authoritarianism and oppression was contrasted with a moment of uprising, an 'episode of radical political opening' (Whitehead 2015: 19).

At the start of the Arab uprisings, the EU's neighbourhood policies, hitherto featuring a 'high degree of stability and stasis', were suddenly presented with a major juncture (Whitman and Juncos 2012: 151). This caught the EU – and other international actors – unprepared and surprised (Goodwin 2011). One interviewee told me (Interview PO28):

> As anybody else we were surprised. We always knew that change would come. But we were surprised first by the moment, we were surprised by what triggered it and we were definitely surprised by the kind of avalanche effect that it took.

To the European Union, the fact that the movement spread to Egypt was especially important, as interviewees confirm, because Egypt is an 'incredibly important player in the region, for the entire Union' (Interview PO16), a 'key country [of which] everyone agrees it is important that [it] succeeds in order to have a spill-over effect in the region' (Interview PO15).

The Arab uprisings painfully showed the discrepancy between the stated goals of the ENP – stability, prosperity and democracy – and the status quo. The tools to achieve these goals, such as a policy dialogue, trade cooperation and financial support under the principles of conditionality, were shown to be insufficient. EU governments became aware that the geopolitical landscape in the southern 'neighbourhood' was changing rapidly, and that policy had to be adjusted to new actors and dynamics. One official commented the EU 'knew that some countries were more democratic than others. But we found out these countries were dictatorships' (Interview PO15). The EU's initial reaction was therefore cautious and slow, as if awaiting the outcome of the Egyptian and Tunisian revolutions before it spoke out (Khalifa Isaac 2012; Pinfari 2013). As I will describe further below, the tide began to turn as the Arab uprisings progressed.

Overall, the Arab uprisings constituted a critical juncture for the ENP, as they loosened the constraints on its structure, within which only a 'routine review' of the Policy was planned. They also allowed various actors to propose policy innovations and reforms. As such, they opened multiple possible futures, 'the determination of which [depended] on the particular political dynamic and power relations when new institutions are established' (Sorensen 2015: 25).

Key actors

In Chapter 1 I explained that an important step in dissecting the process of policy change consists in identifying who the key actors were and how they perceived the critical juncture. At the European level, I identify the EEAS and the Commission as key actors in this case.

This identification is based on the institutional set-up of the ENP discussed in a previous section of this chapter, as these institutional arrangements and their plasticity determine who was governing the ENP, who was managing it, who was taking decisions and also what power the member states had to shape the ENP. The institutional arrangements put the EEAS and the Commission at the head of the ENP's day-to-day management, with the European Council as the primary decision-maker. Despite the Council having this role, I do not regard it as a separate key European actor in the process by which the ENP was changed, first because it consists of the member states, and thus is difficult to separate analytically from the key actors at the member state level; second because its role in the ENP reform process was *pre* and *post hoc*: it requests a reform, which starts the process of policy change, and once a revised policy has been developed, it adopts that policy formally. In between, its role in the decision-making process is limited.

At the European level, the key actors thus were the EEAS and the Commission. Although they are separate institutions and do not necessarily have the same position on all occasions, in the course of the 2011 and 2015 ENP reforms their policy preferences are impossible to disentangle, as they jointly led the formal reform process, producing joint consultation papers. Interviewees, especially those at the delegations, confirm that the Commission and the EEAS ran the reform process in conjunction. The European Parliament is excluded from my analysis because, although in the past it has played a role in urging the Commission and EEAS to push ENP reform, the EP does not hold decision-making powers over the ENP and its role during the process of deciding on ENP reform was negligible.

At the member state level, the key actors in this critical juncture were France, Germany, Spain and Italy. Historically, France, Spain and Italy have often been identified as key actors in the Mediterranean region, although Italy is described by some as a smaller player in Euro-Mediterranean policy (Kausch and Youngs 2009; García and de Larramendi 2002; Gillespie 2000). Italy's main priorities in the Mediterranean were historically to secure energy supplies, and to foster relations with the individual states in the region. Although it gained in importance after 9/11, Italy has histori- cally played a smaller role than Spain and France, especially in the EMP (Bicchi and Gillespie 2014: 241; Pace 2005: 80; Böttger 2008; Balfour 2007).

In 2008, France spearheaded the UfM during a summit co-chaired by the then French President Nicolas Sarkozy and Egyptian President Hosni Mubarak. To France, an important goal of the UfM was to reiterate its leading role in the Mediterranean, and to rally EU resources towards the south (Delgado 2011).

Germany, finally, has been less visibly present than the southern European member states, and is not historically connected to the region in the same way as France, Spain or Italy, but is nevertheless an increasingly important actor in EU relations with the Mediterranean (Ratka 2012). 'The Mediter- ranean region is our task in Europe', said Chancellor Angela Merkel at the dawn of the French Council Presidency. 'France has a lot of Mediterranean coast, we do not have Mediterranean shores … This does not mean that Germany has no interest in the Mediterranean region' (Merkel 2007). The German government has become more interested in the region gradually, especially in the diversification of its energy towards solar and wind options (Jünemann 2007). Germany was finally able to emerge as a key actor early in the critical juncture because France, Spain and Italy were initially scrambling to correct their initial responses to the Arab uprisings, such as the endorse- ments of Berlusconi, the diplomatic gaffe of French Foreign Minister Alliot-Marie and the Spanish statement that indigenous forces should take the lead in their countries' transition (Ratka 2012).

To summarise, the four key actors at the member state level are identified as France, Germany, Spain and Italy. This has been confirmed by several interviewees. These actors are not necessarily the European states that were most vocal in the wake of the Arab uprisings: the United Kingdom, for instance, was similarly outspoken in supporting the Arab revolutionaries. This case study, however, assesses the Arab uprisings as a critical juncture for the ENP. Neither the UK nor other member states took as active a role in reforming the European approach to the 'neighbourhood' as these four countries, which is only these four key actors are studied in this chapter.

As choices have to be made, in this book I selected actors without whom an assessment of the ENP reform rounds would be incomplete.

Perception of the critical juncture, preferences for policy reform

The next step is to describe the dominant perception of the critical juncture and the preferences for policy reform that the key actors held, as well as how they tried to shape the process of changing foreign policy. Table 2.1 provides a summary of the main perceptions of the key actors, which will be elaborated below.

European Commission and EEAS

The Arab uprisings that swept across the MENA in the winter of 2011 caught the EU by surprise. While, initially, the European response was timid and slow, throughout February 2011 the Union institutions increasingly engaged in a display of self-criticism regarding the EU's previous approach to the region.

The Arab uprisings were perceived as a watershed moment for EU relations with the region, as leaders drew parallels between the Arab uprisings and the fall of the Berlin Wall in 1989, and signalled a strong sense of urgency as well as a need for radical reform in various speeches and statements (Ashton 2011a, 2011b, 2011c; Barroso 2011a, 2011b; Van Rompuy 2011b;

Table 2.1 Summarised perceptions of the critical juncture

Actor	Crisis as	Stance regarding ENP reform
France	Opportunity to strengthen/modify ENP	Change player
Germany	Opportunity reiterate normative dimension of ENP	Status quo player
Spain	Ambivalent, overall opportunity to strengthen its own role in ENP/alternative policy frameworks	Moderate change player
Italy	Threat to security; opportunity to strengthen 'European solidarity'	Moderate change player
European Commission/ EEAS	Opportunity to reiterate the ENP	Moderate status quo player

Füle 2011). On 4 February 2010, Council President Herman Van Rompuy was the first to explicitly call for ENP reform, when the European Council tasked the High Representatives and the Commission 'to adapt rapidly the instruments of the EU' (European Council 2010). The Council stated it was 'determined to lend its full support to the transition processes towards democratic governance, pluralism, improved opportunities for economic prosperity and social inclusion, and strengthened regional stability'. On 23 February 2011, HR/VP Catherine Ashton asserted that a 'fundamental review' of the ENP was needed, to 'revamp and renew the Neighbourhood Policy in light of the new challenges we face', making it 'more ambitious' (Ashton 2011d).

In a response to the political developments, the Commission presented the 'Partnership for Democracy and Shared Prosperity for the Southern Mediterranean' (hereafter: Partnership) as a first step towards ENP reform, on 8 March 2011. This statement serves as an important source for identifying the policy preferences of the EEAS and the Commission in the process by which policy changed. Throughout the Partnership document the Commission claimed that its response to the Arab uprisings would entail a novel and strategic approach to the changing circumstances in the southern 'neighbourhood'. It is described as a 'qualitative step forward in the relations between the EU and its Southern neighbours' (European Commission and HR/VP 2011a: 2), intended to demonstrate the EU's commitment to the democratic transition, as well as its adaptability: '[the EU] needs to support wholeheartedly the wish of the people in our neighbourhood to enjoy the same freedoms that we take as our right'. In the Partnership document, the HR/VP and the Commission announced the ENP reform agenda. 'A radically changing political landscape in the Southern Mediterranean requires a change in the EU's approach to the region', they argued (European Commission and HR/VP 2011a: 3), following this with the argument that the ENP should be 'focused, innovative and ambitious, addressing the needs of the people and the realities on the ground' (European Commission and HR/VP 2011a: 5). Yet although the EU purported to break new ground with its revision of the ENP, the proposals for ENP reform by the Commission and EEAS in the Partnership do not deviate substantially from the *status quo ex ante*. The Partnership maintains the old notion that democratic transformation goes hand in hand with trade liberalisation and the development of a liberal market economy.

What the EU deemed necessary was an amplification of previous policy: the new approaches should focus on even deeper economic integration, even broader market access and closer political cooperation. Political and economic reforms must continue to 'go hand-in-hand' and, like before, 'the EU should be ready to offer greater support to those countries ready to work on [a] common agenda, but also reconsider support when countries depart from this track' (European Commission and HR/VP 2011a: 5).

Overall, in both its perception of the critical juncture and its preferences for ENP reform the EU – through the words the EP, its Commissioners and its HR/VP, and in its policy documents (Ashton 2012; Barroso 2011b; Malmström 2011) – was seeking a consonance between the causes and goals of the protestors (which it refers to mostly as being democracy and freedom) and what the EU had been trying to promote hitherto in the countries where the Arab uprisings took place. It thereby framed the Arab uprisings as a display of a yearning for more Europe. When we look beyond rhetoric towards the policy proposals, to the Commission and the EEAS, at the dawn of the reform episode the Arab uprisings were presented as revealing a deficiency in the previous implementation of EU policy, rather than a mistake in its design or its foundations. Table 2.2 summarises the policy preferences for reform of the European institutions, which are considered status quo players.

France

The French government was knocked off balance at the dawn of the uprisings as it had initially supported the Tunisian authorities. French Foreign Minister Michèle Alliot-Marie had even offered President Ben Ali of Tunisia material support and expertise with riot control in the early days of the uprisings in Tunisia (*Le Monde* 2011).

Because a stable economic environment in Northern Africa is important to France, given its various commercial interests in the region, it had always been reluctant to devote more than just words to the importance of democratising authoritarian states in the 'neighbourhood' (Schäfer 2011; Delgado 2011). As the Arab uprisings progressed, France shifted towards supporting the demonstrators. The uprisings were perceived by the French government as an opportunity to rally support to reinforce the southern dimension of the ENP, as well as to strengthen alternative policy frameworks. Alain Juppé, then Minister of Foreign Affairs, went so far as to call the Arab uprisings a 'tremendous opportunity' when speaking to the French Senate, requiring the West to respond 'without hesitation' (Juppé 2011c).

In its perception of the critical juncture, the French government explicitly linked the Arab uprisings to the necessity of ENP reform, and of fostering better synergies between the ENP and the objectives of the UfM. Juppé later spoke of a historical moment, a 'rendez-vous with history' in French and EU relations with the Southern neighbourhood (Juppé 2011c). France started to invest considerable time and energy putting itself forward as a regional leader, especially focusing its attention on the UfM. 'Who does not see the

Table 2.2 (How) should the ENP be modified?

Actor	Desired level(s)	Substance	Directionality
Germany	Meso	**Conditionality: stricter** - Limit funding where progress is not satisfactory - Make half of funding conditional **Amount of overall funding: stable, slight increase** Funding sources: no change **Funding focus: democracy, human rights** **Overall focus:** normative elements ENP, liberalisation, conditionality, no increased regional focus	0

France	Macro, meso, micro	**Conditionality: less strict**
		 - Rather greater differentiation/flexibility
		 Amount of overall funding: increase
		 - Improve offer towards the South
		 Funding sources: diversify, expand
		 - Increases resources available, draw on CFSP budget, reallocate development funding towards ENP
		 - Reinforce Mediterranean dimension ENP
		 - Possible use of EU structural funds, increase contribution maximum for regional fund
		 Funding focus: South
		 - Mediterranean dimension, better distribution towards south
		   - Civil society
		   - Political reform
		 Overall focus:
		 - Macro-strategy for Southern Mediterranean
		 - Amplify project-based UfM
			++

Table 2.2 (How) should the ENP be modified? (Continued)

Actor	Desired level(s)	Substance	Directionality
Spain	Macro, meso, micro	**Conditionality:** less strict – supports France - Rather greater differentiation/flexibility Amount of overall funding: increase - Improve offer towards the South **Funding sources:** diversify, expand – supports France - Increases resources available, draw on CFSP budget, reallocate development funding towards ENP - Reinforce Mediterranean dimension ENP - Possible use of EU structural funds, increase contribution maximum for regional fund **Funding focus:** South – supports France - Mediterranean dimension, better distribution towards South - Civil society - Political reform **Overall focus:** - Supports French priorities - Not outspoken until after ENP reform - Enhanced cooperation with Morocco and Tunisia - Focus on security, trade, migration	+

Table 2.2 (How) should the ENP be modified? (Continued)

Actor	Desired level(s)	Substance	Directionality
Italy	Mainly meso	Conditionality: not clear Amount of overall funding: increase - Economic growth, social development, possibly through a Mediterranean 'Marshall Plan', which would require significant resources Funding sources: not clear Funding focus: South **Overall focus:** South, irregular migration - accelerate work UfM - enhance cooperation/enhanced status for Southern Mediterranean states - support with refugee issues	+
European Commission/ EEAS	Macro	**Conditionality:** stricter (on paper) - Supposed novel, strategic approach: more for more (conditionality), democracy promotion at core of new approach. **Amount of overall funding:** increase committed yet an overall limited real increase for Arab uprisings countries (see **Error! Reference source not found.**) Funding sources: not outspoken **Funding focus:** stable, socio-economic **Overall focus:** presenting a new offer - New deal for all partners, even the one where there was no Arab uprising - 'more Europe, not less'	0

0= no deviation from status quo, 0/+= very little deviation from status quo, += deviation from status quo, += significant deviation from status quo pertinence of the Union for the Mediterranean to respond to the demands of the people?' Sarkozy told a group of French ambassadors. 'The moment has come to revive and rebuild it' (Sarkozy 2011). The French priority regarding the ENP was to adapt the instruments of the EU as rapidly as possible to the developments in the Arab uprisings.

In February 2011, along with Spain, Greece, Malta, Cyprus and Slovenia, France presented a non-paper on ENP reform, amongst other things calling for a 're-evaluation of the European offer to its Southern Partners' (Alliot-Marie et al. 2011: 2), an important step in the ENP reform process. In the non-paper, the countries suggest that several EU foreign policy instruments be modified in a 'macro-regional' strategy, similar to the Baltic Sea Strategy. By referring to the discrepancy in EU support per capita between Tunisia and Moldova, the letter implies that there should be a shift in funding from the east to the south. There was also debate surrounding the strengthening of the UfM, and on its relationship with the European institutions. In the non-paper, France and its partners intended to create strong links between the objectives of the EU and the objectives of the UfM (Alliot-Marie et al. 2011: 1–5), making it a change player, as summarised in Table 2.2.

Germany

Most analyses of Germany's role in the wake of the Arab uprisings focus on its decision to abstain on UN resolution 1973 on Libya, marginalising itself in the EU (Miskimmon 2012; Brockmeier 2013). Its decision was indeed criticised both domestically and abroad. But in the reform of the ENP, Germany clearly emerged as a key actor. This research classifies key actors as change players or status quo players in reform. I consider Germany to have been a status quo player, especially in comparison to other key actors.

Despite its relative activism and the reinvigorated German pursuit of bilateral partnerships with the Mediterranean countries in the wake of the Arab uprisings (Behr 2012c), its policy preferences for ENP reform consist of reiterations of the trade-oriented, normative dimensions of the ENP, preferring trade over aid and preferring the ENP to remain a rule-based policy of socio-economic integration between the EU and partner countries, as further detailed in the next section. Germany clearly put forward its own vision of the European policies following the Arab uprisings. German Chancellor Merkel stated there was a 'historic European obligation to stand by the people who are now on the streets of North Africa and parts of the Arab world for freedom and self-determination' (Merkel 2011). The German policy preferences regarding ENP reform diverged from the French position.

This is why, following the non-paper issued by the French (mentioned in the preceding subsection), German Foreign Minister Guido Westerwelle proposed an alternative set of policy propositions, rallying the support of various European countries for it. He proposed to apply greater democratic conditionality in the funding of the ENP, improve attention to human rights and the rule of law, and called for the further liberalisation of agricultural trade with the countries in the Mediterranean (Behr 2015: 42; Westerwelle 2011b). The Germans suggested a stricter application of conditionality, with up to half of the money to be allocated depending on reforms, and a limitation of budget support to countries that are not making enough progress.

The German propositions went against the proposal backed by France and Spain, which instead proposed a geographical distribution of resources, in response to the Arab uprisings (Behr 2012c). The German proposals underscore human rights and economic liberalisation. 'For the political awakenings [in the Arab region] to succeed, political developments and economic and social progress must go hand in hand', said Westerwelle in his speech to the German Bundestag (Westerwelle 2011a).

When France was in the process of leading the establishment of the UfM, Germany had acted as a veto-player, leading a group of countries that argued that the UfM – which was limited to southern nations – should involve the entire EU (Bicchi 2011: 7). 'It cannot be', Chancellor Merkel had stated earlier, 'that some countries establish a Mediterranean Union and fund this with money from EU coffers' (*EU Observer* 2007). Later, in 2011, it was agreed that France, Germany and Spain would contribute half of the UfM's funding, while the other half would be funded by the EU.

Overall, the German policy preferences reflect its intentions at the time of being a force behind the democratisation of the region – breaking with its former connivance with the region's autocrats. The German proposal underscores human rights and economic liberalisation. In direction, which as discussed in Chapter 1 is an important element of assessing policy change, the German proposals do not deviate significantly from the *status quo ex ante*. It opposed a redistribution of resources in the ENP and its proposals reflect a wish to reinforce the existing normative and socio-economic dimensions of the ENP, and apply an existing EU foreign policy instrument – conditionality – more strictly.

Spain

Spain's policy was long characterised by support for a strong and unified European policy towards the Mediterranean region, its ambition to further develop relations with Morocco and a general awareness of it being a border country in the Mediterranean (García and de Larramendi 2002; Gillespie

2000). This last point meant that, in practice, Spain cooperated closely with the authoritarian executives in North Africa, keeping the opposition parties largely at bay (Soler i Lecha 2012: 9). The uprisings took the Spanish government by surprise, calling into question its previous policies premised on authoritarian stability (Planet and Larramendi 2013: 125).

Although it had avoided manifest support for the Middle Eastern and North African (MENA) autocrats in the early days of the Arab uprisings, Spain was slow to react to them, much like France. The visits of President José Luis Rodríguez Zapatero and Foreign Minister Trinidad Jiménez, and their overt support for the transition processes in these countries, were an attempt to compensate for this (Echagüe 2011; *El Mundo* 2011). Zapatero promised limited funding in terms of credit lines and financial assistance to the electoral process in Tunisia (I. X. Legislatura 2011a: 5). After the presentation of the Partnership document in March 2011, the State Secretary for Foreign Affairs Yáñez-Barnuevo García stated that 'in the Government's view, such measures are only part of what Europe's response to the challenges posed by democratic revolutions in the Arab world should be. That the instruments and initial initiatives are reformed is not enough in order to address the historical challenges of an unprecedented magnitude we now face' (I. X. Legislatura 2011a: 6), suggesting Spain would push for further-reaching reforms.

Instead of becoming a leading player in the European reform process, however, Spain focused on an adaptation of current EU policies towards MENA countries. On paper, it supported the European reform process. One of its priorities was to *adapt* the existing instruments and initiatives within the framework of the ENP and the UfM (I. X. Legislatura 2011b; I. X. Legislatura 2011a; emphasis mine). Spain co-signed the French non-paper, and it supported the French policy preference for strengthening the southern dimension of the ENP, but none of its actual policy preferences deviate greatly from the *status quo ex ante*. As the Spanish State Secretary for Foreign Affairs García underlined (I. X. Legislatura 2011a: 6): 'we must emphasise that the reforms now under way in the Euro-Mediterranean Partnership with the aim of supporting democratic transitions in the Arab world do not imply a change of objective but rather a reinforcement of the instruments that we have at our disposal'.

In all, after an ambivalent initial reaction Spain was a moderate change player in the ENP reform process, for which the critical juncture was an opportunity to boost support for the southern Mediterranean while increasing its own relevance in the European institutions (Echagüe 2011). But most of its support was on paper. It aligned with France in the latter's reform efforts as it was one of the most important co-signers of the French non-paper, but as Echagüe wrote (2011: 2), Spain's response to the Arab uprisings was reactive and timid: 'the fact remains that Spain stood on the side-lines until the autocrats were overthrown and only then became a cheerleader for the process of reform'.

Italy

Italy's geostrategic interests in North Africa and President Silvio Berlusconi's personal relationship with some of the Arab leaders in North Africa meant that in the very early days of the Arab uprisings Italy was reluctant to advocate a change to the European approach. This altered as the influx of refugees crossing the Mediterranean towards Italy caused that country to pursue a 'European' approach, hoping to rally European support to deal with the refugee flows. The impact of these events will be described in more detail in the next section of this chapter.

The Italian Parliament stated in a report on the ENP (that was only published in 2012) that it 'is necessary that [Italy] will in time position itself in front of a revolution that is about to profoundly change relations with the Arab world' (Commisione I. I. I. Affari Esteri e Comunitari 2012: 5). What characterises Italy's perception of the critical juncture, as well as its policy preferences in ENP reform, is its focus on the migration and security aspects of the Arab uprisings. 'Europe must act quickly', stated Italian Minister of Foreign Affairs Franco Frattini early in the crisis, 'or this "arc of crisis" will lead to more illegal immigration, terrorism and Islamic radicalism' (Frattini 2011). This focus on migration and security was prompted by the sudden rapid increase in refugee flows, which forced Italy to seek EU support to deal with the problem early on in the process that led to ENP reform. Italy made a formal request for support to the EU regarding the 'extraordinary migratory situation in the Pelagic Islands' (Frontex 2011). Although it did receive support in the form of a Frontex mission a mere few days later, it called for more 'European solidarity' to tackle the influx of migrants from North Africa, and in various ways tried to strong-arm the EU into providing additional backing.

Throughout the spring of 2011, the influx of refugees dominated the Italian agenda. The Italian Parliament made an inventory of where the ENP was falling short, concluding that it mainly lacked a multilateral dimension, having long suffered from 'reappropriation by member states'. Foreign Minister Frattini outlined the Italian priorities for reform, as summarised in Table 2.2 (Frattini 2011). To the Italian government, the critical juncture presented both a threat and an opportunity: a threat in the sense that Italy perceived the Arab uprisings as a crisis to its internal security, fuelled by the refugees arriving on its shores. Yet at the same time, the subsequent window for reforming the ENP opened by the critical juncture enabled Italy to put the issue of curbing illegal migration prominently on the reform agenda and to amplify the European resources available to combat the problems Italy was encountering. 'The current crisis', wrote the Italian Minister of Foreign Affairs in February 2011, 'can be a stimulus to redirect the UfM towards the concrete tasks announced when it was launched' (Frattini 2011).

Overall, Italy's policy propositions deviate from the status quo in the sense that they would require a significant amplification of European resources, as well as a reconsideration of the role of the UfM – converging with France and its allies in the February 2011 non-paper. But aside from the statements by Frattini, Italy did not comment overtly on the direction a reformed ENP should take, and it was not part of the group that proposed a non-paper on ENP reform, led by France. Its focus on dealing with the refugee flows significantly constrained its willingness and ability to take part in ENP reform. Italy had declared a state of emergency after receiving 51,811 refugees in nine months, with Frattini calling the refugee flows a 'biblical exodus' (*Der Spiegel* 2011; Maccanico 2011).

To recapitulate, the key actors in this critical juncture were eager to remain active in the political landscape after the Arab uprisings, while searching to strike a balance between the demands of the Arab revolutionaries and their own perceived interests. Yet the actors' attitudes to ENP reform differ, both in perceptions of the critical juncture and in policy preferences for ENP reform. They all declared a desire to reform either the macro-ambitions of the ENP, the policy objectives or the policy tools.

The non-paper propagated by France, followed by Spain and a host of other countries, which called for a pivot towards the south, increased funding, a more flexible ENP, greater differentiation and a strengthened UfM, was an important step in the reform process. Germany countered the non-paper with a range of policy propositions of its own, putting human rights and economic liberalisation at the core of its plans, pursued through more stringent conditionality. Table 2.2 summarises how key actors believed the ENP should be modified.

Temporal contingency: the impact of events

In this section, I aim to relate the temporal developments to the changes made to the ENP during the 2011 reform round, in order to demonstrate that the policy changes that followed the process of reform were in part shaped by the particular temporal context. Table 2.3 summarises how temporal developments impacted the ENP reform process.

Table 2.3 Summary of impact: temporal contingency

Temporal development	Impact on foreign policy change
Structural:	
- Decade-long cooperation with authoritarian regimes	- Apologetic attitude among actors, questioning rationale 'old' ENP
- Securitisation of the Mediterranean region	- Rhetorical innovations and variations on ENP to demonstrate commitment to
- The historical development of the ENP from the Enlargement process	transitions and reform ('deep democracy', 'more for more', '3M's)
	- Continued linking of migration and security, mobility and security
	- Continued focus on socio-economic development
Conjunctural:	
Financial and economic crisis	Reduced political bandwidth, increased refugee flows
Liminal:	
- Rapid spread of the Arab uprisings	- Increased salience of the issue of Euro-Mediterranean relations, and of the ENP
- Influx of refugees	- Increased urgency for ENP reform

In the very early days of the Arab uprisings, both the EU-level and the member state actors were wary to act or speak immediately in favour of a particular changed policy course. This caution was partially rooted in uncertainty about how the rapidly changing situation would play out, and partially in a long tradition of cooperation with the authoritarian regimes in the countries where uprisings took place, with which many EU member states had historically fostered close ties, both politically and economically. As late as mid-January 2011 the Mediterranean member states blocked the EU Council from taking a tougher stance against Tunisia (*EU Observer* 2011). Around the same time, French President Sarkozy defended Tunisian President Ben Ali and the co-President of the UfM Hosni Mubarak. Frédéric Mitterrand, culture minister in Sarkozy's government, had stated Tunisia was not an 'unequivocal dictatorship' while Minister of Agriculture Bruno Le Maire said that Ben Ali had done a lot for his country, which 'is not a country that has known any real difficulties' (Chrisafis 2011; *EU Observer* 2011). French Foreign Minister Alliot-Marie even offered Ben Ali material support and French expertise with riot control (*Le Monde* 2011). German Chancellor Merkel herself had earlier declared that a transition in Egypt led by Mubarak was possible, a suggestion that had to be walked back after his downfall (Schumacher 2015b: 561). Italian Prime Minister Berlusconi, finally, went as far as stating he hoped 'that in Egypt there can be a transition toward a more democratic system without a break from President Mubarak, who in the West, above all in the United States, is considered the wisest of men and a precise reference point' (Reuters 2011).

Four months before the revised ENP was presented, the EU thus found itself in a situation in which 1) the ENP was on a path-dependent trajectory, not envisaged as changing any time soon; and 2) the key actors were generally reluctant to speak out against the incumbent authoritarian regimes, both member state actors and EU actors. Several turning points served to disrupt this path-dependent trajectory.

Spread of the uprisings to Egypt

Over the six weeks between mid-January and late February (when reform of the ENP was announced) there were several political developments. The most important was the rapid spillover effect of the demonstrations and the subsequent fall of Ben Ali in Tunisia. After he fled to Saudi Arabia on 14 January 2011, within sixteen days protests erupted in three different countries: Egypt, Yemen and Sudan.

Overall, in my interviews EU officials working on the southern Mediterranean remarked both on this rapid spread of the Arab uprisings, and the fact that they arrived in Egypt so quickly and so profoundly. For the EU, hitherto reluctant, these developments constituted a turning point. 'We basically had a big event in North Africa', states one senior interviewee closely working on the issue, 'and the political schemes which had the support of the EU in Tunisia, in Libya and in Egypt were suddenly put into question with these uprisings, and … there was a simply the willingness, if I may say simply, to be on the right side of history' (Interview PO22).

Egypt is described by interviewed officials as a 'key country in the region' (Interview PO15) and 'a cornerstone in the Mediterranean and of the Arab world' (Interview PO19). It was when Mubarak's regime became increasingly untenable and Europe's credibility and influence in the region had reached a low point, that the EU and the member states agreed that urgent reform was necessary: 'everyone [agreed] it is important that Egypt succeeds to have a spillover effect in the region' (Interview PO15). Another senior interviewee argued that 'the situation in the region being as unstable as it [was], we could not [let Egypt] fall either into political or economic disarray … Overall, the common view of the EU28 was that Egypt was too big to fail', and that a change of course was necessary (Interview PO19).

The rapid spread of the Arab uprisings and the developments in Egypt greatly increased the sense that ENP reform was urgent, as becomes clear from the flurry of action in response to events. The 4 February 2011 Council Conclusions invited the HR/VP to link the ENP and the UfM to the transformation processes in the region (European Council 2011b: 15). Three days after Mubarak resigned in Egypt, on 14 February, a non-paper was put out on European action in the southern 'neighbourhood' by France, Spain, Malta, Slovenia and Cyprus (Alliot-Marie et al. 2011). Little over a week later, Germany presented an alternative plethora of proposals and circulated a 'room document' at a Foreign Affairs Council meeting where the French-led non-paper had been due to be discussed. Germany was wary of tilting the ENP balance towards the south and favoured instead an approach of 'limited and conditional funding, and more trade', contrasting with the general approach of southern member states who wished more funding for the south, while remaining wary of opening up agricultural markets (Ratka 2012: 61). It also implied – countering the French-led non-paper – that the Mediterranean dimension should be reinforced within the existing budget (Westerwelle 2011b; Behr 2015: 42; Ratka 2012). Two days after the German room document, on 23 February 2011, Ashton announced that a 'fundamental review of the European Neighbourhood Policy' was needed (Ashton 2011d). Meanwhile the President of the Council declared in a video message that the EU 'want[s] to turn this Arab Spring into a true new beginning' (Van Rompuy 2011b) and a day later argued in the Council that the EU should rapidly adapt its instruments in light of the developments in the southern 'neighbourhood' (Van Rompuy 2011a).

Influx of refugees crossing the Mediterranean

Secondly, the rapid influx of refugees fleeing the unrest and political instability across North Africa and the Maghreb further stimulated the urgency for ENP reform. Many refugees fled Libya where the uprisings had evolved into a deadly conflict between Muammar Qhadafi and rebel militia during the last two weeks of February. The developments in the Mediterranean encouraged traffickers operating in Tunisia to use routes towards Calabria and Apulia, increasing the burden on Italy. A hitherto-record number of 58,000 refugees arrived in Europe across the Mediterranean in 2011, of which the vast majority (97%) arrived in Italy (UNHCR 2012). In the period between January and August 2011 more than 51,811 refugees arrived in Italy, prompting it to declare a state of emergency (Maccanico 2011).

The discourse surrounding the issue hardened in Europe. Italian Foreign Minister Frattini went so far as to call it a 'biblical exodus' (*Der Spiegel* 2011). The sudden influx of refugees prompted a very quick response by the EU: within a matter of days, it launched a Frontex mission. This greatly increased the salience of the Arab uprisings to EU member states as its consequences were now also felt on European soil. The sudden rise in the number of refugees had two concrete consequences for ENP reform. First, it encouraged member states who had hitherto remained reticent to speak out against the authoritarian regimes in MENA states, and for European reform; Italy was one (Frattini 2011).[2] The influx of refugees thus mobilised actors in supporting EU-wide action. Second, it encouraged further securitising of the issue of EU relations with the Mediterranean. Worries over refugee flows towards the EU, and the burden this would put on some member states, quickly made their way onto the policy agenda. As we shall see, in the revised ENP presented a few months later mobility, border management and migration were crucial elements.

Policy output

The previous sections have described how, in the wake of the Arab uprisings, there was what Hall would refer to as a breakdown of the old paradigm. The old rationale for the ENP was seriously questioned, as leaders across the EU drew parallels between the Arab uprisings and 1989, signalling a need for reform in various speeches and statements (Ashton 2011a, 2011b, 2011c; Barroso 2011a, 2011b; Juppé 2011a). One interviewee told me there was 'a sense of guiltiness' (Interview PO20) and the EU stated it no longer wished to be 'a passive spectator' (European Comission and HR/VP 2011b: 2). Sweeping changes to the ENP were announced, explicitly in the statements of actors at the European level (Ashton 2011a, 2011b, 2011c; Barroso 2011a, 2011b; Füle 2011). The European Union insisted it was to 'take the clear and strategic option of supporting the quest for the principles and values that it cherishes' (European Comission and HR/VP 2011b). The HR/VP stated that the EU's response should be 'built on the need to acknowledge past mistakes and listen without imposing' (Ashton 2011a).

These statements signalling a break with the past reflect Hall's description of paradigm change as occurring when policymakers reassess not just the goals of the existing policy, or the instruments used to attain these goals, but rather the very nature of the problem that these policy goals are meant to address (Hall 1993: 279). Indeed, the EU's policy response to the Arab uprisings overall shows it was eager to draw on an array of policy instruments, including the appointment of a Special Representative (EUSR) for the southern Mediterranean (European Council 2011a), the (*ex post*) imposition of sanctions and asset freezes, and (as we have studied in this chapter) a revision of the ENP that was presented as a new response to the developments in the 'neighbourhood'.

Table 2.4 Summary of changes to the ENP after the 2011 reform round

	Policy level		
	Macro	Meso	Micro
Policy goals	Abstract policy aims - Democracy promotion: 'Deep democracy' (0) - Inclusive economic development (0) - Support for democratic transitions (+) - Strengthen the two regional dimensions of the ENP (0/+)	Policy objectives - Supporting socio-economic development (0) - Integrating partners in global market (0) - Intensification of political and security cooperation (+) - Political reform: establishing or reforming efficient institutions (0) - Strengthen civil society (0) - Reinforce basic laws and human rights, good governance, reform of judiciary, combat corruption (0) - Border security (0/+)	Policy targets - extend mandate of EBRD (+) - border controls at expense of mobility (0) - migration management (0/+) - conflict management (0) - enhanced sectoral cooperation, notably rural development (+)
Policy means	Policy implementation preferences - Money – increased financial incentives (0/+) - Mobility – the prospect of mobility partnerships allowing easing of some visa restrictions (0) - Markets – greater access to European markets (0)	Policy tools - 'More for more'; funding conditional on progress (0) - Market liberalisation (0) - Negative conditionality ('less for less') (+) - Conditional financial and technical assistance (0) - Mobility partnerships (0) - Visa liberalisation (0)	Policy tool calibrations - Clearer benchmarks to mark progress (+) - SPRING program (0/+) - Civil Society Facility (0/+) - European Endowment for democracy (+) - Encouraging member states to increase EIB lending (+) - €1.2 billion additional aid and investment 2011-13 budget (0/+)

0= no deviation from status quo, 0/+= very little deviation from status quo, += deviation from status quo

Table 2.4 shows, however, that barring the various declarations signalling the need for a reformed European approach, and a changed European paradigm to 'rise to the historical challenges in [its] neighbourhood' (European Commission and HR/VP 2011a: 1), substantive policy changes to the policy settings, method or goals are virtually absent. The 'new response' offers minor adjustments, and some revised policy instruments, while the overarching policy paradigm as well as the bulk of the meso-level policy objectives remain the same (Schumacher 2015a: 389–90).

Some first-order and second-order changes did emerge. Examples are new policy instruments such as the SPRING programme and the Civil Society Facility, or additional funding, although their principles and their underlying logic are far from new. 'Despite assertions of a paradigmatic shift in the EU's approach to democracy', argue Teti, Thompson and Noble (2013: 61), 'the conceptual structure of these documents maintains unaltered the substantively liberal model for both development and democratisation.' The ambitions for policy reform were directed mainly at the macro level of policy and were mainly symbolic in nature, using concepts like 'deep democracy' as a purportedly new approach (Ashton 2011c). At the meso level, 'more for more' was presented as a change of tack by the EU, which would put norm diffusion back at the forefront of the ENP. But the underpinnings of these revised approaches do not break significantly with the *status quo ex ante*, and in the case of 'more for more' and 'deep democracy' are little more than cosmetic rebranding.

This case study has thus shown that there might be room for an additional form of change, which might be dubbed rhetorical change (Boin, t'Hart, and McConnell, 2009) or 'symbolic change'. As many interviewees told me, the EU is not made to deal with the type of crisis the Arab uprisings represented. It moves slowly and is generally inertia-prone. Symbolic measures that signal its support are thus helpful because they show that the EU is 'doing something' (Interviews PO19, PO20). Because symbolic changes are not part of traditional accounts of policy change, Chapter 4 dives deeper into how we might conceptualise these forms of policy change that fall outside the traditional typology.

Conclusion

This chapter started off by outlining various political institutional initiatives regarding EU relations with the Mediterranean. It argued that the way in which the policies towards the southern 'neighbourhood' are organised bears testimony to the 'plastic' nature of institutions, which constrain key actors and their policies yet at the same time allow actors to mould them to their purposes. They have had an enabling role because the Commission's historical lack of autonomy in relations with neighbouring countries before 2004, followed by the later technocratic and trade-oriented nature of the ENP, left member state actors room to pursue political institutional initiatives, both bilaterally and multilaterally. The various overlapping institutional initiatives – i.e. the EMP, the ENP and the UfM – show this room for policy entrepreneurship. At the same time, the simultaneous existence of these sometimes overlapping institutions has constrained actors, leaving these institutions underfunded and unfocused.

Moreover, this chapter demonstrated the plasticity of institutions in the 'neighbourhood', underlining the way in which the French government has tried to mould the European institutions focused on the southern 'neighbour-hood' towards its 'own' UfM initiative for the region, bringing the UfM onto the ENP reform agenda time and again. It used the 'elastic stretch' of the ENP to advance its own agenda. It formed a coalition with five other member states in the wake of the Arab uprisings around a non-paper in which the UfM was put forward as a crucial element of the EU's policies towards the south. While France may not have been successful in reviving the UfM, its attempts demonstrate the malleability of the institutions governing European policies in the 'neighbourhood'.

The European actors framed the Arab uprisings as an opportunity to reiterate existing ambitions. The Commission built the narrative that what was needed as a response to the Arab uprisings was more of the same goals, better executed and better implemented. If anything, the Commission seems to have been strengthened in its belief that it had been doing the right things, but simply not enough of them. The Arab uprisings, in this view, exposed a deficiency in the previous implementation of EU policy, rather than a mistake in its design or its foundations. In expressing this view, the policy preferences of the Commission and the EEAS did not substantially deviate from the *status quo ex ante*.

The key member states, meanwhile, disagreed over the course of action to take. At the member state level they diverged over both perceptions of the critical juncture and policy preferences for ENP reform.

When the Arab uprisings occurred, the EU thus was both too committed to its policy approach to the 'neighbourhood' to step away from it, and too greatly exposed to ignore the developments. As a result, small policy adjustments to the policy goals and tools were combined with grand symbolic gestures. Both the structural impact of the temporal context and the liminal impact of the temporal context played a role in producing this outcome. Historically, all key actors had long fostered close relationships with the authoritarian regimes that were now being toppled. Too often, policy deals had been made in exchange for access to energy resources, or for cooperation on high-stakes issues, such as combating irregular migration, fighting Islamist terrorism or managing refugee flows. When it all came down in the early months of 2011, symbolic pledges and a new lexicon focused on 'deep democracy' were an attempt to deal with this historical connivance, this supposed lack of legitimacy when it came to the demands and desires of the revolutionaries. These demands thus were rephrased as a call for more Europe, more 'European-style' democratic development, allowing the EU to propose the response: deep democracy and 'more for more'.

No less important here was the decade-long commitment to socio-economic development and market liberalisation as a means to achieve political freedom and democracy, which was used in the 'neighbourhood' much as it had been in the enlargement process. The Commission had managed the ENP, which had distinctly political goals, in a technocratic way, using markets and trade as levers, just as it had managed the enlargement process earlier. But these structural and long-term historical developments interacted with 'liminal' events, happenings that perforated the structure of 'neighbourhood' relations, if only temporarily. Over the six weeks between mid-January and late February 2011 (when reform to the ENP was announced) there were several political developments. The rapid spread of the Arab uprisings; the fact that they reached Egypt, a crucial country for Europe and in the region, and the influx of vast numbers of refugees fleeing the uprisings greatly and quickly increased the salience both of the ENP and of the region, and the urgency of ENP reform.

Notes

1   The powers of the European Parliament are legislative, budgetary and advisory. It needs to provide consent for EU enlargement, agreements with third countries, and opinions on Commission proposals (the consultation procedure). On foreign policy, the Parliament is to be kept informed by the HR/VP.
2   Helpfully, at the same time, increased access to supplies from Russia and Norway lessened Italy's immediate dependence on North African energy supply (President of the Council of Ministers Italy 2011: 42).

3

Foreign policy change after the Ukraine crisis
Changing the Neighbourhood Policy
once more

The critical juncture in Europe's relations with its Eastern neighbours commenced ten days before the Vilnius Summit of November 2013,[1] where Ukraine was about to sign an Association Agreement (AA) and a Deep and Comprehensive Free Trade Agreement (DCFTA) with the EU. Both are core parts of the European Neighbourhood Policy and provide an agenda and priorities for political and economic reforms.

Until August of that year, it appeared as if the Ukrainian government led by President Viktor Yanukovych was moving steadily towards the signing of both documents, but mounting structural problems were set to collide in a Ukrainian domestic context characterised by severe financial and economic trouble. In November 2013, Yanukovych decided to postpone signing the AA – purportedly in order to leverage Russian support, eventually received in the form of a bail-out in December – but also under severe Russian pressure to not sign (Freedman 2014: 19). Demonstrations and rallies followed, by the many Ukrainians who supported a landmark EU deal over closer ties with Moscow and who regularly clashed with pro-Russia demonstrators.

The Ukrainian refusal to sign the agreements exacerbated an already unstable chapter in EU relations. The political and military crisis which unfolded after the Vilnius Summit was the culmination of a series of events and developments that had been looming under the surface for over a decade (Cadier 2014; MacFarlane and Menon 2014; Sakwa 2014). Within a few months the country descended into a full-scale geopolitical crisis, with the Russian military supporting the insurgency in eastern Ukraine and the Crimea (R. Allison 2014). At the end of February 2014, President Yanukovych fled the country as the Ukrainian parliament voted to remove him from office. Around the same time pro-Russian gunmen seized buildings in Simferopol, the capital of the Crimea. On 16 March 2014, an overwhelming majority of Crimean voters supported joining Russia in an illegal referendum regarding the future status of the territory. Despite challenges to the legality of the referendum (R. Allison 2014), this ballot was followed by the Russian annexation of the peninsula, widely considered a fundamental breach of international law, the Helsinki Act of 1975 and the terms of the 1994 Budapest Memorandum (Paul 2015). The variety of means that Russia had deployed to put pressure on Ukraine to not sign the Agreement, followed by its role in the escalation of the military conflict, called into question member state perceptions of EU–Russia relations (Nitoiu 2016).

This chapter focuses on change to EU foreign policy that took place in the wake of the Ukraine crisis, zooming in on how the EU reformed the ENP. Like Chapter 2, it starts with an account of how the ENP institutions have historically faced eastwards. I shall explain that the main institutional 'effects' of the ENP and its historical development were threefold. First, the ENP has long focused on trade and socio-economic development. Second, the ENP towards the east has been quite technocratic and focused on processes (of legal approximation and meeting benchmarks). These two effects are a direct consequence of the ENP's development from the enlargement process. Finally, the way in which the ENP historically has been governed has made the institutions quite plastic – able to both shape and be shaped by the decision-making process.

In this particular case this plasticity meant that actors derived decision-making powers and significant leeway from the ENP institutions that enabled them to subsequently steer and guide the neighbourhood policies by taking a pro-active approach. The Eastern Partnership (EaP) bears testimony to this room for policy entrepreneurship. In this particular crisis, moreover, the technocratic and trade-oriented approach of the European institutions combined with this institutional plasticity meant that Germany, France and Poland, rather than the European institutions, quickly took the leadership in resolving the political crisis in the 'neighbourhood', dealing with the political dimension of the Ukraine crisis in meetings that later laid the groundwork for reform of the ENP.

This chapter subsequently describes how temporal contingencies fed into the changes made to the ENP in 2015. It explains how, at the dawn of the Ukraine crisis, neither the European actors nor Germany were convinced that this crisis was one that necessitated ENP reform. But four months after the Vilnius summit, the first ENP reform proposal was made by Germany, France and Poland, followed by the presidency passing to Jean-Claude Juncker, eager to reform the ENP.

To explain how this occurred, the chapter details how several political developments served as important turning points in the reform episode. It identifies as crucial events first the failed Vilnius summit and the subsequent demonstrations that were violently repressed, which mainly served to greatly increase the salience of the neighbourhood region and of the ENP. Second, the deal with and flight of Viktor Yanukovych formed an important turning point in the sense that it marked the re-emergence of the Weimar Triangle taking the leadership in a crisis, which later turned out to be a stepping stone for ENP reform. Third, the annexation of the Crimea constituted a crucial turning point, as it was around this time that the European institutions moved from being status quo players regarding the ENP towards becoming change players (albeit moderate).

The actions of Russia in Ukraine, and the breaching of international law, equally served to make the neighbourhood policy even more salient and ENP reform more urgent. This was exacerbated by the tragedy of the shooting-down of flight MH17 over eastern Ukraine in the summer of 2014. It compounded the changing stance of the key actors, who thenceforth were all eager to reform the ENP.

This chapter describes how these temporal contingencies fed into the policy changes made to the ENP, first in the forging of a shared declaratory commitment to a strategic overhaul of the policy, in order to better deal with the uncertainties stemming from the region. It finally concludes with a discussion of the output of the policy change process.

Institutional set-up and historically created arrangements

Since the collapse of the Soviet Union a dense net of institutional and legal frameworks has been cast over the post-Soviet space. Unlike the EU's southern 'neighbourhood', this includes integration initiatives offered by an actor other than the EU: Russia's strong commitment to institutionalising its relations with the post-Soviet space has led to a variety of integration efforts in the region in parallel to the EU's efforts (Dragneva and Wolczuk 2013).

While a large number of these initiatives have been unsuccessful, they have proved to be a challenge for the Union. EU policies are conditional and require significant political efforts from partner countries. The higher the political and economic costs of approximation with the EU, the greater the temptation to engage with a different power that does not subject its aid to such conditions, especially in a strenuous political climate. Its use of conditionality differs greatly from that of the EU, but Russian support to Ukraine is not unconditional. The crucial difference, however, is that while the EaP offers a catch-all approach, Russia is keen to exploit the particular vulnerabilities of the countries to which it offers support.[2]

EU relations with its eastern neighbours have been covered by the ENP since 2004, as discussed in Chapter 2. The EaP, which falls under the umbrella of the ENP, was launched in 2009, aimed at revamping EU relations with the region (Korosteleva 2012: 7). One of the aims of the EaP was to address a number of problems that emerged from the ENP, which was said to be too much 'one-size-fits-all' and to not address the idiosyncratic features of the different ENP countries, particularly those towards the east. The EaP was concluded with the EU's neighbours Ukraine, Moldova, Georgia, Belarus, Armenia and Azerbaijan in Prague in May 2009. The goals, instruments and institutional operating procedures of the EaP remain those of the ENP.

The state of European relations with its eastern neighbours at the dawn of this critical juncture was thus one of overlapping institutional initiatives and frameworks that were managed by the European Commission and the EEAS. These institutional frameworks mainly aimed both at establishing a free trade area and at legal approximation between the EU and its eastern partners. This trade-oriented relationship with the eastern 'neighbourhood' created a conviction that the EU's project, if not beneficial, would be at least neutral to Russia. As a senior official I interviewed (Interview PO5) expressed this:

> The EU did not appreciate that Ukraine joining the AA and DCFTA had become an existential threat for the Russian elite, as it thought that Russia had nothing to lose by Ukraine signing the DCFTA. Yes, Sergei Glazyev [a Russian advisor to Putin] was getting increasingly active in Ukraine in the months leading up to the AA, making bogus statements about the negative impact of the DCFTA on Ukraine … but no one would take them seriously.

How plastic is the policy area?

In Chapter 2 I detailed the institutional effects of the ENP and its historical development. Its focus on trade and socio-economic development, and on processes, are a direct consequence of the ENP's development from the enlargement process; and the way in which the ENP historically has been governed has made the institutions quite 'plastic'. They both structure and shape the political world *and* are shaped, re-designed and re-moulded by capable actors.

We have seen active policy entrepreneurship by member states in European policies in the 'neighbourhood' (Bicchi 2002; Copsey and Pomorska 2014). Poland, along with Germany, has long advocated a differentiation between the 'European' neighbours to the east and the states in the Mediterranean. It has tried to convince its European partners that countries like Ukraine and Moldova would be best served by being offered the prospect of EU membership. Because this track has not succeeded the Polish government has continued to invest its efforts in further deepening the EU's institutional framework *vis-à-vis* the east (Marcinkowska 2016). The EaP was a consequence of a joint initiative by Poland and Sweden in 2008. It followed the launch of the UfM in 2008 and was intended as a highly ambitious partnership with particular ENP countries to the east, aimed at revamping EU relations with the region (Korosteleva 2012: 7).

Interviews I have carried out confirm that, especially before the Ukraine crisis, leadership of the eastern relations of the EU was delegated to Germany, Poland and occasionally Sweden; according to one senior interviewee, '[Poland may have] wanted a bolder approach towards Russia, and pushed for the Eastern Partnership, but [overall] the situation was kept low-level and in the hands of these few member states along with the Commission. The situation was stable and everybody was happy' (Interview PO4). This room for policy entrepreneurship and policy leadership by a member state willing to take the lead is an indication of the plasticity of the ENP. In this particular crisis, moreover, the approach of the European institutions combined with this institutional plasticity meant that Germany, France and Poland quickly took the lead in resolving the political crisis in the 'neighbourhood', rather than the European institutions, as I shall describe below.

The critical juncture

As mentioned earlier, in November 2013 it had appeared as though the Yanukovych government was moving steadily towards signing the agreements with the European Union. Stewart (2014: 25) argues that this was because the AA could be used by the Ukrainian leadership as a means to increase the country's leverage and bargaining power with Putin, showing it disposed of alternatives to Eurasian integration. Mykola Azarov, then prime minister of Ukraine, stressed in January 2013 that the signature of the Agreement was one of the priorities of his government, and that he was personally coordinating the implementation of the EU–Ukraine Association Agenda (Delegation of the European Union to Ukraine 2014).

The Russian Ministry of Foreign Affairs (2014b) had earlier detailed how in 2013 Russia put Ukraine under pressure before the Vilnius summit, as the Russian leadership had 'explained' to Ukraine that further EU–Ukraine association, in the form of the AA, would have 'economic consequences'. The extent of these consequences was not specified but it is clear that Russia tied its material assistance directly to Ukraine's choice whether to sign it. Sergei Glazyev indicated as much in Yalta in September 2013 when he said that Ukrainian authorities would make a default by Ukraine inevitable, and that if Ukraine were to sign an AA with the EU Russia would not extend any help: 'signing this treaty will lead to political and social unrest ... The living standard will decline dramatically ... there will be chaos' (*The Guardian* 2013b).

President Yanukovych accordingly decided to forgo signing the Agreement with the EU in Vilnius. Media reported the EU was 'stunned' by this course of events (*The Guardian* 2013a; Euractiv 2013). Pierre Vimont, Executive Secretary at the EEAS, later stated that the EU 'never really had any clear warning, on behalf of the Russians, that this [Agreement] was unacceptable to them, for many years' (House of Lords 2015: 54). Demonstrations, rallies and counter-protests followed, which turned increasingly violent. Within a few months the country descended into a full-scale military and political crisis, with the Russian military manoeuvring on its borders, supporting insurgency in eastern Ukraine.

The illegal referendum and the subsequent annexation of the Crimea in March 2014 came as a shock to many scholars and decision-makers alike. It was the first time since the Second World War that a country in Europe had seized the territory of another European country. But the Ukraine crisis presented a critical juncture not just for EU–Russia relations, but also for the ENP in particular. Although it was not the underlying cause of the Ukraine crisis, the ENP had been a proximate cause of the events that unfolded from late November 2013 onwards. Russia had arguably attempted to frustrate the EU's efforts to deepen its relationship with Ukraine through the ENP and the EaP long before the Vilnius Summit took place (Casier, Korosteleva and Whitman 2014: 4). The Ukraine crisis as it occurred was not the unique reason for reforming the ENP in 2015, as it compounded the effects of a variety of other crises, but the ENP reform was without a doubt in part a response to the Ukraine crisis. As HR/VP Federica Mogherini stated in a joint speech with Commissioner Johannes Hahn (European Commission 2015d): 'we need to review our policy, our way of working, our partnership with the countries of our region … In particular because as our region is in flames, both to the east and south, we have to use all the potential of our bilateral relations with partners in the region to have an effective impact on our region.' At this press conference, Mogherini was asked whether the neighbourhood policy had often been naïve and whether Brussels had underestimated the Russian response to Ukraine's association with the EU. In reply, she offered a 'timid *mea culpa*', saying that while she did not want to be over-critical, 'the new Commission could "clearly see the negative limits" of the policy so far' (Euractiv 2015d).

Yet it was only in late March/early April 2014 that actors at the European and at the member state level connected the Ukraine crisis to the need to reform the ENP. As the crisis unfolded in 2014, criticism of the EU's 'neighbourhood' strategy was on the rise, ushering in a temporary loosening of the constraints of structure. In February 2015, the UK House of Lords accused the EU and the UK of a 'catastrophic misreading' of the Ukraine crisis in an extensive report on the crisis and EU–Russia relations (House of Lords 2015). The EU's supposed misunderstanding of Russia's intentions in Ukraine, as well as the Union's half-hearted technical propositions to engage with a struggling partner, had allegedly sowed the seeds of the current crisis. Other EU countries similarly concluded that they had lacked intelligence capabilities, and simply did not have enough Russia experts, a feature plaguing many European countries in the post-Cold War era. Media and experts outlined how the EU had supposedly failed to fully appreciate Russia's increasing desire to shrug off the humiliation of the 1990s and understood insufficiently how it increasingly conflated the EU's integration proposals for the region with NATO expansion and, more broadly, Western expansionism (*Der Spiegel* 2013b; House of Lords 2015; MacFarlane and Menon 2014; Sakwa 2007).

Partially as a response to increasing calls for a more forward-looking and strategic approach towards the 'neighbourhood', the EU initiated a review of the ENP. The role of agency in the shaping of the ENP was heightened: the goal of the EU was to 'consult as widely as possible both with partners in the neighbouring countries and with stakeholders across the EU' (European Commission and High Representative for Foreign Affairs and Security Policy 2015a: 10). The 2015 review was meant not only to re-examine tools and instruments, but to review the very foundations on which the ENP was built. It started with a consultation process led by the Commission and the EEAS, which was open to input from civil society. The consultation process led to 250 responses from EU institutions, member states, non-governmental organisations (NGOs), think tanks, partner countries, agencies of the United Nations (UN) and other partners (European Commission and High Representative for Foreign Affairs and Security Policy 2015b).

Key actors

Germany, France and Poland emerged as the key actors from the very beginning of the ENP reform episode under scrutiny. This is due primarily to Germany's and Poland's historical commitment to the eastern neighbourhood, as well as the fact that the Ukraine crisis was not just an ENP crisis, but a full-blown geopolitical crisis on European borders, resolution of which was not left to the European institutions, but to the countries of the Weimar Triangle: Germany, France and Poland. Initially established in August 1991, the Weimar Triangle had been a symbol of reconciliation between its three members after the fall of the Berlin Wall. It provided for annual consultations on European policy. Mounting disagreements over the decade before the crisis however – over the war in Iraq, the Treaty of Lisbon and bilateral disputes among the three countries – had planted discord, until the events in Ukraine ignited the Triangle's temporary revival in 2014 (Bendiek 2008; Koopmann 2016). Although some argue their joint appearance at the foreign ministers' meeting in Kiev in February 2014 'had the appearance of being an ad-hoc event without substantial strategic thought' (Koopmann 2016: 11) in the early days of the critical juncture the Triangle temporarily re-emerged as the crisis manager in the conflict.

Because the Triangle countries took the lead in resolving the political and military conflict, they repeatedly met 'minilaterally'.[3] From these meetings resulted the first detailed proposal to reform the ENP on 1 April 2014 (Foreign ministers of the Weimar Triangle 2014) one day after the leaders of the three countries had met to discuss the situation in Ukraine. They were the first to propose ENP reform at this juncture and left an important mark on the reform agenda (Wright 2018).

As an illustration of the key role played in this critical juncture by Germany and France in particular, take the events in June 2014, during the days leading up to the European Council meeting. By this time, it had become clear that Russia had neither honoured nor taken any steps to attempt to honour the ceasefire pronounced by Ukraine. In accordance with the Council decision of March 2014, this should have triggered new sanctions. Seibel (2017) writes how the Council gave Russia three days to meet its obligations and to achieve 'rapid and tangible results in de-escalation', under the heading 'further significant restrictive measures' (European Council 2014a: 12). As a testimony to the power of these two key actors, no such sanctions were imposed since Chancellor Merkel and President François Hollande conducted a telephone conversation with Ukrainian President Poroshenko and Russian President Putin, and agreed to support Putin in extending the ceasefire (Seibel 2017: 277).

Among the other actors that were considered key players but dismissed were Sweden, the United Kingdom and the European Parliament, Sweden because of its role in propelling the EaP and its general proactive involvement in the neighbourhood under the foreign affairs leadership of Carl Bildt. After the Swedish general elections of late 2014 and the subsequent new 'feminist foreign policy strategy', however, the country paid less attention to Russia and the eastern 'neighbourhood' (Government Offices of Sweden 2015). The new government's early struggles coincided with the conflict in Ukraine. Although Sweden remained actively engaged with the Eastern Partners, it did not play a key role in the 2015 reform episode (Schmidt-Felzmann 2015). The United Kingdom, although traditionally one of the 'Big Three' in EU foreign policy, was initially hesitant in the Ukraine crisis and its government 'has not been as active or as visible on this issue as it could have been', according to the House of Lords (2015: 29). Most of the

United Kingdom's involvement was within the Group of Seven and within the UN General Assembly, and focused primarily on imposing sanctions on Russia, on the Crimea annexation and, later, on condemning Russia after the MH17 tragedy. It was not actively involved as a key player in the process of ENP reform. At the European level, I do not include the European Parliament in this analysis. During the 2011 ENP reform round after the Arab uprisings, the Parliament's Committee on Foreign Affairs had issued a resolution (Ashton 2011c) urging the EU to revise the ENP. Additionally, despite having no decision-making powers, members of the EP had frequently aimed to influence EU's policies towards the Arab uprisings (Reinprecht and Levin 2015: 6). During the 2015 reform process, however, internal divisions over the course of EU policy towards Russia within the Parliament, as well as the political and military escalation of the crisis, distracted attention away from the decision-making process on ENP reform according to Kati Piri, Member of the European Parliament (MEP) (Interview PO33). EP discussions prioritised the political dimensions of the Ukraine crisis, the Euromaidan demonstrations and EU–Russia relations (Euractiv 2015a; Nitoiu and Sus 2017).

Perception of the critical juncture, preferences for policy reform

After having identified the key actors during this critical juncture, the analysis turns towards explaining how these key actors perceived the critical juncture and what changes they proposed to the ENP. As I did in Chapter 2, I will evaluate whether each actor was a change player or a status quo player in the reform process, as summarised in Table 3.1 and elaborated further below. Then I will describe how the key actors tried to shape the European Neighbourhood Policy building on these preferences, which allows me to answer the first research question.

Table 3.1 Summarised perceptions of the critical juncture

	Crisis as	Stance regarding ENP reform
Germany	Threat to status quo	Moved from status quo player to moderate change player
France	Opportunity to modify ENP	Moderate change player
Poland	Opportunity to strengthen ENP	Change player
European Commission and EEAS	Threat to status quo	Moved from status quo player to moderate change player

European level

In the early days of the Ukraine crisis, European actors were quick to support the Ukrainian protestors on the 'Euromaidan'. Then President of the European Commission José Manuel Barroso declared his solidarity with the protestors at a speech in December 2013, stating that '[w]hen we see in the cold streets of Kiev, men and women with the European flag, fighting for that European flag, it is because they are also fighting for Ukraine and for their future' (Barroso 2013).

Despite this expressed support for the protestors in Ukraine, the European Commission and the EEAS did not link the crisis to the need for ENP reform until well into the Ukraine crisis, nor did it substantially modify its approach to the region (Interviews PO23; PO24; PO26; PO27). Throughout this period, from the November 2013 Vilnius Summit until the summer of 2014, the Union continued to pursue the same policy goals with the same instruments as before the Vilnius Summit. It thus favoured the status quo. This was visible in the statements and actions of the European institutions at the time. Initially, the European actors focused on defending the ENP, which was framed as an agreement to undertake mutually beneficial socio-economic reform. Such agreements between the EU and Ukraine were at no point intended to have a detrimental effect on Russia or its policies (Füle 2013), because neither the European Commission nor the EEAS perceived the neighbourhood as an area of geopolitical competition (Interview PO35):

> The EU has a radically different way of thinking compared to the Russians. [It] believes that cooperation in the neighbourhood is not just desirable, but necessary. Multilateral cooperation and international agreements are the best way forward for everyone ... That has been the biggest shock here ..., the fact that the Russians perceive this so differently remains impossible for the EU to fathom.

Signals indicating Russia did perceive the EU's policies as problematic, in the light of its wider approach to its near neighbours, were either not picked up, or not recognised as a result of a failing European policy agenda. As one EU official working closely on this issue commented (Interview PO24):

> We conduct our policy taking into account what is our interest, what is the interest of the country in question ... We are not insensitive or blind to the concerns of others, but it cannot be so that the concerns of others direct our policy. And we don't say no to a marriage with a person we love because the guy from the other village disapproves of it. The world doesn't work like that.

As the crisis started, late in 2013, the EU maintained that the door of the ENP remained open to Ukraine, making it clear it wished to pursue the

ENP as it was. This resulted in Ukraine, Georgia and Moldova signing the AA on 27 June 2014. As one Commission official expressed this status quo approach, the period between the Vilnius Summit and the spring of 2014 was 'just a parenthesis', and there was no 'change in terms of policy, at least not in terms of policy instruments ... What was on the table ... is the exact same Association Agreement which was supposed to be signed in Vilnius, [and which] was signed in June six months later. So not a single comma was changed in the Agreement' (Interview PO23).

Initially, the EEAS and the Commission thus perceived the crisis as an incident, and carried on the plans that were already on the table, as confirmed by the interviewees at DG NEAR and at the delegations in Kiev and Moscow. This reluctant stance only altered slightly when the new cabinet of Commissioners took office on 1 November 2014, eager to put forward ambitious projects and plans for action or reforms at the start of their term. The new President Juncker made review of the ENP a priority of his cabinet's first year (Carp and Schumacher 2015: 2; Politico 2014). As the crisis in Ukraine continued to escalate, the EEAS and the Commission moved towards encouraging policy change. They jointly launched a review of the ENP in 2015. Juncker went as far as declaring the review of the ENP would be one of the major objectives of his Commission (Carp and Schumacher 2015: 2; Politico 2014).

The incoming DG NEAR Commissioner Hahn had himself stated it was his 'priority to ensure that the ENP is fitter for purpose and that it contributes more effectively to preserving Europe's security and values', while repeatedly referring to the escalation of the conflict in Ukraine. 'To achieve this', Hahn had told the European Parliament when they were scrutinising him for office, 'it is clear that the ENP must be further adapted to and targeted on our neighbours' individual situations and needs' (2014: 4).

On 4 March 2015 the HR/VP and the European Commission jointly launched a consultation paper, 'Towards a new European Neighbourhood Policy' (2015b). I identify the preferred policy preferences of the European actors for ENP reform based on this paper, summarised in Table 3.2. It indicates that to the EEAS and the Commission there were indeed increased challenges in the European 'neighbourhood' which demanded an ENP that is 'fit for purpose' (European Commission and High Representative for Foreign Affairs and Security Policy 2015b: 3). As the HR/VP stated in the accompanying press release, 'we need a strong policy to be able to tackle these issues. We also need to understand better the different aspirations, values and interests of our partners. This is what the review is about if we are to have a robust political relationship between our neighbours and us' (European Commission and High Representative for Foreign Affairs and Security Policy 2015b).

Still, the policy preferences of the European actors regarding policy change remained conservative. The consultation document shows that the Commission and the EEAS did not wish to change the underlying logic of the ENP – that is, its focus on the promotion of socio-economic development and good governance as a means to achieve greater political association and economic integration between the EU and its partners. Rather, they preferred to revise the modalities through which these goals are pursued, and the pace and countries with which these goals are pursued. According to another senior EU official, the words 'greater differentiation' and 'more ownership' had always been present in EU documents on the 'neighbourhood', but this was the first time the EU was genuinely committed to it: 'we always wanted to have the member states on board, and to diversify, but now we are really trying to make it happen' (Interview PO17). The policy aims and instruments preferred by the Commission and the EEAS thus did not deviate substantially from the *status quo ex ante*. It is '*how* instruments should be used' that is seen to be the basis for the review (European Commission and High Representative for Foreign Affairs and Security Policy 2015b: 3, emphasis mine).

Germany

Although repeatedly operating together within the Weimar Triangle, Germany, France and Poland did not perceive the Ukraine crisis on similar terms. Despite its active role in resolving the political conflict that resulted from the crisis (i.e. forging a European consensus on sanctions and, together with France, facilitating dialogues which included Russia and Ukraine) Germany did not immediately link the crisis in Ukraine to a need to reform the ENP. In her speeches up to early March 2014, German Chancellor Merkel argued her government was in favour of continuing the track towards signing the Association Agreement with Ukraine. It was not proposing an ENP reform episode or a change of approach towards Ukraine, explicitly saying that the Neighbourhood Policy was about modernisation, not geopolitics (Bundesregierung 2014; Pond and Kundnami 2015; Wright 2018).

It was only in late March/early April 2014 that the German government shifted position, as evidenced by the materialisation of the German policy preferences for ENP reform in five points, as summarised in Table 3.2. First, Germany was in favour of a more 'political' ENP, possibly through linking it to the CFSP. Strengthening and expanding the role of the HR/VP and bringing the ENP under full control of the HR/VP had been a long-standing policy preference of the German government ('Deutschlands Zukunft Gestalten. Koalitionsvertrag zwischen CDU, CSU und SPD 18. Legislaturperiode' 2013: 116). Second, Germany preferred a stronger differentiation of the ENP, tailoring it more to the requirements and achievements of each

Table 3.2 (How) should the ENP be modified?

Actor	Desired level(s) of policy change	Substance	Directionality
Germany	Macro, meso, micro	**Instruments: no change** - Main tools and instruments should remain the same: socio-economic reforms, conditionality – but a stricter and more coherent application - ENP should become 'more political', possibly through greater link with CFSP - 'more political' ENP, thus more strategic thinking about Action Plans, although the focus remains socio-economic development **Differentiation among partners:** - Greater differentiation **Greater flexibility:** supports Weimar proposal, not outspoken as to how **Leading role ENP:** greater role EEAS **Neighbours of neighbours:** - More political ENP - Greater differentiation - Greater role EEAS **Funding:** stable **Overall focus:** ENP as socio-economic development instrument	0/+

Table 3.2 (How) should the ENP be modified? (Continued)

Actor	Desired level(s) of policy change	Substance	Directionality
France	Macro, modest meso-proposals.	**Instruments:** change of tack - 'more political' ENP = more focused on current crises and challenges - Less stringent pursuit of conditionality when partners are crucial for stability and security Differentiation among partners: - Greater differentiation, strengthen Mediterranean dimension Greater flexibility: - More flexible and adaptive ENP to respond to crises - Flexible use of funding **Lead in ENP:** greater role EEAS Neighbours of neighbours: not antagonize Russia Funding: - Stable ENI, Additional budget for crisis management Overall focus: - Keeping Eastern and Southern ENP dimension unified - Crisis management	0/+

Table 3.2 (How) should the ENP be modified? (Continued)

Actor	Desired level(s) of policy change	Substance	Directionality
Poland	Macro, meso, micro	**Instruments:** improve and reinforce framework - 'more political' ENP = reinforced **Differentiation among partners:** supports Weimar proposal on differentiation - Focus mainly on the East Greater flexibility: yes - ENPs should be strengthened, more ambitious and 'active' - More political and strategic ENP - Reiterate Eastern dimension, reconfirmation of EU commitment Lead in ENP: - Commission to retain leadership over ENP **Neighbours of neighbours:** Not giving Russia more leverage **Funding:** Not outspoken, but for its strengthening efforts increased ENI would be needed Overall focus: Amplify ENP, especially towards East	+

Table 3.2 (How) should the ENP be modified? (Continued)

Actor	Desired level(s) of policy change	Substance	Directionality
European Commission/ EEAS	Macro	**Instruments: no change** - Reassessing how ENP *current* instruments should be used more wisely **Differentiation among partners:** - Greater differentiation **Greater flexibility: yes, not in funding** - It promotes a more flexible ENP - Does not want greater flexibility in funding **Leading role ENP:** not outspoken, EC presumably in favour of EC retaining leadership, EEAS to increase its own role **Neighbours of neighbours:** - In some cases, cooperation necessary **Funding:** stable **Overall focus:** socio-economic development, stability	0/+

0= no deviation from status quo, 0/+= very little deviation from status quo, += deviation from status quo, ++= significant deviation from status quo

partner (Bundesregierung 2015). Third, it did not advocate a change of the ENP tools and instruments, but rather a stricter and more coherent application of them, mainly of conditionality (Fix and Kirch 2016: 16). Fourth, Germany reiterated that the ENP was not a pre-accession stage for its partners, while finally, it wanted there to be a greater role for the 'neighbours of the neighbours', that is, Russia, as Merkel reiterated that the 'neighbourhood' initiatives were not a matter of 'either/or, either moving closer to the European Union or complying with Russia's wish for closer partnership with these states' (Bundesregierung 2015).

France

While the Ukraine conflict cast doubt on the relationship that had developed between Paris and Moscow since the early 2000s, the French interests in a stable relationship with Russia had implications for France's perception of the critical juncture. The French initial response to the Ukraine crisis was cautious (Euractiv 2013; Riols 2013). France moderately argued in favour of a revision of the European approach towards the 'neighbourhood'.

In their critique of the ENP, the reform proposal submitted by the French National Assembly stated that the 'bureaucratic management of the ENP, without political vision, is in part responsible for the eruption of the political crisis in Ukraine' (Assemblée Nationale 2015: 3). It also argued that 'given the failure of the ENP to attain its objectives, despite multiple reform attempts, it is imperative for the EU to build anew the ENP in order for it to be able to be useful in attaining political stability, economic development and promoting the values of peace and democracy'.

The main reform preferences of the French government, as summarised in Table 3.2, were as follows. First, it wanted increased flexibility of the ENP, making it more adaptable to the specificities of the partner country in question. Second, France wanted to keep the Eastern and the southern dimensions unified, so as not to compromise attention towards the southern 'neighbourhood'. Third, it advocated that conditionality attach fewer strings, a more 'political' policy; a budget for the management of crisis in the 'neighbourhood' on top of the ENP budget, which should remain unchanged; and finally a stronger relationship with the 'neighbours of the neighbours', converging with Germany on this, mainly focusing on energy, development and security cooperation (Assemblée Nationale 2015; De Hoop Scheffer and Quencez 2015; Nougayrède 2015; Sénat 2015).

Overall, France can be considered a moderate change player. To both France and Poland, the crisis presented an opportunity to change the ENP. France's main focus, as identified above, was on strengthening the ENP's Mediterranean and security dimensions, especially in the wake of the war in Syria and the increasing insecurity over terrorist threats. A focus on the southern dimension of the ENP also allowed France to remain involved in the reform process, whilst abstaining from focusing on the 'Russia question' too much.

Poland

I identify Poland as a change player in the 2015 ENP reform episode, although it differed in opinion from its Weimar partners regarding the substance of some of the changes. To the Polish government, the Russian incursions in Ukraine and its aggressive stance towards the EU showed that the ENP, especially the EaP, needed to be significantly strengthened. The Polish perception of the crisis was that it was caused by Russia turning against the West (Szeptycki 2020; Sakwa 2014).

Accordingly, it argued that the conflict in Ukraine called for a united European response that would confirm the EU's commitment to the region, as exemplified in speeches by its foreign minister Grzegorz Schetyna (2015). Schetyna argued that 'the source of instability [in the eastern 'neighbourhood'] is the lack of a European perspective and reforms, not the other way around … It [Europe] should reaffirm that the EU is ready to continue its ambitious cooperation not only with Ukraine, but also with Moldova and Georgia, and to engage in new initiatives with Armenia, Azerbaijan, and Belarus.' Its priorities for ENP reform, as summarised in Table 3.2, were thus a reconfirmation of the EU's commitment towards its eastern neighbours (Buras 2015a, 2015b). Additionally, the Polish government stated that the DCFTAs that had already been signed with the EU's partners needed to be ratified and implemented as quickly as possible. Poland was much more wary than the other Triangle members of giving Russia any more leverage in the EU's policies towards its eastern neighbours (Euractiv 2014). A further point of contention was the fact that both France and Germany expressed a desire to integrate the ENP and the EaP more with the CFSP, with the EEAS in the leading role rather than the Commission. Poland preferred the ENP to remain under the leadership of the Commission.

Weimar Triangle

Despite their diverging approaches to the critical juncture and ENP reform, the Weimar countries met on 31 March and 1 April 2014 to discuss 'how they can work together to inject fresh impetus in the EU' (*Auswärtiges Amt* 2014b). Their meeting exemplifies how these three member states took the lead not just in solving the conflict in Ukraine, but also in ENP reform: the goal of the meeting was explicitly 'to develop new foreign and European policy initiatives beyond day-to-day politics' (*Auswärtiges Amt* 2014b).

On 1 April 2014, the Triangle proposed a review of the European Neighbourhood Policy. Overall, their proposal suggests that the original rationale of the ENP should be maintained, but that the ENP should allow the EU to be flexible when faced with crises or unexpected developments. Making it more flexible, and more political through increasing the role of EEAS, should enable the EU to better respond to the crises in the 'neighbourhood'. The proposal started by acknowledging that 'the original rationale for developing the ENP – building an area of stability, shared prosperity and common values – remains stronger than ever. At the same time, the ENP has to adapt to these changes and rise up to the challenges and opportunities created by this new context' (Foreign Ministers of the Weimar Triangle 2014). Second, it reiterated ENP policies that were already in place, such as a stronger compact with the neighbours of the EU, enhanced trade and deepened economic integration.

The main deviation consists in giving an increased political profile to the EEAS – something only Germany and France had wanted given its more intergovernmental set-up compared to the Commission – whilst reassuring Poland and other EU member states that the 'insight, expertise and tools [of the European Commission] remain indispensable for the success of the ENP'. Second, the statement advocates additional attention to improving the crisis management capacity in the 'neighbourhood' of both the EU and the ENP partner countries.

To achieve this aim, EU financial assistance had to become more flexible. Although the proposal is clear that the European Neighbourhood Instrument (ENI) budget should not be increased, since the €15.4 billion budget for the 2014–2020 period was already 'a significant commitment', the Triangle argued that much of the ENP funding was long-term, adding that the EU 'should increase its flexibility to allow for speedier and more strategic delivery of support … a substantial proportion of neighbourhood funds should be available at shorter notice so that the EU can react to new developments on the ground'. This reflects the fact that the EU was faced with increasing crises both within and outside its borders, and a desire to be able to respond to these more quickly. Third, while the 'more for more' principle stands, the Triangle argued that the ENP should be more tailored and more differentiated, and should 'take into account [the] political realities in which our partners operate', a French priority. Finally, the group's suggestion of reaching out to the 'neighbours of the neighbours' and promoting regional integration was something both France and Germany had wanted, although it stated that 'the EU will continue not to negotiate its relations with its neighbours with third partners', clearly referring to Russia (Foreign Ministers of the Weimar Triangle 2014).

Overall, the proposal echoes a compromise among the three states, in which the Polish demands are the least reflected: although the ENP should become more political, the EEAS should be more important, and although the EU has to 'step up its game' in the 'neighbourhood' as Poland insisted, it must do so with the same amount of funding, whilst using this same funding for a better ad hoc crisis response.

Temporal contingency: the impact of events

The EU always said, 'we should not see this as a zero sum game'. But if we look at the events, we can see that it did end up playing one. If we really want to understand the backlash, and the subsequent problems, we should pay special attention to the events that happened early [in] 2014.
Kati Piri, member of the European Parliament, interviewed June 2015

The temporal context of the 2015 ENP reform episode consisted of a stream of (unanticipated) events and crises. The economic and financial crisis evolved into a Eurozone crisis that had repercussions for the governance of the EU at large. First, the EU's economic strength has historically been not merely a key enabler of the tools of economic policy, but itself a crucial element of that policy. Additionally, over and above the reduction in political bandwidth available for external relations, the economic crisis had a direct impact on the foreign policies of the member states and the EU as a whole, as the resources devoted to external relations had to be cut.[4]

Finally, the crisis had consequences for the constellation of power within the EU as the Ukraine crisis erupted. The French economic decline persisted and was paralleled by its retreating global influence (ECFR, 2014), which some maintained got worse under the ailing French President Hollande (*Der Spiegel* 2013a) while Germany's authority over the resolution of the Eurozone crisis was asserted. In German policy circles, the notion that with 'new power comes new responsibility', and that 'Germany will have to take the lead more decisively and more often', has become a cautious consensus (Cafruny 2015; Stiftung Wissenschaft und Politik and The German Marshall Fund of the United States 2014).

This increasing willingness to take the lead was echoed by the German Minister of Defence in a 2016 White Paper on German security policy (Bundesregierung 2016). During the previous reform round of 2011, the rhetoric of promoting democracy and good governance had taken centre stage, as one interviewee argued: 'when there is a certain development, you jump on it, and you have suddenly an overfocus *[sic]* on it. [After the Arab uprisings] the ENP was suddenly perceived as an instrument to promote democracy and civil society' (Interview PO31). But by the time the Ukraine crisis broke out this mindset appeared firmly in the past, as the context had significantly altered.

In the wake of that crisis several political developments are important to consider when assessing the ENP reform episode. At the dawn of the crisis, neither the European actors nor Germany was convinced that this crisis was one that necessitated reform of the ENP. France was hesitant to act, while only Poland signalled an eagerness to reform the ENP. Four months after the Vilnius Summit, however, a first ENP reform proposal by Germany, France and Poland was on the table. This was followed by the investiture of the Juncker presidency on 1 November 2014, eager to reform the ENP. How did this transformation occur? I argue there were four main turning points in the critical juncture opened by the Ukraine crisis:

1) the 'Euromaidan' demonstrations that followed the Vilnius Summit and their violent escalation;
2) the deal with Yanukovych and his subsequent ousting;
3) the annexation of the Crimea and
4) the tragic downing of flight MH17.

From the Vilnius summit to the Euromaidan

In the wake of Yanukovych's decision to suspend the signing the of the AA after talks between the prime ministers of Ukraine and Russia, an estimated 100,000 protestors gathered at Kiev's Independence Square on 24 November 2013 (BBC News 2013). They waved European flags and started using the hashtag #євромайдан (Euromaidan) on social media; 'Euromaidan' means 'European Square', and indicates the pro-European leanings of many protestors. The demonstrations turned violent a few days later, reaching a critical point when Russian President Putin announced on 17 December 2013 that Russia would invest $15 billion in Ukrainian government securities. It would also reduce prices for Russian gas imports by around one-third (*Bloomberg Business Week* 2013). The deal was interpreted as 'a blunt confirmation that Yanukovych had no intention of giving in to the innovative protest movement that had put his government in crisis by demanding that the country look west toward Europe instead of becoming a Russian ally once more' (Diuk 2014: 9).

Protests escalated and on 22 January the first casualties were reported. The refusal to sign the AA was an important moment of the temporal context under study, mainly because Yanukovych's decision and the subsequent violent protests created a moment of heightened contingency in which the previous policy course of the ENP started to lose legitimacy. For the time being (until February 2014, see below), this did not yet affect the key actors' stances on possible ENP reform. President Hollande for example stated 'the partnership remains open' (*Financial Times* 2013), while President of the Council Van Rompuy also said 'the offer is still on the table' (*The Guardian* 2013a). Chancellor Merkel, likewise, told Ukraine 'the invitation stands' (Merkel 2013). At this time, the issue of ENP reform, or an assessment of the role the ENP itself had played in causing this crisis, were not yet on the agenda. However, as the following will show, this was set to change in February and March of 2014.

Yanukovych ousted

The protests continued over January and February, during which the Ukrainian president passed anti-protest laws, further antagonising the protestors in Independence Square (*The Guardian* 2014b). Thursday 20 February 2014 was the most violent day of the protests thus far and multiple casualties were reported (*The Guardian* 2014a). Appalled by the deteriorating situation and the violence used by government forces, the EU imposed its first sanctions against Ukrainian officials, including 'asset freezes and visa ban against those responsible for human rights violations, violence and use of excessive force' (European Council 2014b). Meanwhile, the Weimar Triangle re-emerged for the first time, as the foreign ministers of Germany, France and Poland attempted to negotiate a deal between the Yanukovych government and the opposition (*Auswärtiges Amt* 2014a). Agreement was reached on 21 February 2014, when the foreign ministers of the Weimar Triangle and Yanukovych, in the presence of Russian diplomat Vladimir Lukin, signed a deal seeking an end to the bloodshed in Ukraine, including a call for new elections no later than December 2014 (Sikorski et al. 2014). It was an important moment that marks the beginning of a proactive leadership by these three key member states to de-escalate the crisis, which later turned out to be a stepping stone for ENP reform. The following day, however, the Ukrainian parliament voted to remove President Yanukovych from office and he fled the country.

The key actors at the European level welcomed acting prime minister Arseniy Yatseniuk and reiterated their commitment to Ukraine (Barroso 2014; Füle 2014), while the Russian leadership expressed shock and worry at the course of events, and at the ousting of their ally Yanukovych (R. Allison 2014: 1257).

The annexation of the Crimea

The third turning point, the annexation of the Crimea, was crucial. On 1 March 2014 the Federal Council of the Russian Federation authorised the deployment of Russian armed forces in Ukraine in order to 'protect the interests of Russia and of Russian-speakers in Crimea and in the entire country' (European Parliament 2014).

The use of Russian forces on Ukrainian soil in the Crimea breached the 1997 treaty containing the bilateral status of forces agreement between Russia and Ukraine (R. Allison 2014: 1263) and sparked outrage among the European actors. HR/VP Ashton stressed that this violation of Ukrainian sovereignty was unacceptable (Ashton 2014); Martin Schultz, President of the European Parliament, condemned the violation of human rights in Ukraine (*Deutsche Welle* 2014). France and Germany, along with other EU member states, expressed their concerns about the violation of Ukrainian sovereignty and territorial integrity, while the Baltic countries and the Visegrad Group countries drew analogies between the annexation of the Crimea and their own histories of Soviet occupation (Bloomberg 2014; Visegrad Group 2014).[5] Poland also forcefully condemned the 'Russian aggression' (Ministry of Foreign Affairs 2014) and requested NATO backup (*Financial Times* 2014). Media sources, meanwhile, mused about the resemblance that events in Ukraine had suddenly taken to the Cold War (Charap and Shapiro 2015; Levgold 2014).

Around this time the European institutions moved from defending the ENP status quo towards becoming very moderate change players. The Commission and, to a lesser extent, the EEAS had hitherto been convinced that European integration with the post-Soviet region was beneficial to Russia. Kati Piri, an MEP I interviewed, referred to the EU as 'super-naïve' when it came to Russia (Interview PO33). This naïvety seemed to turn around in the wake of the Crimea annexation and over the course of 2014. Another interviewee stated that the EU had 'never imagined that Russia would resort to military force in Europe without a clear financial interest; that seemed an idea from the past. The EU did not properly anticipate how far Russia was going to fight back in Ukraine' (Interview PO28). Yet another policy official commented that '[the EU] did not realise that we were dealing with a dictatorship, taking decisions based on temper. Not the way rational countries operate. We thought Russia was a normal country' (Interview PO24).

Two weeks after the annexation, the foreign ministers of Germany, France and Poland met in Berlin and Weimar to discuss the Ukraine crisis. Their meeting signalled the first time since the eruption of the crisis that the possibility of reforming the ENP was proposed. Initially, the Triangle discussed 'how they can work together to inject fresh impetus in the EU', underlining that the crisis in Ukraine went beyond the scope of the ENP (*Auswärtiges Amt* 2014b). Within a few days, the three countries presented their first blueprint for ENP reform, tying reform into their preferred EU crisis response (Foreign Ministers of the Weimar Triangle 2014). The Russian intervention in Ukraine had served to make the Neighbourhood Policy even more salient and reform of it more urgent. This was exacerbated by the tragedy of flight MH17, shot down over Eastern Ukraine on 17 July 2014 killing all 298 people on board. Van der Pijl (2018: 1) cast this catastrophe as a prism which refracted the broader historical context in which it occurred 'in a rare moment of clarity'.

The shock event impacted on the attitudes both of decision-makers and of the general public towards the Ukraine crisis and the actions of Russia over the summer of 2014. It compounded the changing stance of the key actors, triggering the imposition of new sanctions against Russia and providing fresh impetus to reform the ENP after the summer of 2014 (Toal and O'Loughlin 2017). Merkel, for example, stated that the downing of the aircraft showed that 'the Ukraine crisis is by no means solely a regional issue. No, this example shows us: it affects all of us' (Merkel 2014).

Table 3.3 summarises how the events I have described fed into the process of reforming the ENP.

Policy output

The temporal contingencies described in the previous section thus first played a role in forging a shared declaratory commitment to a strategic overhaul of the ENP, in order to better deal with the uncertainties stemming from the region. A clear rhetorical break with previous policy was announced.

This declaratory commitment to policy reform, shared by virtually all actors, meant that most of the reforms of the ENP addressed its grand ambitions: making the ENP 'more political', more focused, increasing differentiation and ownership and, most of all, increasing the focus on stability and social and economic stabilisation (European Commission and High Representative for Foreign Affairs and Security Policy 2015a). Where article 8 of the TEU had obliged the member states to establish 'an area of good neighbourliness, founded on the values of the Union', the revised ENP firmly focused on the challenge of stabilising the 'neighbourhood', building on 'our genuinely shared common interests'. To do this, '[t]he ENP will take stabilisation as its main political priority in this mandate (European Commission and High Representative for Foreign Affairs and Security Policy 2015a).

In order to achieve these macro policy goals, the main policy implementation preferences were differentiation and flexibility. These concepts were presented as the 'hallmark of the new ENP' (European Commission and High Representative for Foreign Affairs and Security Policy 2015a: 2), aimed at improving the cooperation between the EU and third parties. Rather than

Table 3.3 Summary of impact: temporal contingency

Temporal development	Impact on ENP reform
Structural:	
1. The historical development of the ENP as a technocratic, trade-oriented order (rather than as a political instruments)	- EU actors long did not perceive the neighbourhood as an area of geopolitical competition - Initially, the ENP is not connected to the crisis - Room for policy entrepreneurship, creating key actors (e.g. Poland) with high commitment to the Eastern neighbourhood - Emergence of member states as key actors to tackle the political crisis in Ukraine, allowing them to set the tone for the ENP reform process
Conjunctural:	
1. Eurozone crisis 2. Escalation of conflict in the European neighbourhood 3. Rising German leadership, weakening France (and UK) 4. Ukraine not just a crisis of the ENP, but a political and military crisis	- A more pragmatic and securitised narrative that captures this temporal context - Increased salience of neighbourhood region - Important role for the Weimar Triangle, first in political resolution and then in propelling ENP reform
Liminal:	
1. 'Euromaidan', escalation of violence 2. Ousting of president Yanukovych 3. Crimea annexation, Russian troop involvement, spread of violence 4. MH17 plane disaster	- Bringing key actors together, enabling them to form an opinion on ENP reform 'minilaterally' - Increased urgency of ENP reform - Increased focus on stabilisation - Grand symbolic pledges to a revised ENP

a one-size-fits-all policy the Commission argued it should put forward different partnership styles, in which those who want a more transactional relationship with the EU will get a different 'menu' in the ENP (European Commission and High Representative for Foreign Affairs and Security Policy 2015a: 2; Hahn 2015). At the same time, the EU would be more flexible in its use of the ENP, to enable it 'to respond to ever changing needs and circumstances'

(European Commission and High Representative for Foreign Affairs and Security Policy 2015a: 3). Except for the prominence of stability, none of these grand changes appear to be very specific, nor are they all new. Greater differentiation, more flexibility and more ownership featured in the 2011 review of the ENP (European Commission and High Representative for Foreign Affairs and Security Policy 2011a: 1, 2, 8, 19–20). These vague and ambiguous macro-policy ambitions have the advantage of not requiring agreement among actors regarding the exact direction and level of policy changes. But they do have a strong symbolic element, showing the actor in question is 'doing something' and on the 'right side of history' and thus are rewarding, especially in the capricious temporal context of the 2015 ENP reforms.

The proposed changes were indeed presented as significant breaks with previous policies. DG NEAR Commissioner Hahn even said that with the reform, 'the ENP has to become a real postmodern foreign policy' (Hahn, 2015). In wording, the overall macro-ambitions of the 2015 ENP thus appear to signal a clear break with previous macro-ambitions, e.g. the 2011 commitment to 'deep democracy', which has altogether disappeared from the 2015 ENP language. This is a clear reflection of how priorities have changed over the five years just pastowing to the rapid succession of developments during 2014. Yet as I will show, despite these rhetorical breaks with the past the ENP remains largely unchanged when we assess its policy goals (the meso-level of policy) and its policy targets and tool calibrations.

The proposals changed very little of the policy tools and targets, even though it was expected the EU would step away from its enlargement methodology in which reforms were leveraged through market access and closer cooperation. 'The "Enlargement light" toolbox', argued DG NEAR Johannes Hahn, 'has been too wide' (Hahn 2015). The tools to achieve the political aims of the revised ENP remained mainly economic: the EU would continue its commitment to its partners' approximation to the EU's *acquis* through the use of AAs and DCFTAs, supposed to lead to a gradual economic integration with the European market. This approximating with European standards requires long and painful reforms, with only visa liberalisation as a potential short-term incentive.

Funding for the ENP, a total of €15.4 billion over the 2014–20 period, remained stable; of this €5 billion was reserved for five frontrunners: Georgia, Ukraine, Moldova, Tunisia and Morocco (European Commission 2016c, 2015e; Koenig 2016: 13). Overall, the revised, overarching policy ambitions did not seep through to the level of policy tools and targets because the various actors differed greatly regarding the changes desired. Only France and Poland proposed substantial changes to the directionality of the policy, though the two actors disagreed on the new direction itself; amongst other things France suggested a greater focus on the south and crisis management; and Poland suggested a significant strengthening of mainly the eastern dimension of the ENP.

The revised macro-level ambitions were not accompanied by meso-and micro-level changes to the ENP because the three actors differed greatly regarding these levels of policy. Table 3.2, which summarised the way in which the countries thought the ENP needed to be reformed, shows that only France and Poland proposed substantial changes to the directionality of the policy, but as we have seen they disagreed on the new direction itself. One of the consequences of this disagreement among key actors was 'constructive ambiguity' in policy change, a term which Dingley (2005: 1) used to describe the Belfast Declaration, meaning 'a form of words that all could sign up with because each party could interpret them differently'. For example, the proposal did not spell out how the EaP and the UfM were supposed to fit within the ENP framework. In an apparent gesture to Poland and France, the revised ENP states the EaP and the UfM are to be strengthened (European Commission and High Representative for Foreign Affairs and Security Policy 2015a: 18). It does so by admitting that previous initiatives for intraregional cooperation had failed, and calling for more 'ad hoc meetings' and for thematic frameworks to reinforce relations between the neighbours (European Commission and High Representative for Foreign Affairs and Security Policy 2015a: 18). Despite these declarations, however, the commitment to the UfM in particular is vague: the EU merely committed to 'give priority, wherever suitable, to the UfM in its regional cooperation efforts' (European Commission and High Representative for Foreign Affairs and Security Policy 2015a: 18). Similarly, the preference for a more political ENP was shared by all three key actors and made it to the final ENP reform document. But despite its prominence, its exact meaning and consequences for the policy objectives and tools remained unspecified.

This is where we see the impact of temporal contingencies on policy change. Vague and ambiguous overarching policy ambitions, such as more focus, more differentiation, ownership and more stability, have the advantage of not requiring agreement among actors regarding the exact direction and level of policy changes. But I have already pointed out their strong symbolic element and the rewards they thus offer. Chapter 4 dives deeper into how we might conceptualise such constructive ambiguity, a form of policy change that falls outside the traditional typology.

Table 3.4 summarises the main policy changes at the macro, meso and micro-level that can be observed in the 2015 ENP document.

Table 3.4 Summary of changes to the ENP after the 2015 reform round

	Policy level		
	Macro	Meso	Micro
Policy goals	Abstract policy aims - Stabilisation (economic and political) (0/+) - More 'political' ENP (+)	Policy objectives - inclusive socio-economic development (0) - security sector reform (+) - improved crisis response capacity (+) - 'legal and safe' mobility (0/+)	(main) Policy targets - conflict prevention (0) - counterterrorism (0) - border management (0) - combatting 'irregular' migration, human trafficking and smuggling (0/+) - job creation (0) - good governance (0) - people-to-people contacts (0)
Policy means	Policy implementation preferences - differentiation (0) - flexibility (0) - ownership (0) - pragmatism (0/+) - step away from Enlargement methodology (+)	Policy tools - economic means to political aims (cf. AA's, DCFTAs) (0) - deepen EaP and UfM (0/+) - grouping interested neighbours in frameworks (+) - flexible deployment of ENI (+) - improved partnerships on energy security and climate (+) - funding conditional on progress (0)	Policy tool calibrations - ENI stable at €15.4 billion (0) - tailor-made reporting (+) - thematic reports that track development (+)

0= no deviation from status quo, 0/+= very little deviation from status quo, += deviation from status quo

Conclusion

This chapter describes how historically developed rules and practices in the EU's relations with its neighbours resulted in a long unwillingness to regard the eastern 'neighbourhood' as a site of geopolitical contention. This affected the ENP reform process by delaying the process of reform since, initially, the European actors did not think a revision of policy was necessary.

It also created an environment in which Germany, France and Poland could emerge as key actors in the ENP reform process, through dealing with the political dimension of the Ukraine crisis in meetings which later laid the groundwork for reforming the ENP. Next to assessing this impact of institutions on the process of policy change, this historical institutionalist analysis explicitly situates variables in their appropriate temporal context, seeing policy outcomes as contingent on their temporal context. Rather than specifying which events were more important than others, or nuancing how important each event was in causing a certain outcome, my focus was on demonstrating the role the key events or turning points played in the decision-making process. In the second part of this chapter, I therefore demonstrated that the particular forms of change made to the ENP would have been different if the temporal context had been different.

At the dawn of the Ukraine crisis, neither the European actors nor Germany was convinced that this crisis was one that made reform of the ENP necessary. But four months after the Vilnius Summit, the first proposal was submitted by Germany, France and Poland, shortly before Juncker, eager to reform the ENP, took over the presidency. To explain how this occurred, I described how several political developments served as important turning points in the reform episode. I identified as crucial events first the failed Vilnius Summit, the subsequent demonstrations and their violent repression, which mainly served to greatly increase the salience of the eastern 'neighbourhood' and that of the Neighbourhood Policy. Second, the deal with and flight of Viktor Yanukovych was an important turning point in the sense that it marked the re-emergence of the Weimar Triangle, taking leadership in the Ukraine crisis, which later turned out to be a stepping stone for ENP reform. Third, the annexation of the Crimea proved crucial, as it was around this time that the European institutions moved from being status quo players regarding the ENP towards becoming (albeit moderate) change players. The actions of Russia in Ukraine, and the breaching of international law, equally served to make the Neighbourhood Policy even more salient and ENP reform more urgent. This was exacerbated by the shooting-down of MH17 over eastern Ukraine later that summer. This compounded the changing stance of the key actors, who after the summer of 2014 were all eager to reform the ENP.

I described how these temporal contingencies fed into the changes made to the ENP, first in terms of forging a shared declaratory commitment to a strategic overhaul of the policy, in order to better deal with the uncertainties stemming from the region. In the wake of the Ukraine crisis, which presented a severe challenge to European policies in the eastern 'neighbourhood', a clear rhetorical break with previous policy was announced, mainly visible in the policy's macro-ambitions, which had to become more political, stability-oriented and more focused. Differentiation and flexibility were presented as the hallmark of the new ENP.

However, as this chapter shows, neither the rhetoric nor the declared ambition for reform in response to these events was matched by a major revision of actual policy objectives or policy tools. The high sense of urgency as a result of critical events prompted a declaratory commitment to reform and revised grand ambitions, but a *de facto* continuation of the bulk of the policy tools and instruments. The revised ENP continues to embody technocratic logic, which is now complemented by a more pragmatic and securitised narrative, reflecting the temporal context. This chapter thus found that, as a result, policy change took the form of constructive ambiguity: policy agreements and changes that all actors can sign up to because they can be interpreted differently, or because grand statements are not followed by meso- and micro-level policy changes. Chapter 4 will explore the notion of constructive ambiguity and the other forms of policy change.

Notes

1 Parts of this chapter have previously been published in *Geopolitics* (Ikani 2019).
2 As it did for example when it strong-armed Armenia into not signing the AA with the EU by selling artillery and rocket launchers worth $1 billion to Azerbaijan in 2013 (Reuters 2013).
3 'Minilaterism' is a term introduced by Kratochwil, referring to 'the creation of core groups and the multilateralisation of their agreements'. In the EU context it refers to the practice of convening and negotiating in small groups of member states – such as the Weimar Triangle – rather than convening the entire Union in order to facilitate or speed up decision-making (1993: 468).
4 Eight EU countries (Bulgaria, Denmark, Finland, France, Germany, Italy, Portugal and the UK) all undertook a real-terms decrease in the 2015 defence budget, while only two countries with very modest armed forces (the Netherlands and Spain) foresaw no change (Fleurant et al. 2016).
5 The Czech Republic, Hungary, Poland and Slovakia.

4

Conceptualising EU foreign policy change

When after the Ukraine crisis, Judy Dempsey of Carnegie Europe asked a group of experts the question 'Is the ENP doomed?', a senior advisor at the German Marshall Fund replied that the Policy should not be maintained as it 'has failed to achieve its goal of building a ring of well-governed states to the EU's East and South' (Dempsey, 2015). Another expert stated that 'the EU still has to figure out how its own Eurocentric considerations can serve countries whose populations are struggling simply to achieve security, stability, and better living conditions', while yet another analyst argued that 'the EU's aversion to change even in separate policy areas threatens to trigger indifference in the Union's neighbours'.

This study takes issue with such claims. They not only neglect whether eleven years would be enough for any policy to achieve such ambitious aims in this particular region, but do not consider *why* the EU would be unable to change its policies. This should be a crucial question – especially since the EU is a composite actor in which decision-making powers on the degree and type of change are scattered among different institutions and member states operating at different levels. If 'the' EU is Eurocentric, or if 'the' EU has an aversion to change, why? How did this come about? Have there been change processes, and what were the key impediments? Equally important is the question: has there really been no change at all?

Chapters 2 and 3 gave in-depth accounts of how and under what conditions critical junctures may produce policy changes. This chapter develops a typology of EU foreign policy change. What kinds of policy change did we see, at what level did they take place, what was their actual substance and why was this the particular output of the decision-making process? To develop a typology appropriate for studying change at the European level, in this chapter I shall first address the shortcomings of existing conceptualisations of policy change for the assessment of changes in EU foreign policy. My starting point is the different kinds of policy change we observed in the ENP reform rounds. Specifically, in the light of the findings in Chapters 2 and 3 I shall consider the shortcomings of the widely used, cumulative typology of change proposed by Hall, which divides policy change into three levels or 'orders'. Then I shall argue why two categories, symbolic change and constructive ambiguity, provide a complementary perspective on the variation in policy change outputs for the EU.

The traditional, cumulative typology

Peter Hall (1993) proposed to distinguish three levels or 'orders' of change. First-order changes, Hall suggested, consist of calibrations to policy instruments. These changes are mainly incremental. Second-order change is one step up from such incrementalism, involving changing policy instruments that pursue similar goals as a result of past experiences. Finally, third-order changes involve shifting policy goals and a shifting hierarchy of goals behind the policy.

First- and second-order changes, according to Hall, were instances of 'normal policymaking', a process of adjusting policy without challenging the terms of the overarching policy paradigm (Hall 1993: 279). When faced with anomalies, his argument goes, policymakers constantly pursue first- and second-order changes to policy, seeking to correct the problems that occur. But when anomalies and problems are not solved using the policies within the existing paradigm, or keep occurring, the evidence of repeated failure breaks down the authority of that paradigm. Third-order change thus occurs when first- and second-order changes are tried and tested, yet prove unable to combat the impending challenges. The core question for Hall was not whether paradigm change would take place after current policy fails, but rather how a new policy paradigm emerges (Oliver and Pemberton 2004: 419). He argued that, when first- and second-order changes fail to address anomalies, a 'marketplace of ideas' would emerge, in which actors seek new solutions for persisting problems, while at the same time advancing their own interests and ideas on how to move forward. Interactions between the actors engaged in policy change may eventually result in a new policy paradigm taking over. This happens when policymakers reassess not just the goals of the existing policy, or the instruments used to attain these goals, but rather the very nature of the problem that these policy goals are meant to address: the policy paradigm (Hall 1993: 279). Hall (1993: 278) calls this 'social learning', 'a deliberate attempt to adjust the goals or techniques of policy in response to past experience and new information'.

Whereas for first- and second-order change the rationale of policy is not questioned, third-order change thus challenges precisely this policy rationale. Figure 4.1 summarises how policy change occurs, according to Hall.

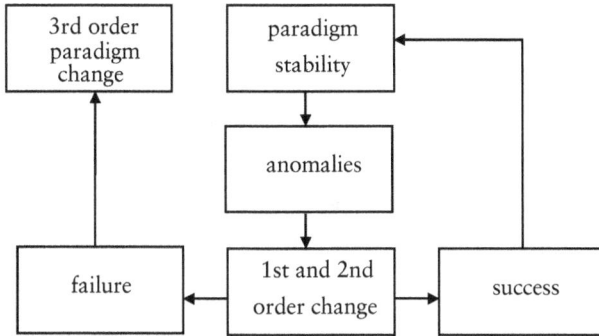

Figure 4.1 Policy change according to Hall (1993)

Hall's typology, like those of Hermann (1990) and Rosati (1994) in the field of foreign policy analysis, follows the logic of a cumulative scale, the Guttman scale. First- and second-order changes need to be 'completed' before third-order change can occur. Third-order change thus always implies second- and first-order change, and second-order change always implies first-order change (Hall 1993: 293). His typology has since became mainstream in assessments of policy dynamics.

Table 4.1 summarises what we should expect policy change to look like if we categorise policy changes using Hall's typology. First-order changes would concern the micro level of policy, and would not present a significant deviation from the status quo before the critical juncture. Second-order changes would imply revised micro- and meso-level policy, adjusting the policy objectives and policy tools. These would deviate slightly from the *status quo ex ante* in the sense that adjustments to policy instruments are made, but since policy pursues the same goals as before, second-order changes remain a coherent development of past policy. Third-order change, finally, entails a revision of the micro, meso and macro levels of policy, the policy aims, ambitions and the main preferences for policy implementation. Only third-order change as Hall qualifies it entails a significant deviation from the status quo; only this order of change questions the previous policy rationale, and floats new ideas regarding the goals of the policy and the nature of the problems it addresses (the policy paradigm), to be contested and eventually adopted (Hall 1993: 279).

Chapter 2 has shown how in the wake of the Arab uprisings there was what Hall would refer to as a breakdown of the old paradigm. The old rationale of the ENP was seriously questioned: Neighbourhood Commissioner Štefan Füle lamented that too many policy officials 'fell prey to the assumption that authoritarian regimes were a guarantee of stability in the region' (Füle,

Table 4.1 Policy changes that fit within the typology proposed by Hall (1993)

	Level	Substance	Directionality away from status quo ex ante
First-order change	micro	Policy adjustments, calibrating targets and settings	0
Second-order change	micro, meso	Adapting policy instruments, objectives	0/+
Third-order change	micro, meso, macro	Changing the policy goals/aims Restating policy ambitions; changed conception of the problem, of 'how the world works'	+

2011). One official I interviewed told me there was 'a sense of guiltiness, a feeling of shared responsibility, sharing the burden of what happened in the last 40 years in the region ... We were in a guilty attitude' (Interview PO20). French Foreign Minister Juppé (2011b) spoke of a 'rendez-vous with history' when referring to the Arab uprisings and the appropriate response by Europe, while German Chancellor Merkel stated there was a 'historic European obligation' to stand by the protestors (Merkel 2011), with her Minister of Foreign Affairs Westerwelle suggesting the ENP should be applied much more strictly in order to let the political awakenings succeed (Westerwelle 2011b). The EU no longer wished to be 'a passive spectator' (European Commission and High Representative for Foreign Affairs and Security Policy 2011b: 2).

Sweeping policy changes to the ENP were announced, explicitly mentioned in the statements of actors at the European level. HR/VP Ashton concluded that a fundamental review of the ENP was needed, which was echoed by key member states agreed on. She stated that the EU's response should be 'built on the need to acknowledge past mistakes and listen without imposing' (Ashton 2011a). These statements signalled a break with the past, reflecting Hall's description of paradigm change – which occurs when policymakers reassess not just the goals of the existing policy but rather the very nature of the problem that these policy goals are meant to address (1993: 279).

And indeed the revised ENP of 2011, the 'New response to a changing Neighbourhood', includes a revision of the macro-ambitions of the Neighbourhood Policy. One of the most crucial changes at the macro level was the commitment to 'deep democracy' (Ashton 2011c), which was presented as a new and comprehensive approach to build a democracy of the kind 'that lasts' (European Commission and High Representative for Foreign

Affairs and Security Policy 2011a: 2). In order to achieve this, the Commission and the HR/VP proposed a strategy of '3Ms' – money, mobility and markets – in a policy with benefits in these three areas for member states who 'go further and faster with reforms' (European Commission and High Representative for Foreign Affairs and Security Policy 2011b: 5). These policy changes proposed for the 2011 revision to the ENP are mainly directed at the macro level, signalling a changed perception of the nature of the problem. The title of the 2011 ENP review, a 'New response to a changing Neighbourhood', confirms the perception that the 'neighbourhood' had altered, that the problems were somehow new, that the changing dynamics in the region would 'require [the EU] to look afresh at the EU's relationship with our neighbours'. Not just the problem had changed; so had the EU's solution to these problems: 'the EU needs to rise to the historical challenges in our neighbourhood' (European Commission and High Representative for Foreign Affairs and Security Policy 2011a: 1).

But despite the allusions made to a profound revision of the ENP, the statements and declaratory commitments to a change of paradigm were not substantiated with significant changes to the policy objectives, means, tools or calibrations. In other words, third-order change was not preceded by first- and second-order changes. This is where policy change in the two cases studied in this book departs from Hall's typology.

Additionally, many of the 'revised' macro-ambitions in both new ENP documents do not consist of actual departures from the *status quo ex ante* when we assess their directionality. An example is the 'more for more' principle presented in the revised ENP of 2011. One senior EU official hailed this principle as new, even calling it a 'fourth 'M', referring to the '3Ms' HR/VP Ashton presented as a response to the Arab uprisings.[1] Yet if scrutinised in detail, the 'more for more' scheme proposed in the 2011 reform round built forward on the same notion that financial assistance should be conditional upon democratic reform. This has been a cornerstone of the original ENP in 2004.

These 'false' paradigm changes, where at a rhetorical level the EU committed to a revised policy but did not follow up with changes at the meso and micro levels of policy (i.e. policy tools, objectives and specific policy targets) are not well explained by the traditional typology proposed by Peter Hall.

The ENP revision of 2015 similarly displayed signs of a breakdown in the belief in the old policy paradigm guiding the ENP, as detailed in Chapter 3. Commission President Juncker asked DG NEAR to make recommendations for improving the ENP, arguing '[r]eform means change. I want us all to show that we are open to change and ready to adapt to it' (2014a: 1). DG NEAR Commissioner Hahn later stated the EU had indeed to revise the tools of the past, saying 'the "Enlargement light" toolbox has been too wide', and that 'the ENP has to become a real postmodern foreign policy' (Hahn 2015), without specifying what exactly this would entail.

The French Parliament (Assemblée Nationale 2015: 3) stated that the 'bureaucratic management of the ENP, without political vision, is in part responsible for the eruption of the political crisis in Ukraine'. It also argued that 'given the failure of the ENP to attain its objectives, despite multiple reform attempts, it is *imperative for the EU to build anew* the ENP in order for it to be able to be useful in attaining political stability, economic development and promoting the values of peace and democracy' (2015: 3, emphasis mine). Even Germany, among the key actors the least convinced that the *status quo ex ante* needed to be radically altered, propagated a profound rethink of the ENP against the backdrop of events in Ukraine and the rest of the neighbourhood (*Auswärtiges Amt* 2015). The authority of the previous policy paradigm, and its crucial features such as the enlargement logic it embodies, were thrown into question – as we would expect when paradigm change occurs.

And again, the revised ENP of 2015 initially appears to reflect a change in policy course. The 2015 ENP document does not mention conditionality once, suggesting a quite radical break with one of the oldest tools in the EU's foreign policy toolbox. It states that the incentive-based approach of 'more for more', to which the EU had so adamantly committed itself a mere four years earlier, 'has not proven a sufficiently strong incentive to create a commitment to reform, where there is not the political will' (European Commission and High Representative for Foreign Affairs and Security Policy 2015a: 5). As a result, one EU official with years of experience working on the ENP called the 2015 ENP 'the end of values in EU policy' (Interview PO18). The EU claimed to embark on a new strategy with the revised ENP, one that reprioritises the EU's activities and that introduces new ways of working (European Commission and High Representative for Foreign Affairs and Security Policy 2015a: 2). In the words of Commissioner Hahn (2015): 'in the light of structural problems and turmoil in many parts of the neigh-bourhood, we have to take a hard look at the policy and ask self-critically: is it working? Is it delivering? How can we do better? Because we have to do better, in our own interest!'

Yet again and despite these statements suggesting a break with previ-ous policy, it would be incorrect to argue that this breakdown of the old paradigm represented third-order policy change, in which both first-order changes and second-order changes were attempted and completed. Rather, the first- and second-order policy instruments and their settings remain stable. Conditionality remains a crucial tool of the ENP and for the disbursement of ENI funding: the actual implementation of the reforms in ENP countries 'will continue to guide the allocation of funds under the ENI umbrella programme, in line with the incentive-based approach' (European Council 2015b). The ENI number 232/2014 the Council Conclusions refer to makes 10 per cent of the total funding conditional upon 'progress in implementing mutually agreed political, economic and social reform objectives' and partner countries' commitment to 'deep and sustainable democracy' (European Parliament and European Council 2014, article 4b and 4c).

These examples show how the policy changes that can be observed in the 2011 and 2015 reform rounds are not fully captured following the traditional typology. They are not accurately described as first-, second- or third-order changes. They do not follow the process described in Figure 4.1. Not all policy change is substantive, progressive and tangible in nature. Policy changes may cut across these traditional categories, containing elements of all three orders of change, as well as elements that fit none of these categories. The problem is not that the policy changes are merely mislabelled in this three-order typology, but rather that the three-level conceptualisation of policy change following a cumulative scale offers an inaccurate description of the policy process leading towards the particular policy outputs we observed.

After having mapped the substance and directionality of the changes made to the ENP in the reform rounds described in Chapters 2 and 3, it thus appears that this traditional typology falls short of conceptualising the kinds of policy change observed in the ENP reform rounds of 2011 and 2015. What we have observed rather are policy changes that in terms of wording consist of changed macro-aims, ambitions and changed conceptions of 'how the world works' – which in the traditional typology would occur during third-order change, after first- and second-order changes had been completed. Yet neither have we seen first- nor second-order changes 'completed' before the policy aims and goals were revised, nor do the proposed policy changes deviate substantially from the *status quo ex ante*.

This is quite important because Hall specifies that third-order changes to the policy paradigm are necessarily preceded by 'simultaneous changes in all three components of policy' (1993: 279). What we have seen instead are rather policy changes that are 'third-order' in rhetorical presentation, whilst representing minor, first-order changes and occasionally second-order changes in substance and directionality. How to explain such changes?

Towards an improved conceptualisation of policy change

Based on the findings in Chapters 2 and 3 and the theoretical framework advanced, this research proposes to complement the existing, three-level typology of policy change with two analytical categories: symbolic policy change and constructive ambiguity.

Symbolic change

Chapters 2 and 3 demonstrated how the plasticity of the institutional arrangements in areas of EU foreign policy, such as the European Neighbourhood Policy, has allowed key players to emerge at the member state level in the immediate aftermath of a critical juncture. This research divided the key players in the reform process into actors who see the critical juncture as an opportunity to revise the status quo on one hand, and actors who are invested in containing the status quo on the other. In the decision-making process that follows the critical juncture, the change players seek to delegitimise the *status quo ex ante* and try to put forward policy changes that fit their preferences, while the status quo players are invested in maintaining the *status quo ex ante*. Usually, one would expect either policy stalemate or incremental adjustment to follow such a standoff, especially because even the change players may disagree amongst themselves on the nature of the policy changes desired (Hart and Tindall 2009: 31).

This research has shown, however, that in some instances after a critical juncture *symbolic policy change* is more likely to follow from the decision-making process. The notion of symbolic change as a result of crisis has previously been examined in public policy studies, and is sometimes dubbed 'rhetorical' change. Scholars found that, in a post-crisis situation with pressure from the public to reform, there is often a willingness to take immediate and visible steps, to show that action is being taken in order to avoid future, similar crises. Despite these 'accommodating gestures', the core values and policies remain intact (Boin et al. 2005; Boin, t'Hart and McConnell 2009; Drennan and McConnell 2007; t'Hart and Tindall 2009; Rose and Davies 1994). And indeed, this study has shown that not all policy adjustments are substantial in nature. They do not always involve actual changes to policy goals or the way in which those are attained. Sometimes adjustments are made to the way the policy is formulated, without this change in wording being accompanied by substantive changes to settings, methods, goals or the paradigm. Symbolic policy change thus can be an important outcome of EU foreign policy change.

An important factor in determining the outcome of policy change is the particular temporal context in which the reform process takes place. Events that take place within the particular context can a) increase or decrease the salience of the issue area in question; and b) consequently increase or decrease the urgency for policy reform. The sudden increased salience of the issue area – often exacerbated by media attention or public criticism – makes politics as usual no longer an option, and actors feel compelled to commit to urgent reform. When this urgency for policy reform is accompanied by policy preferences that diverge among the key actors, a likely outcome is a substantial gap between the rhetorical commitment to reform on one hand, and actual policy changes on the other, resulting in symbolic policy change, as shown in Table 4.3.

Chapters 2 and 3 indeed demonstrated that the 'liminal' impact of the temporal context, in particular, is related to symbolic changes, because they are powerful engines of a change rhetoric, causing leaders to get 'carried away by symbolism or emotion' (Welch 2005: 56), even when their policy preferences diverge substantially. Liminal events – sudden, contingent 'triggering events' that may constitute turning points within the critical juncture – encourage both change players and status quo players to find a way out of their standoff by providing a mix of noncostly accommodating gestures, rhetorical shifts and symbolic changes to existing policy. Chapters 2 and 3 have shown that such changes or accommodating gestures are mostly directed at the macro level, where arguably they are most visible. In a highly salient temporal context, replete with liminal events that challenge 'politics as usual', it has been shown that even the status quo players chose to engage in a 'radical change' rhetoric. 'Deep democracy' or 'more for more' both represent such symbolic shifts and gestures. These policy changes, however, do not constitute substantive adjustments or deviations from the *status quo ex ante*. In this way the gap between rhetoric and reality regarding what the EU says and what it does in its 'neighbourhood', discussed by other authors (Casier 2013; Warkotsch 2006), also applies to the process of policy change after critical junctures.

Symbolic change thus is a policy revision that is almost entirely rhetorical in nature, often taking place at the macro level. The wording signals a shift in policy aims, objectives and often even the underlying paradigm, but in practice it is not substantiated with first-, second-, or third-order policy changes. A good example was the 'more for more' strategy of the ENP after the 2011 reform, ostentatiously announced as a new step change in the Neighbourhood Policy, which was now to focus on promoting democracy. Meanwhile, the financial envelope of funding actually conditional upon democratic reform (the Support to Partnership, Reforms and Inclusive Growth [SPRING] funding) was a mere €500 million for 2011–13: 7 per cent of the total ENP budget for those years. Meanwhile, the eventual policy changes did not break substantively with many of the pre-Arab uprisings policies at the micro or meso levels, but instead consisted of a 'rebranding of existing initiatives' (Echagüe, Michou and Mikail 2011: 330), a rewrapping of old policies in new rhetoric.

Chapter 3 has shown that the process of 2015 ENP reform likewise featured symbolic reforms. The reform episode was to a large extent shaped by its temporal context. After the Vilnius Summit in late 2013, when Viktor Yanukovych decided to postpone signing an AA with the EU, media reported the EU as 'stunned' by the course of events (Euractiv 2013). The subsequent annexation of the Crimea in March 2014 was a crossing of the Rubicon, a breach of international law involving Russian troops that drew sharp criticism across Europe, ushering in momentum for reform, which was again exacerbated with the downing of flight MH17 during the summer of 2014. Overall, these events constituted a temporal context within which actors were eager to demonstrate a commitment to reform. As a senior EU official commented to me:[2]

> I would say we are perhaps running the risk of being behind the events a little bit, each and every time. We move decisively in one direction or another, we had a decisive move towards democracy [after] the Arab Spring, and we were following it as the EU with our ENP revision, factoring it into our approach. Then we had the big instability in the east in the context of [the] Ukraine [crisis] and the south in the wake of the Arab Spring and now we are factoring the need of stability in our policy.

To summarise, according to Hall third-order change is paradigmatic, marked by 'radical changes in the overarching terms of policy discourse' (Hall 1993: 279). Chapters 2 and 3 showed that such radical changes in the terms of policy discourse may occur *without* there being a radical alteration in the policy tools, objectives or implementation preferences themselves. They showed that there are situations in which symbolic changes to the macro-ambitions of a policy can be easier to achieve than changes to policy tools, objectives and calibrations. Declarations do not often require unanimity, whilst they do have a strong symbolic element, showing the actor in question is doing something and on the 'right side of history'. Changes to policy tools and objectives, however, do actually require both institutional agreement and the commitment of resources, which is especially complicated in the European institutional context.

Constructive ambiguity

The second analytical category this book proposes is *constructive ambiguity*. The term has been attributed to Henry Kissinger, who used it as a negotiating technique during the 1970s. It is referred to as 'the deliberate use of ambiguous language in a sensitive issue in order to advance some political purpose' (Berridge and James 2003: 51). In negotiation, it implies pushing for an ambiguous text that provides opportunities for advancing the interests of all negotiating parties (Elgindy 2001). It has been used to define international agreements, e.g. by Dingley describing the Belfast Declaration (2005: 1) as 'a form of words that all could sign up with because each party could interpret them differently'.

The notion of policy ambiguity has been explored in public policy studies, although even there sparingly (Edelman 2001; Moynihan 2006; Palier 2007). Bruno Palier uses the term 'polysemy' in his work on the evolution of the French pension system, which he argued was highly resistant to change, characterised by far-reaching institutional lock-in effects. Polysemy literally means the co-existence of multiple meanings for a word or phrase. According to Palier, in order to be viable and to accommodate both left-wing and right-wing parties as well as employers and trade unions new measures had to be polysemic in order to garner support from divergent interests, bringing together contradictory interpretations around the broadest agreement possible.

Ambiguous propositions can be identified when vagueness surrounds the meaning of adopted measures, and divergent interpretations of the solutions that are adopted 'lie[s] right at the very heart of their political functionality' (Palier 2007: 99–100). Ambiguity is strategic in circumstances where clarity would face strong opposition (Jegen and Mérand 2014: 183).

In this book, I use constructive ambiguity as a term to identify EU foreign policy changes which are viable because, owing to their vague formulation, they mean different things to different key actors, leaving significant room for interpretation.

Ambiguity is sometimes presented as a constraint on policymaking or as a means of postponing conflict into the future. Others see ambiguity as a form of 'incomplete contracting' (Farrell and Héritier 2005: 277), i.e. actors moving forward with a political project while disagreeing over its implementation, thereby delaying the decision on change. Finally, some scholars (Edelman 2001: 80) see it as a conspicuous political communication strategy, a way of concealing conflict. In this sense it would obscure the incomplete contracts, presenting them as actual policy outcomes.

But this book argues, in tune with the work on ambiguity of the past decade in policy areas other than foreign policy (Best 2008; Jegen and Mérand 2014; Moynihan 2006; Palier 2005, 2007) that instead of conceptualising ambiguity as an outcome of policy change which implies stalling and deadlock, ambiguity is better understood as a constructive technique of governance. It facilitates agreements which aggregate different and even contradictory interests, often concerning new measures. Constructive ambiguity as the outcome of a policy change process is thus not the postponement of a strategy, but can be a strategy in and of itself, a way to move forward despite disagreements. Ambiguity, thus, can be a politically functional outcome of policy change.

The notion of such constructive ambiguity has been studied in other areas of EU policymaking. Stanley Hoffmann addressed the notion of ambiguity in the construction and integration of the European Union. 'There has always been most progress', he argues (1995: 131), 'when the Europeans were able to preserve a penumbra of ambiguity around their enterprise, so as to keep each one hoping that the final shape would be closest to his own ideal, and to permit broad coalitions to support the next moves.' The extant literature, however, posits that political entrepreneurs generally shy away from pursuing constructive ambiguity because of the associated risks. Coalitions built around ambiguity and vague proposals, authors such as Jegen and Mérand (2014) or Hoffmann (1995) argue, are hard to sustain. Chapters 2 and 3 in this study, however, seem to indicate that constructive ambiguity does occur quite frequently in EU policymaking. This may be due to the particular nature of EU decision-making, which is scattered across a variety of institutions and which brings together twenty-seven member states. The test-drives in Chapter 5 further engage with this notion of constructive ambiguity in order to assess to what extent it is a politically viable strategy in EU foreign policymaking.

Unlike for symbolic changes, the temporal context is less relevant in determining this particular outcome of policy change than the constellation of preferences among the key actors. Ambiguous agreements are likely to be reached when key actors share neither a common vision of the policy changes desired, nor the same interest in those measures (Palier 2005: 131). When actor preferences diverge, ambiguous changes provide a politically viable alternative to first- and second-order changes. They allow decision-makers to 'muddle through' (Lindblom 1959), despite disagreement. A good example is the proposition in the 2015 revised ENP to make the ENP 'more political', reflecting the EU's interests better (European Commission and High Representative for Foreign Affairs and Security Policy 2015a: 4), which was both ambiguous and constructive. It was ambiguous because it did not mean the same thing to all of the key actors. To Germany and France this meant a greater role for the EEAS. France also was eager to make the ENP more adaptable to the crises with which Europe is faced from time to time, through an additional budget provision for the management of crisis in the 'neighbourhood'. A 'more political ENP' to France also meant a less stringent pursuit of conditionality in a more political, EU-interest-based policy focused on crisis management and security. Finally, to Poland and also to the Commission, making the ENP more political essentially meant strengthening the policy through a greater commitment by the EU: fewer bilateral policies, more EU-wide activity. Poland did not wish to see a greater role for the

EEAS. There thus was a divergence in policy preferences. At the same time, the push for a more political ENP was constructive, as it aggregated the different and diverging interests of the key actors. It was a policy change of which the Commission and the EEAS, Germany, France and Poland had all argued in favour. Here we find that the use of the notion of a more 'political' ENP was ambiguous, in which divergent interpretations and a vagueness surrounding the meaning of the measure made the policy change politically viable. It indeed became one of the four major changes during the 2015 ENP revision.

Other examples of constructive ambiguity are the fleeting reference to the UfM in the 2015 ENP revision. In an apparent compromise to Poland and France, the revised ENP states that the EaP and the UfM are to be strengthened. The revised document states the EU intends to 'give priority, wherever suitable, to the UfM in its regional cooperation efforts' (European Commission and High Representative for Foreign Affairs and Security Policy 2015a: 18). It is not spelled out how the UfM is supposed to fit into the new ENP and the document explicitly calls for the meetings to be ad hoc. It is precisely because of the document's ambiguity that it received nominal support from all actors involved. ENP changes with greater clarity (e.g. a greater role for the EEAS) would probably have failed to rally the agreement of all parties involved or would have resulted in diluted compromises. And whereas 'to give priority wherever suitable to the UfM' arguably can be called a diluted compromise, it was a compromise that made the revised ENP more palatable to actors in favour of a stronger UfM.

Constructive ambiguity is more than a theoretical concept that allows us to better capture the outcomes of policy change processes. It directs our attention to a frequent and important outcome of EU policy change processes. Understanding the way in which European decision-makers deal with critical junctures and other policy challenges requires an understanding of their efforts to create constructive ambiguities as a technique of governance that offers a way out of stalemate. Table 4.2 summarises the two analytical categories that are thought to provide an additional analytical layer through which the institutional changes made to the ENP in the wake of two critical junctures can better be understood.

Most likely outcomes of change

In Chapters 2 and 3, I explored two factors that, I argue, explain the kinds of change we may expect after critical junctures: institutional plasticity – the way institutions allocate authority and structure decision-making; and the temporal context surrounding a critical juncture. First, the institutions of

Table 4.2 Symbolic change and constructive ambiguity

	Level	Substance	Directionality away from status quo ex ante
Symbolic change	Macro	Changed rhetoric and a declaratory commitment to new policy, combined with little to no substantial adjustments to policy	0
Constructive ambiguity	Micro/meso	Deliberately ambiguous and vague policy changes, that are constructive because they allow for different interpretations and thus garner support from diverging interests	0/+

the policy area under scrutiny and their plasticity determine who the key actors are and what room they have to shape policy change. The way in which the policy area under scrutiny is governed, moreover, can exacerbate the consequences of diverging member state preferences, because foreign policy change in the EU setting hinges on member state agreement. Radical and substantive policy adjustments need to be approved by all member states. As one interviewee told me, 'the EU is entangled in its own procedures. It is heavy machinery. By the time we found the right tool, things change' (Interview PO15). Another senior EU official called the EU a slow-moving 'super tanker' (Interview PO22).

Chapters 2 and 3 found that the dispersed institutional basis for EU foreign policymaking in areas such as the ENP, the technocratic approach the Commission has historically taken and this heterogeneity in member state preferences together provide fertile ground for more ambiguous policy changes, which carefully play into diverging policy preferences, not only because they are easier to agree upon, but also because the plastic institutional structures provide room for such ambiguity.

The second explanatory factor was temporal contingency, as this study underlines that policy change happens not in a vacuum, but is embedded in a particular temporal context, and is shaped by the structural, conjunctural and liminal features of this context. The structural impact of time refers to how the historical development of the policy area under study determines who the key actors are, what their power is and what kind of institutional

Table 4.3 Most likely policy change outcomes

Temporal context	Policy change preferences about the substance/level of change	
	Convergent ————————➤ Divergent	
Non-salient ↓ Salient	First or second-order (incremental) change	No change or Constructive ambiguity
	Third-order paradigm change	Symbolic change (possibly accompanied by first-order change)

landscape they need to navigate to manage policy. The conjunctural impact of time refers to the wider, medium-term political conjuncture in which the policy reform takes place. We have seen in both Chapters 2 and 3 that the policy reforms described took place in a context of European crisis. In the 2015 reform of the ENP, the immediate temporal context consisted of a stream of (unanticipated) events and crises, ceaseless high-level summitry, often without satisfying results, and political fragmentation across Europe. The political bandwidth available to devote to ENP reform was drastically limited for many actors.

Finally, the liminal impact of the temporal context refers to the several triggering events that shape the decision-making process. It has been argued that decision-makers perceive certain events, developments or dates as 'decision points', which greatly amplify the salience of the event, making leaders more strident in their willingness to propose policy changes. The statements made in the wake of the Arab uprisings by Commission President Barroso, Neighbourhood Commissioner Füle and HR/VP Ashton and detailed in Chapter 2, which had a strong whiff of *mea culpa*, underline the perceived salience of the Arab uprisings, and contrast their initial wariness to publicly support the Middle Eastern protestors. They show the increased sense of urgency that reform of the European approach towards the southern neighbours acquired over time, which played an important role in transforming the 'regular' ENP revision, planned in 2010, into a revision of the ENP's grand ambitions.

The liminal impact of the temporal context can be further amplified by the broader conjunctural and structural context in which policy change takes place. For example, the focus on stabilisation that became apparent in the 2015 reform round was partially in response to the events taking place in Ukraine. But the broader temporal context was one of increasing security threats emanating from the European 'neighbourhood' in the wake of the Arab uprisings, such as the continued Syrian war and the rapid influx of refugees from North Africa and Syria, exacerbating existing worries over European security. While these structural and conjunctural features of the temporal context might not by themselves have sufficed to prompt this particular policy outcome to occur, they served to amplify the impact of liminal events taking place during the critical juncture on the decision-makers. They were important in structuring the historical episode in which the ENP was substantially reshaped.

The issue of salience and its impact on decision-making has been discussed by other authors, some of whom focus on salience at the mass level – when issues become salient to citizens (Jacobs and Weaver 2015: 448), while others study the salience perceived by decision-makers (Capoccia 2016b: 1112; Welch 2005: 56; Baumgartner and Jones 1993: 129–30). The shared argument is that institutional reform can become decidedly salient as a result of 'triggering events' (Capoccia 2016b: 1112). The critical juncture is among events that make the temporal context more salient, as it throws into question 'normal' policymaking, which becomes subject to criticism and revision. The events hit at the heart of the existing policy area, exposing its deficiencies (Boin, t'Hart and McConnell 2009: 98), opening 'different paths to the future that were hitherto unforeseen, unimagined or simply unacceptable' (Alink, Boin and t'Hart 2001: 290).

An important finding in this previous research into salience and decision-making, which resonates in the findings of this study, is that a sudden high salience of an issue area need not result in substantive policy changes. For one thing, this may be because salience is often ephemeral (Kingdon 1995: 198). Where the mobilisation that it brings about is hard to sustain over time, actors with power over the reform agenda may shelve or delay reforms (Capoccia 2016b: 1112). Crucial in this research, moreover, is the fact that the effect of salience on the policy process is mediated by institutional constraints on decision-making. Inertia or minimal policy change are the most likely outcomes when key actor preferences regarding policy change diverge, in a context that is not salient, i.e. a temporal context that falls within the remit of 'normal' policymaking, when there is no increased urgency for reform owing to the occurrence of liminal events.

Incremental first- and second-order change are the most likely outcomes when the key actors' preferences converge, in the same non-salient temporal context. When in a salient temporal context, actor preferences regarding the directionality of policy change converge, there is the possibility of a wholesale revision of the underpinnings of a policy, i.e. Hall's paradigm change, after first- and second-order changes have been tried and tested without success.

Thus far these expectations do not diverge from traditional accounts of policy change (Baumgartner 2013; Hall 1993). But when great demand for political action builds up after several high-impact occurrences and this combines with significant divergences in policy preferences among the decision-makers, paradigm change may not be feasible, where the required agreement among actors to achieve institutional change is not reached. Such situations, I argue, make more likely outcomes that fall outside Hall's typology. Table 4.3 provides a schematic account of the most likely policy outcomes. The following section will outline these more likely policy changes: symbolic change and constructive ambiguity.

Symbolic change and constructive ambiguity do not merely measure or categorise the degree or kind of policy change that follows from the decision-making process. They rather underline that not all policy change is substantive in nature the way first-, second- and third-order policy changes are. But the lack of immediate and substantive policy change does not mean the process of policy change has failed, that symbolic or ambiguous policy changes are 'defaults' in the process of EU foreign policy change, or represent postponed decisions.

Rather, symbolic change and constructive ambiguity represent distinct options or strategies in the policy change process, a different way of responding to critical junctures, especially under certain conditions, that deserve further attention. They thus offer an additional analytical layer for understanding how EU foreign policy change may occur and what specific forms it may take, complementing the three orders of Hall's typology, which we have established do not capture the full story when we think about EU foreign policy change in the 'neighbourhood'. The case studies have shown that we might see elements of third-order change, i.e. a breakdown of the original policy rationale and rhetorical breaks with the previous policy paradigm, combined with first-order adjustments to the substance of the policy. Symbolic change – the rhetorical over-selling of minor or small changes to suit the changing context – and constructive ambiguity – deliberately ambiguous and vague policy changes that are constructive because they allow for different interpretations and thus garner support from diverging interests – are especially useful in a European context in which agreement must be reached by a variety of actors with diverging interests.

Conclusion

After having mapped the level, substance and the directionality of policy changes made to the European Neighbourhood Policy in the 2011 and 2015 reform rounds in Chapters 2 and 3, this research has found instances of policy change which are difficult to identify using the threefold typology proposed by Peter Hall (1993). This is either because first-order and second-order policy changes – which are supposed to precede or at least accompany third-order paradigm changes – are absent, or because they constitute a different kind of paradigm change, where the policy rationale is questioned and modified, without the nitty-gritty of the policy undergoing any substantive change.

This book has studied the process of policy change through a historical institutionalist lens. As Chapters 2 and 3 have shown, two historical institutionalist concepts – institutional plasticity and temporal contingencies – have had an important impact on the process of changing policy, and play an important role in shaping its outcome. Primarily, the plasticity of European foreign policy institutions, when combined with a fraught temporal context that may greatly increase the urgency of visible reforms, makes Hall's typology of policy changes quite difficult. As this chapter has argued, in this typology first- and second-order changes occur continuously, while third-order change occurs when these adjustments fail, the old policy paradigm breaks down and a new paradigm replaces the old.

This research has shown that the particular institutional features of EU foreign policymaking, interacting with the temporal context, may alter this process. The institutions governing EU foreign policy, especially those governing the ENP, bring together member states with highly heterogeneous preferences, and constrain policy in this respect. This is something that has been confirmed in my interviews of EU officials, several of which have been cited in the previous chapters. At the same time, the ENP is prone to being moulded and shaped by key actors, because of its technocratic and trade-oriented nature, and its quite weak legal basis. This chapter has described how, under conditions of heterogeneous policy preferences in a highly salient temporal context, *symbolic changes* fare well. They are politically useful because they indicate a willingness to take immediate steps, to demonstrate that action is being taken in order to avoid future crisis while, despite such accommodating gestures, the main features of the policy remain intact. Where symbolic change is often built on grand statements without substantive backing, *constructive ambiguity* can be highly strategic in circumstances 'when clarity would create strong opposition' (Jegen and Mérand 2014: 182). Constructive ambiguity refers to deliberately ambiguous and vague policy announcements, that are constructive precisely because their vagueness allows for different interpretations, enabling them to garner support from diverging interests.

In an attempt to complement the traditional categorisation of policy change into three levels in order to account better for changes made to EU foreign policy, this book thus proposes to add symbolic change and constructive ambiguity to the spectrum of policy changes. While both have been discussed in public policy studies, and constructive ambiguity has been discussed in EU internal policy areas such as the single market, there has been very little attention paid to the role of symbolic changes and constructive ambiguity in the field of EU foreign policy.

The penultimate section of this chapter underlined that symbolic policy change and constructive ambiguity nuance the possible outcomes of policy change because these categories indicate how there may be outcomes of the policy change process that are not substantive in nature, but still may have implications for the future course of the policy. More importantly, rather than measuring the degree or kind of change, they elucidate an (in my view understudied) response that the EU, with its distinct, dense institutional setting (especially regarding its 'neighbourhood') may offer to external challenges. Constructive ambiguity and symbolic change are not defaults on the road to first-, second- or third-order change, but should rather be seen as alternative courses of action that under certain conditions are more likely.

Notes

1 Interview PO19.
2 Interview PO22.

5

Test-driving the analytical framework

This chapter takes the analytical framework presented in this book on three 'test-drives'. As mentioned in the Introduction, combining two in-depth case studies with three shorter test-drives of the theory in this book allows me to flesh out the class of situations which form appropriate testing grounds for my analytical framework. The goal of test-driving my theory in these cases of policy change is to increase our confidence in the analytical steps developed in the previous chapters, by complementing the two case study chapters with additional tests. This also allows me to assess further the design and handling of the analytical framework. Rather than testing a theory through the use of large-n studies, Welch (2005: 9) argues, test-drives have the purpose of judging the performance of the newly developed framework, to assess 'its comfort, its fit-and-finish', whilst keeping the focus on detailed process tracing. The test-drives illustrate the various change outcomes that are possible in the wake of a critical juncture, as well as several reasons for this variety in outcome. They also provide more insight into the conditions under which policy changes are a more likely outcome of the change process, and what the role might be of both temporal contingency and institutional plasticity, the two explanatory factors this book foregrounds. In this way, the test-drives demonstrate how the framework can be used and applied to varying practical instances of EU foreign policy change by those aiming to reconstruct change episodes through historical process tracing.

These test-drives include the changes to EU policy developed in response to rising disinformation coming from Russia in 2014–15, those resulting from the migration and asylum crisis of 2015 and, finally, the EU's policy response to the greater critical juncture in European security which came to the fore in 2014. These cases have been selected for several reasons. A feature they all share is that they concern recent change episodes, in which a variety of different actors was involved at both the European level and the member state level. Students will recognise these episodes as they filled news and analysis sections during their peak. The historical development of the three policy areas differs: policy areas such as migration have deep roots and consist of a variety of policy frameworks and instruments, whereas strategic communication is a relatively new policy instrument with an institutional legacy that is much less strong, historically. A further difference between the cases concerns their time frame. For the first test-drive on the EU's response to rising disinformation, I assess the period from the start of the critical juncture in 2014 until the East StratCom Task Force was launched in 2015. For the crisis in migration and asylum, I focus on 2015 – the year in which the number of asylum seekers entering the EU rose exponentially, and 2016, when the most important policy responses were presented. The last test-drive concerns a longer critical juncture, lasting from 2014 until 2018, with the main policy changes presented in 2017. Allowing this variety in time frames allowed me to explore whether a longer time frame affects the usefulness of the framework. What emerges is that, although in-depth process tracing becomes much more resource-intensive in longer cases, a longer critical juncture does not pose a methodological problem for the application of the framework proposed here.

Finally, the policy changes that emerge as the output of the decision-making process also differ between test-drives, with some encompassing a host of different policy changes across areas (such as migration or security), whilst the EU East StratCom Task Force is a much smaller and more restricted policy area. This allowed me to flesh out the scope conditions under which the analytical framework is most likely to operate optimally. What emerges from the test-drives is that assessing policy change in the wake of crisis is more straightforward when the changes occur within a closely delimited policy framework.

These test-drives, like the empirical studies in Chapters 2 and 3, engage in historical process tracing. They draw on a wide range of policy documents, non-papers, White Papers and speeches, complemented with a review of the secondary literature and semi-structured interviews. Overall, the test-drives are shorter, build on fewer interviews and probe the institutional landscapes of the policy areas in less depth. Yet they helpfully demonstrate the use of the analytical framework in quite different settings, to see EU foreign policy change at work and to serve as a guide for applying this framework to different case studies.

A crisis of disinformation and information operations, 2014–15

> It is very difficult to look for a black cat in a dark room, especially if it is not there. All the more stupid to look for it there if this cat is clever, brave and polite.
>
> Sergey Shoygu, Russian Defence Minister, 2014

In August 1835, the *New York Sun* began a six-part series that described how an English astronomer had discovered a civilisation on the Moon. He had observed scenes of humanoid beavers, oceans and temples on the Moon's surface. Later known as the Great Moon Hoax, the *Sun* claimed that this discovery had been published in the *Edinburgh Journal of Science*, which in reality had ceased to exist a year before the purported publication. The hoax soon turned out to be an attempt to raise the sales of the newspaper, with great success.

Fake news, propaganda and the twisting of information for some form of gain have existed throughout the ages. The terminology has shifted to concepts such as 'information operations', 'perception management' and 'reflexive control' but, in essence, it concerns the coordinated manipulation, collection and use of information to a strategic advantage. The potential of the internet for generating and disseminating false information has accelerated and amplified such actions worldwide. On an average day, for example, 500 million tweets are sent out into the world, whilst encrypted messaging applications such as Telegram represent frontier vectors in the spread of disinformation. The many possibilities for disseminating information have lowered the threshold for actors to engage in mis- and disinformation, and greatly expanded its reach.

In the wake of the Ukraine conflict in 2014, Russian-driven disinformation and information operation campaigns came into sharp focus as an important and disruptive means of conflict. In the official Russian foreign policy discourse, the crisis in Ukraine was framed as a result of Western expansionism: '[the problems in Ukraine] reflected the serious systemic problems in the Euro-Atlantic area, where Western countries have tried to strengthen their own security in the last quarter of a century, without considering Russian interests, in a constant advancement towards the east of its geopolitical space', wrote the Russian Ministry of Foreign Affairs (Ministry of Foreign Affairs of the Russian Federation 2014a). Similar statements were made by Russia's Permanent Representative to the UN, Vitaly Churkin, who at the UN Security Council meeting on 1 March 2015 accused the EU of meddling in Ukrainian domestic issues with the aim of cornering Russia (UN Security Council 1/3/2014). This version of events was also broadcast among the population of the Baltic states, where there are a significant number of Russian speakers. Russia supports a plethora of media initiatives worldwide that support its narrative. The Latvian TV channel PBK broadcast in Russian to 4 million viewers in Estonia and Latvia, which translates to around two-thirds and one-quarter respectively of their total populations at the time (Bentzen and Russell 2015: 4). Other Russian outlets such as Sputnik and Russia Today also operate in the region and beyond.

This test-drive assesses how the rise of strategic disinformation and information operations formed critical junctures for the European Union after 2014, and how the EU has responded in terms of policy change.

The Russian strategy with regard to information campaigns domestically or internationally is not the object of scrutiny in this test-drive. I start from the established assumption that the dissemination of information and propaganda is part of the Kremlin strategy in the region, and during the Ukraine conflict in particular. The Kremlin invested a significant amount of time and money in a communication strategy that puts forward its particular view of the crisis in Ukraine, aimed at swaying public opinion not just in Russia, but also in the West. Shoygu stated that media and information 'have become yet another type of weapons [sic], yet another component of the armed forces' (Interfax 2015) while Dmitry Kiselev – sometimes called the Kremlin's 'chief propagandist' (Bentzen and Russell 2015) – stated that information wars had become the main type of warfare (Yaffa 2014).

In the following sections I shall explain first what the institutional set-up of this policy area was at the time. Then I will explain why the rise of strategic disinformation, and the increased information operations stemming from Russia, created a critical juncture for the European Union. I shall then explain how this prompted a range of policy changes, most importantly the setting up of the East StratCom Task Force.

Institutional set-up and historically created arrangements

Although strategic communications and public relations have deep roots in the private sector, the term only became a focus of governments and institutions in the West around the turn of the millennium. Before that, the term 'public diplomacy' had been used since the beginning of the Cold War.

In the early 2000s, the US government recognised strategic communication as a critical element in public diplomacy and in its military interventions in troubled areas (Hallahan et al. 2007: 8). Around this time, public communication by governmental or semi-private organisations across the EU began increasingly to be referred to as 'strategic communication' in the singular or in the plural (Macnamara and Gregory 2018). Although the term has been expanded as different actors engaged in the practice, it is generally accepted that strategic communication refers to the practice of purposeful communication to advance a mission or goals (Hallahan et al. 2007). A more elaborate definition establishes it as 'a systematic series of sustained and coherent activities, conducted across strategic, operational and tactical levels, that enables understanding of target audiences and identifies effective conduits to promote and sustain particular types of behaviour' (Cornish, Lindley-French and Yorke 2011: 4).

Strategic communications at the EU level were not very developed at the dawn of this critical juncture. The Euronews channel set up in 1993 to promote a European perspective on current affairs does receive European funding, but over the years its varying ownership (among its former owners is Ukrainian media tycoon Dmytro Firtash who has close ties to the Kremlin) meant it never served as an outlet for the Union. Currently 88 per cent of Euronews is owned by the Egyptian billionaire Naguib Sawiris (Stefano 2020).

Within the overall EU communications budget, there was no separate funding line for strategic communications in the Union's external relations, or for strategic communications in general. At the dawn of the critical juncture, this budget was spread over a variety of DGs and institutions, which have varying competences and run varying projects and campaigns. The same goes for EU delegations and EU member state embassies worldwide, as written in a report by the European Union Institute for Security Studies (EUISS), who long engaged in strategic communications 'half-heartedly, as a part-time activity and an afterthought' (European Union Institute for Security Studies 2016a: 30).

How plastic is the policy area?

In earlier chapters I explained that the concept of plasticity holds particular analytical value for students of policy change. What also has been called the 'partial bite' of institutions (Capoccia 2016b; Lohmann 2003) implies that institutions are not intermediaries between powerful actors and outcomes, but malleable, 'plastic'. In other words they can give form to the process of change and take form from it, being both constraining and malleable in the hands of powerful actors.

The policy area of strategic communication is quite plastic. Because there was little previous policy in this particular area, member states such as Latvia were able to take the lead and shape the course of EU policy in the area of strategic communication. This policy entrepreneurship combined with certain temporal factors, as discussed below, to enable the EU to take some steps in this policy field. At the same time however, the decision-making structures of the European Council meant that in order to obtain the necessary member state agreement for a communications task force to be set up, compromises had to be made. The scattered nature of the institutional landscape means institutional innovations enter an arena of multiple actors where supervision and coordination are still lacking. One official I interviewed commented that 'one of the major obstacles is that there are so many actors and parties doing this work and not everybody has the same goal' (Interview

PO54). Thus, member states have had scope to enable and constrain policy change in this policy area.

The critical juncture

Although the concept of 'information warfare' and the strategic use of disinformation rose up the agenda once the Ukraine conflict began, these practices are nothing new. Reflexive control is 'a process by which one enemy transmits the reasons or bases for making decisions to another'. It was developed by the Soviet military in the 1960s (Levefbre cited in Thomas 2004: 238). Pynnöniemi (2019) suggests it may even be traced back to Lenin's 1906 essay 'On guerrilla warfare', which discusses some reflexive control practices. She writes how the colour revolutions in Georgia and Ukraine in 2003 and 2004 respectively underlined again the potential of information-psychological techniques employed by Russia, later further exemplified by the distributed denial-of-service attack on the Estonian government in 2007. After 2014, such practices became used under the umbrella term 'hybrid war'.

These practices had emerged well before the Ukraine conflict started. As early as in 2009, the 'Sandworm' espionage operation started targeting EU and NATO telecommunications infrastructure through 2014 (Unwala and Gori 2015; Zetter 2014). Over the summer of 2013, when Ukraine and the EU were in the final stages of negotiating the Association Agreement, the Russians launched 'Operation Armageddon', targeted at unearthing information about the intentions of Ukrainian government, law enforcement, military and security officials (Lookingglass Cyber Threat Intelligence Group 2015). But the use of information-psychological techniques, such as narrative battles or strategic disinformation – defined as focused efforts to deceive, mislead or confuse (Fetzer 2004: 231) – marked the Ukraine conflict. After the demonstrations in Kiev's Independence Square began, several institutions and media outlets in Ukraine faced cyber-attacks, which destabilised the information infrastructure, attacks which continued into 2014 and also targeted Ukrainian members of parliament (Baezner 2018).

With the departure of Yanukovych in early 2014, the Kremlin lost an important ally in the region, who had blocked NATO accession in Ukraine (as well as deciding against signing the AA with the EU in favour of the Russian-led customs union). Russia from this point accelerated its use of non-military instruments in the Ukraine conflict, drawing on diplomatic, legal and media campaigns, but equally through cyber-attacks, the destabilisation of Ukrainian information platforms and cyber-espionage operations (Unwala and Gori 2015; R. Allison 2014). In February, things began to move more rapidly. Soldiers in uniforms carrying no insignia seized strategic sites across the Crimea, cutting off its communications with the rest of the world (Baezner 2018). At this point it was unclear to authorities in the EU and the USA whether these were actually Russian gunmen or not. Armoured personnel carriers were observed leaving the Russian base in Sevastopol and heading towards Simferopol, then turning back. While at first Russia vehemently denied involvement, Putin later acknowledged that '[o]f course, the Russian servicemen did back the Crimean self-defence forces' (Putin 2014).

The presence of Russian troops and special forces in the Crimea, and the lack of clarity regarding this presence in the West, played an important role in the political developments that followed, including the referendum and the annexation of the Crimea. Putin himself stated that his country 'created conditions – with the help of special armed groups and the Armed Forces ... for the expression of the will of the people living in Crimea and Sevastopol' (Putin 2014). Before it was acknowledged that these had been Russian soldiers, they had been described as 'little green men' and 'polite people' which, according to Kurowska and Reshetnikov (2018: 26), was part of an 'effort to portray them as peaceful and non-interfering in local people's lives'.

Although the level of force used was low, the Russian intervention in the Crimea drew on a wide array of diplomatic, legal and media tools, argues R. Allison (2014: 1258). It used 'multiple small-scale military infringements of Ukrainian sovereignty', and benefited from the 'high threshold that the factual evidence of military action had to cross before western states were ready to accuse Russia of the grave act of military aggression' (2014: 1260). Information operations were an important part of the strategy. Both domestically and abroad, the Kremlin invested heavily in putting forward its narrative of events (Dougherty 2014). This became clearer after Malaysian Airlines flight MH17 was shot down by a warhead launched using a Buk missile system from the eastern part of Ukraine, an area controlled by pro-Russian rebels, on 17 July 2014. The tragic incident became the object of an information war in which disinformation, half-truths and labelling occurred at dizzying speeds, facilitated by social media (Dougherty 2014).

It was not always a singular grand narrative that was directed at swaying the opinion in the EU. Rather, many attempts were aimed at the manipulation of public opinion and the disorganisation of societies by sending out multiple and varied messages tailored to selected audiences across Europe. According to Dougherty (2014: 2–3): the conflict in Ukraine accelerated 'profound changes already under way in the Russian media: the centralisation and mobilisation of information resources in the hands of the state'. This, she argues, provides the Kremlin with the 'means to galvanise public opinion domestically and in the region, as well as forcefully assert Russia's policies, views and – increasingly – values internationally'. A NATO report later concluded that Russia's information campaign against Ukraine was particularly successful during its invasion of the Crimea and eastern Ukraine (NATO Center of Excellence on Strategic Communications 2014).

Although some EU member states had long underscored the importance of the issue, it was only in the spring of 2015 that it gained enough salience that a critical juncture for policy change opened (*The Economist* 2015). In March 2015, the European Council 'stressed the need to challenge Russia's ongoing disinformation campaigns' (European Council 2015a). It requested the HR/VP to prepare an action plan on strategic communication, triggering the start of a decision-making process.

Key actors and preferences for policy reform

The Nordic and Baltic states were key actors at the member state level during this critical juncture, due to their commitment to and expertise in strategic communication. Their importance in this critical juncture and in the process of policy change can be seen by tracing how the policy change landed on the agenda. On 9 January 2015, an informal paper by the ministers of Estonia, Lithuania, the United Kingdom and Denmark urged the HR/VP Federica Mogherini to '[boost] the EU's strategic communications activities'. It was subsequently Latvia that put strategic communication on the policy agenda during its Council Presidency in the first half of 2015. A year earlier, the NATO Center of Excellence (COE) for Strategic Communication had launched in Riga. Latvia's Russian-speaking population amounts to about 40 per cent of the country's total population. There are many Russian channels in Latvia, which the government complained were increasingly targeting this population with propaganda.

Latvia's interests in strategic communication are closely aligned with those of Estonia, Lithuania and Poland (Lieǧis 2015). As a way to counterbalance the Russian disinformation campaigns, the Estonian Ministry for Foreign Affairs had founded the Estonian Center of Eastern Partnership (ECEAP) in 2011. The ECEAP has made strategic communication in the eastern 'neighbourhood' a top priority, and aims to put forward 'strategically planned and wisely executed communication work [that] challenges the spread of false and misleading information in the region and within the EU itself and helps promote the EU narrative in a proactive way' (Estonian Center of Eastern Partnership 2015: 6). Four interviews that I conducted with current and former East StratCom employees confirmed my selection of the Nordic and Baltic states as key actors.

The UK was one of the sponsors of the NATO COE for Strategic Communication, and identifies strategic communications as a key priority. Its focus, however, is mainly on NATO, which is why I have not included it as a key actor orchestrating policy change during this critical juncture (HM Government 2015).

I include in my analysis a group of key actors less prominent in their policy proposals, but more visible in their reluctance to pursue a Europe-wide strategic communications strategy. This group of reluctant countries did not share a stance on Russia nor their views regarding the challenge the information wars stemming from Russia posed to the Union. Some of these countries, for example France, were not against countering strategic disinformation in principle back in 2015, but were sceptical of doing so at the European level. Other countries, such as Italy, Greece and Cyprus, were a lot more sceptical of the need to counter Russian disinformation in general. Since 2015 the stances of these countries have developed further in different directions. However, the focus of this test-drive is on the policies that emerged during the critical juncture, in 2014–15. At that time, these reluctant countries shared an unwillingness to set up a European strategic communications unit countering Russian disinformation, as Task Force officials at the time confirmed in interviews I conducted (Interviews PO45, PO46, PO54, PO59).

A 2017 'Kremlin Watch Report' by European Values – a Czech Republic-based NGO quite critical of Russia – classifies European member states and their concern with Russian information wars. It confirms Estonia, Latvia and Lithuania as players at the forefront of the battle against Russian influence, showing the greatest readiness to respond to the threat across the EU. It considers Denmark, the UK and Germany to be countries who experienced an 'awakening' in this respect (Janda et al. 2017). On 8 January 2015, along with the ministers for foreign affairs of the UK, Denmark, Estonia and Lithuania, the (Latvian) Council President Laimdota Straujuma proposed a non-paper on 'boosting the EU's strategic communications in response to Russia's active propaganda campaign in the Eastern neighbour-hood and certain member states' (Foreign ministers of Denmark, Estonia, Finland, Iceland, Latvia, Lithuania, Norway and Sweden 2015).

At the European level, the European Parliament was an important actor in pushing for more EU-wide action on strategic communications during this critical juncture. In 2014, the European elections had led to an increase in Eurosceptic MEPs who contested EU policies in the 'neighbourhood' as well as EU policy towards Russia. This did not, however, impact on the content of EU resolutions on foreign policy, writes Cianciara (2020), who argues that the European People's Party (EPP) managed to tighten its grip on the EU foreign policy agenda from 2014 onwards. The EPP was generally in favour of more strategic communications efforts.

The EP identified the 'deliberately biased information' spread by Russia in various EU languages as a key problem and started urging the Commission to take measures on strategic communication in January 2015. It did not just advocate for a strategic communications team, however, but requested the Commission and the member states to set up a mechanism to collect, monitor and report assistance provided by Russia to political parties and organisations within the EU, to get a greater grip on Russia's influence over political life and public opinion within the Union and in its neighbours (European Parliament 2015a).

The EP strongly condemned the 'undeclared hybrid war against Ukraine, including information war, blending elements of cyber warfare, use of regular and irregular forces, propaganda, economic pressure, energy blackmail, diplomacy and political destabilisation' (European Parliament 2015b). This made it one of the most vocal actors; it centralised the 'Russian propaganda campaign directed towards the EU, its eastern neighbours and Russia itself', calling for a stronger European response. The Parliament called on the Commission and DG NEAR 'to prepare and present to Parliament within two months a communication strategy to counter the Russian propaganda campaign directed towards the EU, its eastern neighbours and Russia itself, and to develop instruments that would allow the EU and its Member States to address the propaganda campaign at European and national level' (European Parliament 2015b). Many of its resolutions in 2015 concerned propaganda and Russian information activities (Bentzen 2015).

Next to the EP, the EEAS played a key role in this critical juncture as it was tasked by the European Council with writing an action plan on strategic communication, which it published in June 2015, and later with setting up a task force to counter disinformation.

Other influential actors in getting the task force off the ground were the European Council, particularly with the support of Donald Tusk, who aided Latvia in getting and keeping it on the European agenda. Because the Council presidency rotates, and there is overlap between the Council and the member states, it is difficult to disentangle the Council's policy preferences. Based on the findings of my process tracing and the interviews I carried out, I do not consider the European Commission a key actor with independent policy preferences behind the East StratCom policy changes, as it was very much the EEAS who took the lead in this regard. The European Commission did set up its own means to communicate the benefits of the EaP in the 'neighbourhood'.

The EP's strong calls for policy changes in this area were followed up by the European Council Conclusions of March 2015, which tasked the EEAS, together with the member states and the European institutions, to set up an action plan on strategic communication to address the challenge coming from Russia (European Council 2015a). In May 2015, the European Parliamentary Research Service published a document outlining 'Russia's manipulation of information on Ukraine and the EU's response' (Bentzen and Russell 2015). It discusses Russia's media offensive in a very detailed way, covering the Russian use of 'internet trolls', the fabrication of stories or the sugar-coating of political messages in entertainment. While a lot of these outlets operate domestically, the EP Research Service describes the state-owned channel Russia Today as the 'main international media weapon', broadcasting in English, Arabic, French, German and Spanish. Other broadcasters such as Russia Beyond the Headlines and Sputnik are part of a broader media offensive.

At the EEAS, the perception of the critical juncture was a little different. Although some in the EEAS were quite supportive of setting up a task force, people that I interviewed working inside and outside strategic communications state that HR/VP Mogherini (who was head of the EEAS) did not see strategic communication as a priority. As one interviewee summarised it, 'the idea was [just] to have the team somewhere doing something' (Interview PO59).

A non-paper circulated by the foreign ministers of Estonia, Lithuania, Denmark and the UK in January 2015 warned of Russian propaganda, of which 'the objectives are to discredit EU narratives, erode support for legitimate Governments in the region, demoralise local populations, disorient Western policy-makers, and undermine the concept of free, independent, pluralistic media' (Lidegaard et al. 2015). Latvia did not sign this non-paper because it was holding the Council presidency at the time, although it supported its key claims (Interview PO59). During its presidency, Latvia stated its intentions to launch a Europe-wide, Russian-language media outlet which would counter Kremlin propaganda (Euractiv 2015b; *Time* 2015).

During the Nordic-Baltic Foreign Ministers' meeting in May 2015, the ministers of these states expressed their commitment to 'furthering strategic communication, based on facts and openness, and to supporting independent media' as a means to counter the propaganda and disinformation coming from Russia (Foreign ministers of Denmark, Estonia, Finland, Iceland, Latvia, Lithuania, Norway and Sweden 2015).

The group of more reluctant member states was unconvinced strategic communications needed to be dealt with at the European level, especially if the European Commission would take up the issue of strategic communications. Some countries were quite opposed to this. Greece, for example, regularly opposed EU sanctions against Russia as well as other measures that it deemed would alienate Russia (BBC News 2016). In October 2014 the Greek Defence Minister Panos Kammenos even blamed propaganda by the West for causing the Ukraine Crisis: 'western NGOs sponsored by Germany or foundations like the Clinton Institute, provoked the crisis in Ukraine where a *coup d'état* overthrew the legal government' (Dempsey 2015). Some member states in this group, such as France, felt that the money going to the east should rather be spent on countering Islamist propaganda (Interview PO45, PO46, PO54).

Temporal contingency

The analytical framework in this book explains policy change by first taking into account the impact of institutions on the decision-making process, and second by assessing how historical context, political events and their timing affect this same process. I have argued previously that events may both generate and reinforce actor preferences and power relations.

I divided the assessment of the temporal context into three registers: *structural* – long-term historical processes (decades, centuries); *conjunctural* – the medium-term historical context (a few years); and finally *liminal* – particular events and occurrences (days, weeks, months). The structural temporal factors to consider in this critical juncture are the historical experience of the Nordic and Baltic member states, which have long advocated a stronger stance on disinformation coming from Russia, in part due to their sizeable Russian minorities. Estonia, for example, has a long experience with conflict of a hybrid nature with Russia. In 2007, riots broke out in Tallinn after the government moved the Bronze Soldier, a Soviet war memorial, from the centre of the city to the outskirts. Later that year, a wave of cyber-attacks rattled the Estonian government. Although there was no concrete evidence, the Estonian government suggests the attacks were orchestrated by the Kremlin. The year 2007 turned out to be a transformative one for the Estonian awareness of 'information warfare' in its multiple facets, making it a frontrunner in raising awareness of and increasing resilience against propaganda.

Three important conjunctural factors were at play. First was the rise of the practice of 'hybrid war' or 'information war' as conducted by the Kremlin, as described in the introduction to this section. While the practice had been a grievance to the Nordic and Baltic states as well as Poland for longer, it was only during the Ukraine crisis that this use of information and disinformation during conflict received greater visibility. Second, the EU was in the midst of the Greek debt crisis, which had begun in 2009. The multitude of discussions surrounding the European bail-out of Greece at the time, and the fact that countries like Cyprus, Italy, Portugal and Spain were equally rattled by debt crises, had altered the division of power among member states. Some interviewees have argued that member states which were more

Table 5.1 Preferences for policy reform

Actor	Desired level(s)	Substance	Directionality
Nordic and Baltic States supported by i.a. the UK, Denmark, Czech Republic, Poland, Germany	Macro, meso, micro	- Convinced of threat - Suggest strategic communications operations inside and outside EU territory 'deconstructing propaganda proactively' - setting clear EU-wide communications objectives - improving regulation to counter propaganda - provide (Russian-language) alternatives) - supported by EU funding	++
Reluctant member states (including France, Greece, Italy, Cyprus)	-	- Not convinced of threat - Focus on strategic communications outside of EU territory as foreign policy tool - Not supportive of EU funding - Equal focus on communications efforts countering Islamist propaganda	0
EEAS	Macro, meso, micro	- HR/VP sceptical - Focus on strategic communications outside of EU territory towards Eastern Neighbourhood - Key focus on positive narrative EU benefits - Combat disinformation 'where necessary' by raising awareness	0/+
European Parliament	Macro, meso, micro	- Convinced of threat - Focus on strategic communications and 'deconstructing propaganda' within the EU and in the Eastern Partnership countries - Supported by EU funding - Calls for development of a comprehensive, effective and systematic communication strategy - Supports focus on positive narrative EU benefits	+

0= no deviation from status quo, 0/+= very little deviation from status quo, += deviation from status quo, ++= significant deviation from status quo

reluctant to counter strategic disinformation stemming from Russia were in a weaker bargaining position (Interview PO54, PO59). Another important conjunctural factor was the Latvian Presidency. As mentioned, Latvia was an ardent supporter of countering Russian propaganda. The fact that it would be at the helm of the Council at this time, in the wake of the Ukraine crisis, contributed to the window of opportunity to pursue change.

Most liminal events took place in 2014. According to the interviewees, the key events that strongly accelerated the emergence of the East StratCom Task Force were the escalation of the war in the Crimea, the downing of flight MH17 and the heightened disinformation surrounding this tragic incident, and the escalating war in Ukraine. Interviewees confirm that at the end of 2014 and the beginning of 2015, these events had produced a situation in which several important member states began strongly supporting the launch of such a task force. What changed in 2014 and 2015, conclude the interviewees, was that the overall mood towards strategic communication in the EU changed in the wake of the Crimea annexation and the downing of MH17, facilitated by the Latvian presidency.

Policy output

Table 5.2 summarises the policy output which followed the decision-making process. Despite member state disagreement surrounding the necessity of setting up a strategic communications task force, in March 2015 the Council tasked the HR/VP with setting up to prepare an action plan on strategic communication and a communications team (European Council 2015a). Although as mentioned in 'Temporal contingency' above, the temporal context played an important role in this, an important reason member states in the European Council agreed on setting up a communications team was its very modest nature and vague terminology.

Based on the Council mandate, the, EEAS presented an Action Plan on Strategic Communication in June 2015. It stated the objective as being to increase 'public awareness of disinformation activities by external actors, and improved EU capacity to anticipate and respond to such activities' (European External Action Service 2015). It outlined three main objectives:

1) effective communication and promotion of EU policies towards the eastern neighbours;
2) strengthening the overall media environment in the eastern 'neighbourhood' and in EU member states, including support for media freedom and strengthening independent media; and
3) improving EU capacity to forecast, address and respond to disinformation activities by external actors (European External Action Service 2015: 1).

It is important to note that the documents do not define disinformation, nor is there clarity with regards to what 'addressing' such disinformation entails. As a result, 'disinformation' becomes a catch-all term that may mean varying things to different actors whereas clearer terminology and clearer action points would be needed for more nuance and precision in the EU's strategic communications policy (Pamment 2020: 13). Employees who work or worked at the task force that I interviewed describe how this was a product of compromise. One of the interviewees described the task force priorities as an ambiguous construction which embodied 'all the diverging views of the member states' (Interview PO59).

During the decision-making process, the diverging opinions with regard to how the EU should take up strategic communication impacted the final policy output. First, the East StratCom Task Force was not set up within the European Commission, but in the EEAS. Second and following from that, the Task Force could not address strategic disinformation within the European Union, but only disinformation disseminated in the countries outside the Union, such as Ukraine. The lack of clarity surrounding the term disinformation or the appropriate measures to counter such disinformation was exacerbated by the term lacking a firm legal basis (Pamment 2020). These compromises were made to keep aboard the reluctant group of member states. As one EU official commented to me, 'the compromise was that the team would be established in the EEAS. They turned it into a foreign policy issue. They placed it in the EEAS, making it outward-looking. It was also put under the Italian [HR/VP Federica Mogherini], that was important.' Finally, no budget was allocated to the Task Force, which meant that member states had to second their experts to it voluntarily on a rarely used 'cost-free' basis, i.e. the Union would not pay any of their allowances, making it the financial obligation of the member states to second their experts.

The fact that the Task Force was such a consequence of compromise with a lack of terminological clarity has had consequences for its ability to operate. From the beginning, it was under-equipped and under-funded, a problem exacerbated by its unreliable political mandate (Pamment 2020). Among the first countries to second an expert to East StratCom were the countries who had campaigned for the Task Force: Estonia, Latvia, Lithuania, Denmark, the UK, Sweden and the Czech Republic. Only eight full-time employees worked at the Task Force when it started work in September 2015, five of whom were officials seconded on one-year contracts (Euractiv 2015e). While in 2015 around 10 per cent of officials in the EEAS were on secondment (Euractiv 2015e), at the Task Force this percentage was thus much higher (Association of Accredited Public Policy Advocates to the European Union 2016).

The Task Force long lacked the funding and the manpower for more substantive strategic communication measures. As one EU official commented, 'I think that if anyone wanted to think that our boss just wanted to tick a box [doing this], then he would have quite a lot of reason to think that' (Interview PO23). Another interviewee echoed this sentiment: '[within the EU], there were different perspectives on the challenge, and different perspectives on the response. Actors who were not very supportive of going against Russia, they didn't think that anything could be done by a team of seven people.' The same interviewee explained (Interview PO59):

> [The Task Force] was not regarded as some burning, urgent priority from the beginning. It was more like a quick band-aid to make some member states shut up, and move on. The EU is doing such patching up of things often. Sometimes, they make a few big moves. After the migration crisis, it pumped billions in it. Ukraine happened, let's pump billions there. [Strategic communications] was not a billions thing.

The Task Force is a unique actor in the EU. For one thing, its employees were not traditional EU officials, but experts from the field of communication. According to one interviewee, this made them more proactive and less policy-oriented. Moreover, the fact that almost all employees were experts seconded from countries with a history of Russian disinformation meant they were quite aware of their home country's priorities, and of the necessity to raise awareness about disinformation within the European Union. Moreover, despite its lack of funding, some EU actors are quite committed to supporting and sustaining the Task Force. The Nordic and Baltic member states have been very active in supporting the team and seconding their experts, trying to strengthen the task force, and keeping it on the policy agenda.

Conclusion

The East StratCom Task Force consists of policy output which can be classified as constructive ambiguity: policies where vagueness surrounds the meaning of adopted measures, and divergent interpretations of the approaches that are adopted are essential to their political functionality (Palier 2007: 99–100). The contribution the Task Force makes to developing and furthering societal resilience to disinformation from Russia, or its EUvsDisinfo web platform, indeed have important potential in this respect, but suffer from the ambiguous and unreliable commitment made to change policy in this area.

Hooghe and Marks (2002: 7) argue that ambiguity was key to the success of the market program of the Single European Act: 'the fact that it was all things to all actors'. In a policy area of much smaller remit, it becomes noticeable that such ambiguity may be constraining. Vagueness is deeply

Table 5.2 Policy output on strategic communications

	Policy level		
	Macro	Meso	Micro
Policy goals	Abstract policy aims - Increased public awareness of disinformation activities by external actors (+) - improved EU capacity to anticipate and respond to such activities (+) - Support for freedom of the media and freedom of expression (0) - Public Diplomacy Initiatives in the neighbourhood (0) - Supporting pluralism in the Russian language media space (+)	Policy objectives - effective communication and promotion of EU policies towards the eastern neighbourhood (0) - strengthening the overall media environment in the eastern neighbourhood and in EU Member States, including support for media freedom and strengthening independent media (0) - improved EU capacity to forecast, address and respond to disinformation activities by external actors (+) - addressing disinformation where appropriate	Policy targets - communication campaigns targeting key audiences and focused on specific issues of relevance to those audiences, including local issues in Eastern Partnership countries (0/+) - Communication activities on EU funded programmes, projects and activities in the Eastern Neighbourhood (0/+) - development of 'effective networks of communicators' (+)
Policy means	Policy implementation preferences - Increased EU Strategic Communication capacity (+) - coherent with wider EU communication efforts (0)	Policy tools - Use of OPEN Neighbourhood programme (0) - East StratCom team with contributions from institutions and member states (+)	Policy tool calibrations - drawing on 'other current and planned activities, notably ongoing communication activities carried out by the EU delegations and Member State embassies on the ground, the new regional communication programme OPEN Neighbourhood, and communication related to EU projects' (0) - within the existing budget for EU Strategic Communication (0) - 9 full time employees in 2015

0= no deviation from status quo, 0/+= very little deviation from status quo, += deviation from status quo

embedded in the mandate of the East StratCom Task Force. One of its tasks was to 'address disinformation'. Neither the Action Plan on Strategic Communication presented by the EEAS in June 2015, nor the documents on the East StratCom Task Force put out in 2015, define what 'disinformation' exactly means, or how it differs from misinformation, influence operations or foreign interference, for example. Moreover and relatedly, 'addressing' disinformation is a vague action point. Counter-measures to disinformation may include monitoring and reporting on it, overseeing digital platforms, medium- and long-term assessments of disinformation threats, research collaborations, and much more (Pamment 2020: 16–17).

This terminological vagueness on both the threats to be addressed and the measures taken to do so is exacerbated by the fragile political mandate of the Task Force and its even more fragile financing. After funding provided by the European Parliament expired at the end of 2020, a new source of financing would have to be found. Although it is unlikely East StratCom will not find any funding, the financial uncertainty with which the Task Force has been faced since its inception has affected it. Interviewees working at the Task Force were quite vocal about worries regarding this uncertainty, coupled with not having a permanent staff and their dependence on supportive member states. These worries were the same in 2020 as they had been in 2016.

Finally, policy responsibilities regarding strategic communication have become scattered over an even greater variety of institutions since the critical juncture. Interviewees confirm that this means progress towards attaining the goals of the Task Force is slow and sometimes countered by other actors within the EU pursuing different aims.

Ambiguous agreements, I argued in Chapter 4, are the most likely outcome when key actors share neither a common vision of the desired policy changes, nor the same interest in those measures. This critical juncture showed how whilst the Nordic and Baltic states were convinced of the necessity of EU-wide strategic communications, particularly countering Russian disinformation, this conviction was not shared by all key actors during 2015. The salience of strategic communication was not spread evenly over the key actors. When actor preferences diverge, ambiguous changes provide a politically viable alternative to first- and second-order changes. The decision to not focus strategic communications within the EU but strictly outside it, placing the Task Force within the EEAS, reflects such an ambiguous compromise.

Yet at the same time, ambiguous agreements contain potential as they may act as important placeholders, or signposts for future action. As the Task Force starts to gain knowledge about what works and does not work, or whenever for example the Council presidency shifts to a country that has historically supported the Task Force and puts strategic communication back on top of the policy agenda, its role and budget may be gradually expanded. One could also imagine new 'liminal' events occurring which would re-prioritise strategic communication.

The European asylum crisis, 2015

There have been myriad crises in the EU and further afield over the past decade. Many of these have, in one way or another, tied into the issue of migration. In 2015, a migration and asylum crisis emerged for the EU in its own right (G. Falkner 2016; Scipioni 2017).[1] Asylum applications that year stood at a record high of 1.2 million (Eurostat 2016). EU member states such as Italy or Greece were over-burdened by the number of arrivals. Meanwhile the number of deaths among refugees attempting to enter the Union reached historic heights, which made the EU's policies on migration and asylum increasingly unsustainable in 2015 (IOM 2016; Scipioni 2017; Frontex 2016).

During this critical juncture, member states embarked on divergent and sometimes contradictory national policy responses. Germany, in August of 2015, ceased applying to Syrian refugees the Dublin Regulation, which stipulates that asylum seekers must be registered and lodge their applications in the first EU country they enter, a move welcomed by the European Commission as a sign of 'European solidarity' (Dernbach 2015). Shortly after, Germany suspended Schengen arrangements along its Austrian border by reinstating internal border controls. Germany's unilateral decision meant that many asylum seekers got stuck in Austria and Hungary, where the conditions in which they were held were very poor and drove some to crime. By the end of 2015, Austria, Denmark, France, Norway and Sweden had followed Germany, risking the future of the Schengen Agreement.

Institutional set-up and historically created arrangements

The institutional architecture of the EU's migration policy is dense and complex. With the Treaty of Amsterdam, the Schengen *acquis* was incorporated into EU law. The abolition of border controls within a zone of twenty-six countries in what became the Schengen Area necessitated increased cooperation on the EU's external borders.

After European leaders decided in Tampere in 1999 to develop a common asylum and migration policy, the EU gradually expanded its competencies this area. The Tampere Summit Conclusions were the first to recommend the launch of an 'external' dimension of Justice and Home Affairs (JHA), as external issues such as terrorism, crime and security were increasingly seen as linked to internal European policies. The JHA dimension has grown in importance since 9/11, becoming a central priority of the EU in its foreign policy. Wolff (2012: 11) describes how EU relations with its southern neighbours were affected by this internationalisation of JHA policies, as the EU increasingly uses visa policy, technical assistance on migration, counter-terrorism and readmission agreements as tools in its foreign policy.

At the dawn of the critical juncture and to this day, the institutional architecture and the various responsibilities it confers are diffuse. The EU can initiate, legislate and adjudicate common policies on border control, asylum and visa policy. At the same time, writes Lavenex (2016), the EU has widened its migration regime geographically. In 2004 the EU adopted its first Directive under the Common European Asylum System (CEAS), and in 2005 the EU established the Global Approach to Migration and Mobility as the overarching framework of its external migration and asylum policy (DG Migration and Home Affairs 2016). In parallel, the Union strengthened its capabilities to combat and prevent what it calls 'irregular migration' through setting up Frontex in 2005, which coordinates member states' external border controls. The EU's budget for external migration and asylum policy has increased and allowed the Union to create linkages between different issues such as development, asylum and mobility (Lavenex 2016).

Decision-making on migration is done through 'co-decision' between the European Parliament and the European Council, which votes by qualified majority voting (QMV). National governments retain the right to set quotas for the number of migrants from outside the EU they admit, as migration is a policy area of shared competence. Responsibilities in this domain are thus spread over a variety of actors. In 2015 the EEAS was still finding its feet on the issue, while the European Commission had a multitude of DGs working on varying areas touching on migration. When the Commission underwent a reorganisation at the end of 2014, the Home Affairs directorate was renamed the Directorate-General for Migration and Home Affairs (Collett 2015). But migration policy extends beyond the DG HOME portfolio, as it spills over into the areas of employment, education, foreign affairs and development aid.

This scattered nature of migration policy is exemplified by the way the Commission deals with third countries on the issue. If the country is in crisis or conflict, writes Collett (2015), the lead is taken by the Directorate-General for European Civil Protection and Humanitarian Aid Operations (DG ECHO). If development support is needed, DG DEVCO comes to the fore, the DG with a critical mass of financial resources. Third countries closer to the EU would fall under the leadership of DG NEAR, whilst DG HOME manages cross-portfolio priorities and needs, to coordinate migration policy. At the level of the European Council, there is a complex field of various working groups, contact groups and dialogues working on migration. Some of them are geographically focused, mainly those within the Foreign Affairs Council, whilst the working groups preparing the JHA Council are thematic.

How plastic is the policy area?

According to Guiraudon (2003: 265, 277), this heterogeneous 'motley crew' of actors has rendered the field of migration policy 'adhocratic and contradictory'. Scipioni reiterated this more than a decade later, calling migration policy a field of 'low harmonisation, weak monitoring, low solidarity [with a] lack of strong institutions' which made it increasingly unsustainable during the migration crisis (Scipioni 2017: 1365).

Whilst the Lisbon Treaty has empowered supranational institutions on the issue of migration, the policies in this area retained a high degree of continuity, especially since the European Parliament used its new-found responsibility differently than some analysts had expected, rather supporting and reinforcing the more restrictive policies of the European Council. 'In fact, informal negotiations [in this policy area] started so early in the procedure that it became increasingly difficult to differentiate and single out the positions of each EU institution' (Ripoll Servent and Trauner 2014: 1152). The Lisbon Treaty reinforced the agenda-setting role for the European member states, writes Scipioni, which is 'unparalleled in other policy areas' (2017: 1362). This means the role of the Commission as policy initiator was curtailed.

Migration policy is thus an area of shared competence, and the member states have shown in the past they are willing to exercise their power if they deem it necessary. When Germany reintroduced border controls in the autumn of 2015, it used article 26 of the Schengen Borders Code, which grants states the capacity to 'temporarily reintroduce[e] border control at the internal borders in the event that a serious threat to public policy or internal security has been established' (DG Migration and Home Affairs 2020). Moreover, member states do not always implement or comply with the EU roles they adopt in this policy area. A 2014 report on EU return policy, for example, shows numerous instances of such noncompliance (European Commission 2014).

Overall, migration is a relatively plastic area. This is not because the area has a weak judicial basis – as is the case with the ENP, as Chapters 2 and 3 explored – but rather because of a confluence of factors. These include 1) the curtailed role of the European Commission; 2) the absence of a central governing institution, particularly on the Schengen Agreement where there is very little central governance; and 3) the fact that the proliferation of agencies and institutions working on the issue area allows member states, which have historically held a tight grip over migration and asylum policy, to pursue their preferences by venue shopping.

The EU, moreover, lacks credible and effective enforcement mechanisms if a member state should not comply. The institutions are thus malleable for member states. At the same time, the policy area is constraining in the sense that EU institutions retain a power of initiative and, when finding the right coalition, are able to shape the decision-making process. This critical juncture illustrated this constraining power of European institutions when the European Council voted on a politically very 'hot' topic by QMV, rather than requiring unanimity, as will be discussed below. This mutual malleability of institutions and member states makes migration a plastic policy area.

The critical juncture

Although the number of border crossings into the European Union started to surge after the Arab uprisings in 2011, the year 2015 can be identified as a critical juncture in the Union's migration policy. At the time, the civil wars in Iraq, Syria and Afghanistan continued to wreak havoc on the Middle East, whilst the conditions in which refugees were held in countries like Turkey and Lebanon worsened significantly. Media had reported in April that the number of asylum seekers drowning in the Mediterranean could be expected to break all records if the death rates remained unchecked (Kingsley 2015).

The EU was criticised for its haphazard approach to migration by the UN and Amnesty International (Chonghaile 2015). In October 2014, Mare Nostrum, a search-and-rescue programme run by Italy, was replaced by the Triton Programme of Frontex, which operated with a third of Mare Nostrum's budget and which unlike Mare Nostrum focused primarily on border management, not search and rescue, and did not operate in international waters but 30 nautical miles off the Italian and Maltese coasts. It was contended that the decision to end Mare Nostrum was in part to blame for the sharp rise in deaths at sea among asylum seekers trying to enter the EU (Viegas 2015). And indeed, over the course of 2015, over a million asylum seekers tried to reach Europe across the Mediterranean, making it the largest annual number of asylum seekers in Europe since 1985 and five times the number of the year before. A tragic 3,735 of these people went missing, believed drowned. Most arrived in Greece and Italy. Half of the arrivals were asylum seekers fleeing the Syrian civil war, followed by asylum seekers from Afghanistan and Eritrea. As their numbers grew, Greece and Italy were unable to prevent the migrants from crossing their borders northwards, despite the Dublin Regulation, which stipulates asylum applications need to be processed in the first country of arrival.

The asylum seekers did not disperse equally across the Union. Tens of thousands moved through the western Balkans (UNHCR 2015). Germany received the highest number of asylum applications. Other destination countries were Sweden and France. Hungary had the highest number of applicants per 100,000 population (Eurostat 2016). This uneven burden fed into mounting criticism across the Union, where anti-immigrant and Eurosceptic parties had already been on the rise. Germany's unilateral decisions, first to not apply the Dublin Regulation and subsequently to reinstate border controls, further set the scene for recriminations across Europe. Meanwhile, the humanitarian conditions in which asylum seekers were forced to live, as documented on social media and by institutions such as the UN, were systematically poor.

This book defines a critical juncture as consisting of the loosening of the structure, a heightened contingency during the early stages after an event during which agency takes on greater causal importance than the relatively closed nature of later stages. Overall and confirmed by interviewees (Interviews PO58, PO59) and the extant literature (G. Falkner 2016; Scipioni 2017; Lavenex 2015), 2015 constituted such a critical juncture for the EU migration and asylum policy. The sharp rise in asylum seekers entering the Union, the increase in deaths among these asylum seekers and the clearly exposed divisions among member states greatly heightened both the salience of the policy and the urgency for policy reform. While Juncker warned of an 'existential crisis' for the EU, HR/VP Mogherini argued the refugee crisis posed 'a risk of disintegration' for the EU, or of 'committing suicide' if countries tried going it alone (*EU Observer* 2015). The constraints of the structure within which the EU was already conducting a review of its migration and asylum policy (the Agenda on Migration, which was announced at the end of 2014) were loosened, allowing space for key actors to pursue policy reforms.

Key actors and preferences for policy reform

The key actor at the European level was the European Commission, which according to officials in DG Home at the time whom I interviewed, was under great pressure to react to the crisis: 'as Commission, we had to give a signal, we had to come [up] with innovative proposals, as we faced this huge pressure from all these member states from the south [affected by the crisis] so we had to give a signal of EU solidarity. Italy and Greece were blaming us' (Interview PO60). Despite its curtailed role in the area of migration and asylum, the Commission continued to propose myriad policy reforms in this domain over the course of 2015.

The Agenda for Migration in May 2015 provides insight via its key policy preferences during this critical juncture. Overall, the Commission can be considered to have been a moderate change player. Some of its policy proposals, such as the temporary EU relocation mechanism for asylum seekers, were genuine departures from previous policies, as was its suggestion to reform the Dublin Regulation system.

At the member state level, Schimmelfennig (2018) provides a helpful characterisation of member states as front-line, destination, transit and by-stander states. Germany and France were both among the destination states, and are considered here as key actors in this critical juncture. Germany received the highest number of asylum applicants and its government was quite vocal about where it stood. 'If Europe fails on the question of refugees,' stated Angela Merkel in August, 'it won't be the Europe we wished for' (BBC News 2015b). Germany called for a unified European approach, supported by French Prime Minister Manuel Valls. France is also considered a key actor in this critical juncture, although it was less of a destination state than Germany. The French government stated that the French policy proposals, together with those of Germany, fed into the European Agenda for Migration (Gouvernement Français 2015). Although it supported Germany on the necessity of binding quotas for the relocation of asylum seekers, it was more cautious. In a year leading up to a general election, the French government had to placate strong domestic opposition and anti-immigration sentiment, galvanised by Front National leader Marine Le Pen (Chassany 2015).

Germany and France took the lead in this reform episode by first putting forward a joint non-paper (De Maizière and Cazeneuve 2015). Their stance on an important policy issue throughout this critical juncture, namely whether or not the Dublin system had to be reformed, was ambivalent. Initially, both signalled support for the Commission proposals in its Agenda for Migration, which included Dublin reform through a proposal for a permanent common EU system for relocation in emergency circumstances by the end of 2015 (European Commission 2015a: 6). Yet in their non-paper sent out two weeks after the Agenda was published, the states jointly express their commitment to retaining the Dublin system, and argue that any relocation schemes should 'remain temporary and exceptional and should be part of a global approach on migration. The Dublin system must prevail. We are strongly attached to it, as it is an essential pillar of a balanced Schengen area without internal borders' (De Maizière and Cazeneuve 2015). Some commentators have argued this change was political manoeuvring in order to placate increasingly Eurosceptic domestic audiences. France asked to adapt its quota, requesting that asylum seekers already in France be retroactively taken into account, with which Germany concurred (Euractiv 2015c).

Eventually, a year after the first non-paper, France and Germany favoured a reform of the Dublin System in the way the Commission proposed it. In a non-paper, they wrote the 'Dublin system has to be improved to deal with exceptional circumstances through [a] permanent and binding burden sharing mechanism among all member states', followed by the warning that 'if necessary, Germany and France stand ready to proceed on this matter with a group of like-minded partners' (Ayrault and Steinmeier 2016).

Other key actors in this critical juncture are Italy, one of the front-line states, to which 150,000 people crossed in 2015, and Hungary (UNHCR 2015). The two countries had diverging opinions on how the crisis needed to be tackled, as became visible at the September Council summit on the relocation of refugees across Europe. The decision-making process in the wake of the critical juncture shows that they had a less prominent role than the Commission, Germany and France. Italy played an important role in keeping the issue on the agenda and putting forward a number of policy proposals (Euractiv 2015c), although some interviewees claim that, with the benefit of hindsight, they were not very effective. The role of Hungary was chiefly contrarian, as it fiercely opposed the Commission's proposals on a common approach to migration and asylum, as well as reforms of the Dublin system. Interviewees argue that the Hungarian President Viktor Orbán did, however, have a great impact on the narrative on the crisis in Europe: '[his] words about strengthening the protection of external borders, that narrative somehow made it through. Sometimes, he was the one saying things that [other actors] were thinking, but did not dare to say. That's the truth. [His words] played an important role in the narrative in Europe' (Interview PO60).

Greece, another front-line state, is not considered a key actor in this critical juncture. This may seem odd as the islands of the Aegean were one of the main entry points for asylum seekers. Of the refugees and migrants, 80 per cent came to Greece, over 800,000 people in total (UNHCR 2015). The local and national authorities, as well as great numbers of civil society organisations, were operating in Greece to manage the flows of asylum seekers into the country. Yet at the same time, Greece was faced with an unprecedented political, economic and financial crisis which was discussed earlier in this chapter. The Greek economy was crippled whilst there were deep political divisions in the country: in parallel with the migration crisis, Greece was facing the real prospect of defaulting on its €1 billion loans to the International Monetary Fund. It had to agree reforms with its Eurozone creditors to avoid such a scenario, as the media were reporting the threat of an immediate 'Grexit'. Greece finally struck a deal with its Eurozone partners, but this left little room for the Greek government to take a lead in tackling the migration crisis (BBC News 2015a).

Other actors which could have been selected were Sweden, which received a large number of applicants but which did not play a major role in reforming EU policy, and the UK, where the media coverage of the asylum crisis was the most aggressive and polarised according to the UNHCR, and which opted out of the EU quota scheme. The UK did not support EU-wide action to deal with asylum seekers already in Europe. Although it did support strengthening Frontex and combatting human traffickers, it was not a key actor in reforming EU policy (Interview PO58).

At the EU level, Donald Tusk was mentioned by interviewees for having played an important role in gaining agreement for the European response. He is not considered as a separate key actor shaping the policy output here. His impact on the decision-making process and policy output is difficult to trace, owing to the role of Council President and because Council meetings take place behind doors. The European Parliament, conclude interviewees, had less of a role because much of the European response to the migration crisis was operational in nature, where the European Parliament does not have much input. This finding resonates with other scholarly work on the role of the EP during this crisis (Ripoll Servent 2019).

Temporal contingency

Migration to the European Union is as old as the Union itself and the institutional landscape to regulate this process, as well as internal agreements such as Schengen, have impacted on the context within which the 2015 crisis occurred. The structural context of EU migration policy has been detailed above. It was characterised by a scattering of institutional responsibilities over a wide variety of DGs and agencies, the important place of member states carved out in the decision-making process, the curtailed role of the European Commission and the difficulties in enforcing member state implementation of the EU policy course.

In the medium term, the decision-making context was affected by the confluence of crises with which the EU was faced in 2015. The financial–economic crisis, particularly the Eurozone crisis, continued, with the threat of 'Grexit' looming over the EU in spring. 'What remained of the "permissive

Table 5.3 Preferences for migration and asylum policy reform

Actor	Desired level(s)	Substance	Directionality

European Commission	Meso, micro	- Emergency resettlement scheme to relocate and redistribute asylum seekers within the Union based on new distribution criteria
		- 'Asylum package', reforming common European asylum system (CEAS), including:
		- Reform of the Dublin system, by either streamlining and supplementing it with a corrective fairness mechanism or moving to a new system based on a distribution key
		  o suggests permanent relocation mechanism to be evoked in crisis situations
		- Hotspot approach: support Greece and Italy
		- Strengthening Home Affairs agencies
		  o Tripling Frontex capacity on border control and surveillance in the Mediterranean (Triton and Poseidon)
		  o Providing EASO with decision-making powers
		- Evolving Frontex into European border and coast guard system with supranational competencies
		- Establish centres outside the EU to process asylum claims
		- Safe country of origin list
			+

Germany	Meso, micro	- Greater coordination at the EU-level - Supports Commission resettlement quotas scheme, wants it to be mandatory - Warns of EU failure, calling for collective action - Supports processing asylum claims outside the EU - Dublin system has to be improved to deal with exceptional circumstances through permanent and binding burden sharing mechanism among all member states	0/+

Table 5.3 Preferences for migration and asylum policy reform (Continued)

Actor	Desired level(s)	Substance	Directionality
France	Meso, micro	- Greater coordination at the EU-level - Supports processing asylum claims outside the EU - Supports Commission's temporary relocation scheme, wants it to be mandatory - Reluctant to accept asylum seekers from MENA citing security concerns - Dublin system has to be improved to deal with exceptional circumstances through permanent and binding burden sharing mechanism among all member states	0/+
Italy	Meso, micro	- Strong lobby for operational support - Focuses on deterring asylum seekers: proposed to outsource sea patrols to North African countries, funding and training navy in countries such as Egypt and Tunisia - Strongly supports processing asylum claims outside the EU - Calls to change Dublin Regulation	0/+
Hungary	Meso, micro	- Expressed strong preference for non-Muslim migrants - Strongly rejects resettlement quotas scheme supported by Visegrád group: 'any proposal leading to introduction of mandatory and permanent quota for solidarity measures would be unacceptable' (2015), both temporary and permanent - Strict enforcement of Dublin regulation - Wants EU to assist western Balkans with border protection and management	0

0= no deviation from status quo, 0/+= very little deviation from status quo, += deviation from status quo, +±= significant deviation from status quo consensus"',' write Börzel and Risse (2018: 101), 'had been used up during the euro crisis.' At the same time, the Ukraine conflict continued, as did the fraught relations with Russia, whilst the civil wars in Syria, Iraq, Libya and Afghanistan persisted. The multiplicity of crises put a great strain on solidarity within the Union. Even though the migration crisis was a top priority among these crises, the others did reduce political bandwidth.

Among the short-term, 'liminal' political moments and events that impacted on this decision-making process, we can identify, first, the rapid and unprecedented influx in migrants and refugees crossing to the European Union in 2015. In the words of one interviewee, 'we had never seen such big numbers. Numbers that literally overflowed some of the member states. The system was totally over-burdened. This was unprecedented, we never saw that before ... Before, the crises were touching parts of the EU. This was really a crisis literally touching the entire EU' (Interview PO62). Second, the sharp rise in deaths among those crossing the Mediterranean and the Aegean sparked outrage across the Union, bringing the tragedy of the crisis to the public eye. On 19 April, over 800 asylum seekers died when their boat capsized in the Mediterranean. It was the largest single loss of life in the Mediterranean in decades, after which Italian Prime Minister Matteo Renzi urged the EU to no longer 'close [its] eyes and commemorate later' (*The Guardian* 2015). Whilst the EU proposed a ten-point plan to increase financial resources to address the crisis in April, and the Commission presented its Agenda on Migration in May, the number of asylum seekers crossing the Mediterranean routes continued to grow.

Third, the August decision by Germany to cease applying the rules of the Dublin system to Syrian refugees, followed by fourth, its reintroduction of border controls had a domino effect across the Union which dealt a blow to the Schengen system. These events greatly increased the salience of the issue area. The Eurobarometer survey conducted in autumn 2015 shows 58 per cent of the respondents were chiefly concerned over migration, a spectacular jump compared to the years previous (Debomy 2016: 43). A Pew Research Center survey (2016) conducted across ten EU member states early in 2016 found that majorities in each country disapproved of how the EU was dealing with the refugee issue, with disapproval the greatest in Greece and Sweden. But even countries with a low number of applications expressed disapproval of Europe's approach in the survey, illustrative of the politicisation of the issue and the rising popularity of anti-immigrant parties in countries like the Netherlands, France and the UK.

While these structural and conjunctural features of the temporal context may not have been sufficient individually to drive this particular policy outcome, they served to amplify the impact of liminal events taking place during the critical juncture on the decision makers. They were important in structuring the reform episode and amplifying the salience of the issue area.

Policy output

Table 5.4 displays the policy changes made in response to the migration crisis, and the level at and direction in which they were aimed.

The EU response clearly fell short in pursuing far-reaching policy changes. At the macro level, the overarching Union strategy seems to have been, first, one of acceptance of member state unilateralism, which had already damaged the Schengen system (Biermann et al. 2017: 253). Second, the overarching policy course is one of externalisation, concentrating resources and attention on preventing asylum seekers from arriving in the European Union, intercepting them before they arrive. The fiercely criticised EU–Turkey Migration Agreement, for example, consisted of a policy in which Turkey agreed to take back 'irregular' migrants from Greece, in return for which the EU would resettle one Syrian refugee from Turkey. The Partnership for Migration framework, likewise, aimed at reducing migration to the Union by strengthening borders and reinforcing coast- and border guards in departure countries, thereby reducing future arrivals (Collett and Ahad 2017).

At the meso level, the EU managed to agree on several measures, such as the strengthening of Frontex and the EASO. It also established a 'hot spots' approach with additional support for Greece and Italy in registering and processing asylum applications. This approach was a novelty, although it has so far failed to deliver. Member states pledged to send national experts to work in these hot spots, but fell short in sending the number they promised.

Proposals to provide Frontex with supranational competencies (the right to return asylum seekers whose claims were rejected, and the right to deploy guards at EU state borders without consent of the government) were rejected by the Council and the Parliament. In their stead, new regulations allow member states to reintroduce border controls should another member state fail to protect its external borders effectively, which amounts to 'renationalisation rather than supranational enforcement' (Schimmelfennig 2018: 981). The Commission presented seven legislative proposals to improve asylum policy which were at the macro and meso levels. The most ambitious macro-level policy change proposed was to reform the Dublin system 'to better allocate asylum applications among member states and to guarantee the timely processing of applications' (European Council 2019). Exceptionally, the EU had agreed to relocate 160,000 refugees from Greece and Italy across the continent (Politico 2015a). This agreement was reached, however, by the Council opting for QMV on this relocation scheme, which was dubbed the 'nuclear option' by EU officials since delicate issues such as migration would virtually always require unanimity in the Council (Politico 2015b). According to officials I interviewed, this decision to pursue the reforms through QMV had a great impact on the process of deciding to change policy that followed, particularly on the reform to the Dublin system.

Some member states, including Hungary and Slovakia, felt completely sidestepped, making it impossible to reach a deal on reforming the Dublin system. Hungary, a transit state like Slovakia, was fiercely opposed to reforming the Dublin Regulation and wished to opt out of the EU's refugee relocation scheme. It was supported by Visegrad countries, although their power in the Council was significantly undercut. '[QMV] led to a complete blockage of Dublin reform', one interviewee told me. 'Politically, we lost those member states' when the QMV option was pushed through, making reform of the Dublin system impossible (Interview PO60).

EU member states – destination states, 'bystander' countries and transit countries – dug in their heels, leading to a 'Rambo' game in which the states least affected by the crisis professed satisfaction with the status quo, whilst the affected states had to cooperate in order to avoid even worse outcomes (Schimmelfennig 2018; Biermann et al. 2017: 257–8). Although agreement had been reached on some seven chapters, the CEAS reform package fell through because member states disagreed over the package as a whole. Negotiations were stalled, in a deliberate strategy. 'Some [member states] are clear where they disagree with policy proposals', said one interviewee, 'but others show their dissatisfaction by looking at the details, in order to derail the process' (Interview PO62). Although the asylum package was never formally withdrawn, progress on the issues has stalled completely. and A 'New Pact on Migration and Asylum' was launched in 2020, aiming to set forth a new strategy, although at first sight it seems to fall short of that aim (European Commission 2020b).

Conclusion

As mentioned in Chapter 4, when the temporal context is highly salient but the key actors diverge in their policy preferences, symbolic policy changes combined with some first-order changes are a likely outcome of the policy change process. We can witness such a process in this critical juncture. This short case study of policy change in the wake of the migration crisis exposed a policy area of relatively high plasticity, with traditionally a lot of member state power to shape European arrangements, to a period of greatly increased salience. Many of the policy changes in the wake of this critical juncture, particularly those pursued by the Commission, should be seen as measures to 'display institutional, legal and financial solidarity in

Table 5.4 Policy output from the migration and asylum crisis

	Policy level		
	Macro	Meso	Micro
Policy goals	Abstract policy aims	Policy objectives	Policy targets
	- Temporary support in crisis situations (0)	- Temporary relocation of asylum seekers in Greece and Italy (0/+)	- €50 million to relocate displaced persons from outside the EU (+)
	- Reduce migration flows to EU (0)	- Relocation of 22,504 displaced persons clear need protection from outside the EU (+)	- processing asylum seeker registration in dedicated 'hotspots' (+)
	- Upholding international commitments and values (0)	- Dublin system unreformed (0)	- Frontex to be involved in 'joint return operations' (+)
	- securing borders (0)	- European Border and Coast Guard Agency without supranational competencies (0/+)	- Operation Sophia targeting smuggling networks (0)
	- 'creating the right conditions for Europe's economic prosperity and societal cohesion' (0/+)	- Reducing incentives for irregular migration (0)	- Establishment regional base in Sicily for Frontex, Europol, Eurojust and EASO (+)
		- Securing external borders (0)	

Table 5.4 Policy output from the migration and asylum crisis (Continued)

	Policy level		
	Macro	Meso	Micro
Policy means	Policy implementation preferences - Unilateralism by member states (0) - Externalisation of asylum responsibilities and border control using bilateral agreements (0/+) - Integration EU external and internal security toolbox (+)	Policy tools - Migration Partnership Framework to address external dimension of migration through EU-led bilateral partnerships (0/+) - Relocation ad hoc and based on voluntary MS participation (0) - No additional monitoring on implementation (0) - Focus on 'hotspots' in Greece and Italy (+) - Address root causes of migration (+) - Migration deal with Turkey, 'one in, one out' (+) - Boost EU resources devoted to the refugee crisis by €1.7 billion (+)	Policy tool calibrations - Intercepting asylum seekers before they arrive in the EU (+) - Strengthening border guards outside the EU (+) - Expansion EASO budget (+) - Additional €26.25 million in emergency funds for Operation Triton in Italy and Poseidon in Greece for 2015, €45 million for 2016 - Staff expansion Frontex by 60 members - additional pool of EU member state officials (291) to be deployed in the 'hotspots' (+) - bilateral Migration Partnerships with Jordan, Lebanon, Niger, Nigeria, Senegal, Mali and Ethiopia (+) - €3 billion Refugee Facility for Turkey (+)

0= no deviation from status quo, 0/+= very little deviation from status quo, += deviation from status quo

the areas of asylum and external borders policies' in the words of Carrera et. al. (2015: 12). But most of the measures neither address the root causes behind the crisis nor deviate substantially from the previous policy direction (Interview PO61).

This critical juncture opened up space for first-order policy changes, mainly at the meso level. The 'hot spots approach' and the greater support for agencies such as Frontex were first-order changes, consisting of adjustments to existing policy instruments, including increasing the budget to accommodate novel developments. The policy methods were not changed by these developments. The temporary mechanism for the relocation of refugees in Greece and Italy does constitute a second-order change, a first step in the direction of strategic action. The relocation programme, however, was abruptly halted in 2017 by which time only 30 per cent of the number of relocations originally pledged had been accomplished, representing a mere 2 per cent of the arrivals in Italy and Greece since 2015 (Achilli 2018). Similarly, follow-up for the hot spot approach was meagre.

One important but less explicit policy change was the issue linkage that resulted from this migration crisis, which became clear in the Partnership Framework. The Commission had long attempted to link asylum policy and migration policy more to other areas of internal security, to link external and internal security. It had continually been unsuccessful in achieving the linkage it desired. Interviewees explained how this crisis offered an opportunity to do that (Interview PO62):

> There were always attempts to make migration and asylum policy more comprehensive, linking other areas to migration policies. We were never able as DG HOME to pierce through other priorities. Only in 2015, we got at a stage, we got a spot, to pronounce these ambitions [of issue linkage] and to gain support for that. If you look at the Partnership Framework, there are not so many new things. Most of the things had already been suggested before [by the Commission]. But it is the boost that we got behind it, that changed. We simply used the crisis for further boosting the policy development.

But further-reaching policy changes, such as a reform of the Dublin system, proved impossible owing to diverging member state interests. The issue, according to one interviewee, was just 'too political'. That interviewee argues that, due to the politicisation of the policy area, the EU was 'constantly raising more detailed issues to the highest level, things that you would normally have dealt with at the technical level'. This undermined any prospect of transformative policy change (Interview PO62). As another interviewee commented, 'the truth is that all these ideas that were floated for a long time, were not feasible in the end' owing to member state disagreement. 'We did not do what we planned to do. But I think, in the end, it allowed us to make something that allows us today to be better prepared to deal with crisis' (Interview PO60).

The crisis in European security and defence, 2014–18

The year 2014 started with the rapidly escalating conflict in Ukraine (see Chapter 3). In March, after months of increasing violence, Russia orchestrated an illegal referendum to annex the Crimea, which broke international agreements and flouted international law. Meanwhile, Russian President Putin was making threats he could take Kiev 'in two weeks if he wanted to' (Roth 2014), as his country also tightened its grip on Armenia. Scholars and media assessed the threat this posed to Europe as they considered the 'return of geopolitics' (Mead 2014; Duke 2017; Auer 2015). Three months after the illegal annexation of the Crimea, al-Baghdadi proclaimed the establishment of the Islamic State (IS) in northern Iraq. Soon after, parts of Europe were shaken by *jihadi* terrorism linked to IS, with deadly attacks taking place within the span of months in Paris, Brussels and Nice (among other cities).

European security clearly stood at a critical juncture starting in 2014, state interviewees, which is confirmed by the literature (Græger 2016: 478). Security issues during this period moved beyond traditional debates regarding the legitimacy and effectiveness of EU security proposals. Rather, 'the EU's increasing role as a provider of security for European societies moved to the centre of debates on the very *raison d'être* of the European integration project' (Hegemann and Schneckener 2019: 140). Two days after she took office, the new HR/VP Federica Mogherini met with NATO Secretary General Jens Stoltenberg, after which she stated (2014) 'we have a common challenge in front of us: a security environment that is all the more worrying every day'.

This section will test-drive the framework for analysing EU foreign policy change developed in Chapter 1 to assess the policy changes that emerged following this critical juncture.

Institutional set-up and historically created arrangements

Sketching out the institutional set-up for EU security and defence policies is a daunting task for which excellent in-depth and comprehensive accounts exist elsewhere (e.g. Howorth 2014; Whitman and Juncos 2009; Mérand, Foucault and Irondelle 2011). This subsection will briefly set out the key tenets of the historically created institutional arrangements in the field of foreign, security and defence policy which are relevant for understanding this particular critical juncture.

Although the Soviet Union posed a significant external threat at the time European integration was born, the presence of the North Atlantic Treaty Organization (NATO) has long meant that the European Community did not need to be constructed in such a way as to allow for the effective deployment of military force (Simms 2012: 52–3). From the early 1990s, this changed. As Angela Merkel put it, 'while the latter half of the twentieth century was all about security in Europe, the first half of the twenty-first will be about achieving it for Europe' (quoted in Youngs 2010: 5). Institutional developments in the EU's security and defence policy were characterised by a pattern of crisis and response, as described by Peterson and Helwig (2017). The Common Foreign and Security Policy (CFSP) was established in 1993 with the Treaty on European Union, which introduced a 'three-pillar system', with the CFSP as the second, intergovernmental pillar. Decision-making in this pillar was primarily based on unanimity, with very rare exceptions, and member states shared the right of initiative with the European Commission.

The CFSP achievements were limited. The EU's failings in Bosnia at the beginning of the 1990s, followed by the Kosovo war, acted as a decisive catalyst in the creation of the European Security and Defence Policy (ESDP) in the Amsterdam Treaty of 1999 (Shepherd 2009). Ever since, defence and security capabilities have developed steadily. The Council of the European Union's Secretary General and High Representative for Foreign Policy, Javier Solana, was a significant policy entrepreneur guiding the EU through further developments, amongst others by establishing the EU's first strategy document, the European Security Strategy, in 2003. The 'Big Bang' enlargement of the EU in the early 2000s brought issues of collective external action to the fore. With the 2007 Lisbon Treaty, the Common Security and Defence Policy (CSDP) was formed in place of the ESDP, with an expanded remit.

Through the CSDP, the EU made great strides in a process of creating and reforming new civilian and military capabilities. At the start of this critical juncture in 2014, there had been thirty-three ongoing or completed CSDP missions, most of them low-profile civilian missions, of which seventeen had been on the African continent and six in the Balkans. The Libya crisis seriously exposed some of the shortcomings of the CSDP framework, particularly how its decision-making could be heavily constrained by member states. It also brought to the fore the chronic under-investment in defence capabilities as well as disparities in defence spending and research across the Union. Above all, it exposed that the CSDP did not have the full support of all the member states, who proved unwilling to sponsor a CSDP mission within the EU framework to respond to the violence against Libyan civilians.

Intervention under the CSDP framework was not achievable until a late decision in April 2011 to support humanitarian assistance, which 'smacked more of face saving than effective intervention' (A. Menon 2011: 75).

How plastic is the policy area?

To describe institutions as 'plastic' suggests that they are able to give and take form. The more they are able to do both, the more plastic they are. The institutions in European defence are not considered very plastic because although actors (the member states) can shape and remould them frequently to their preferences, so institutions in the field of security and defence can thereby 'take form', they are generally not able to 'give form'.

At the dawn of this critical juncture, this policy area of security and defence was one where member states had the ability to constrain the Union, but not vice versa. A difficulty in formulating European policies in the realm of security and defence had always been the insistence by member states on maintaining control over defence. This has deep historical roots, as nation states in nineteenth-century Europe used war both to provide their citizens with a clear national identity, and at the same time harness that nationalism for the purpose of waging mass war (A. Menon 2017; van Ham 2010: 589).

While a recognition of a need for collective action has led states to collaborate over defence at the European level, nation states that have largely defined their own identity via their ability to provide security feel a continued attachment to the area, which continues to hamper the delegation of real authority to Europe. As the French government wrote in its defence White Paper shortly prior to this critical juncture (2013: 17):

> The specific history of each Member State is reflected in the links forged in every continent, and sometimes in their contrasting visions of the role of military force in international relations. This diversity can be an asset, inasmuch as each country brings its own experience to the common project, but it can also be a source of mutual suspicion and make any hopes of rapid integration appear unrealistic.

Thus EU foreign policy, with its history in the 'intergovernmental pillar' which the member states strictly control, has long been a rigid policy area which was malleable for member states, but not for Union institutions. Under article 41(2) TEU, neither military nor defence operations can be charged to the EU budget, and any mission must be agreed unanimously. The rights conferred on the European security and defence institutions in the treaties have long been extremely restricted. The EU has no means to ensure adequate defence spending by member states, which has resulted in stark disparities in the willingness to invest in and deploy military capabilities. At the dawn of this critical juncture, the plasticity of the policy area was thus quite low.

The critical juncture

This critical juncture, as stated previously, is of a different nature than the Arab uprisings, which were at their most intense for around six months, or the Ukraine crisis, where the first half of 2014 clearly marked a clear departure in previous EU–Russia relations.

The crisis in European security, according to many scholars and practitioners, started in 2014 and continued at a height until around 2018. Despite a broad consensus around this time frame (see the EUISS 2016b consultation with a wide variety of experts on the new EU Global Strategy), it remains disputable mainly because the starting point for the crisis in European security was perhaps not perceived by all actors as such at the time, nor is the end point fixed. From 2014 onwards, however, particularly after the annexation of the Crimea and the Russian threats that echoed along with it, as well as during the rise of IS and the associated terrorist attacks, security was high on the European political agenda, as well as on the European public's mind (Hegemann and Schneckener 2019; Fiott 2020; European Commission 2019; Dennison, Franke and Zerka 2018; European Commission 2017). The fact that Europe was faced with a rapidly deteriorating security environment, against the backdrop of the British referendum decision to leave the EU, created a critical juncture for European security and defence policy.

First, the constraints of the structure loosened temporarily, as the existing institutional arrangements were deemed insufficient to rise to the challenge. In the words of R. Menon and Rumer (2015: 157), the Ukraine crisis 'undermine[d] key elements of the post-World War II political and security arrangements in Europe'. Commission President Juncker had alluded to the necessity of more cooperation in foreign policy and defence during his opening statement to the European Parliament in 2014 (Juncker 2014b). His Commission increasingly drew out security as a key narrative. This allowed the Juncker Commission to put forward several policy proposals in the realm of security and defence of which a few previously had consistently fallen short of member state support. In March of 2015, Juncker even floated the idea of a 'European Army', which 'would convey to Russia that we are serious about defending the values of the European Union'. 'Such an army', he claimed, 'would also help the to form common foreign and security policies and allow Europe to take on responsibility in the world' (Reuters 2015). His words should be interpreted as illustrative of the critical juncture at which the EU stood. The perceived insecurity of the European Union, internal and external, temporarily heightened contingency, meaning there was a broader range of policy options on the table than before or after the juncture, during which the role of agency was temporarily increased.

This critical juncture has, in the words of one author (Sus 2017: 417), 'made the EU more conscious about the salience of the need to develop itself into a more strategic actor with the ability to influence the environment and not to be caught by surprise by events such as the annexation of Crimea or the migration and refugee crisis'. A critical juncture had emerged.

Key actors and preferences for policy reform

One of the key actors during this critical juncture was the European Commission, particularly its President Jean-Claude Juncker. From the day he took office, the contours of a clearly securitised narrative took shape (Sus 2017; Hegemann and Schneckener 2019: 140). In his 2015 State of the Union speech, Juncker underlined a need for unity when it comes to the security of eastern Europe and the Baltic states. He specifically referred to the threat of Russia (2015: 20–21). In the 2015 agenda on security, the Commission clearly defines terrorism, organised crime and cyber-crime as interlinked areas with a strong cross-border dimension, thus needing to be tackled in a shared European framework (European Commission 2015b). In 2016, this narrative is reinforced by Juncker referring to the 'existential crisis' of the European Union in his State of the Union speech. In terms of preferences for policy reform, Juncker and his Commission see a greater role for EU governance in this area, as does the EEAS in its Global Strategy.

An example is Juncker's notion of a 'security Union', as he underlines 'the very real threats to our security at home and abroad' (2016: 7). This idea was first floated a day after the terrorist attacks in Brussels. In August of the same year, Juncker appointed the British Julian King 'Commissioner for the Security Union', to support the implementation of the European agenda on security, which was adopted in April 2015. The Security Union was supposed to urge EU member states 'to move beyond the concept of cooperating to protect national internal security to the idea of protecting the collective security of the Union as a whole' (European Commission 2016a: 2). The Commission also pushed for the creation of a European Security and Defence Union which should 'encourage a stronger alignment of strategic cultures, as well as a common understanding of threats and appropriate responses'. It argued that this would require 'joint decision-making and action, as well as greater financial solidarity at European level' (European Commission 2017: 11). Juncker (2017b) was quite vocal on this in his 2017

State of the Union speech, stating 'by 2025 we need a fully-fledged European Defence Union. We need it. And NATO wants it.'

The EU, 'battered and bruised by a year that shook our very foundation', according to the Juncker Commission, thus had to become 'more united, stronger' (European Commission 2017). During a speech in Prague in June 2017, Juncker reiterated the need for 'systematic defence cooperation and further integration will contribute to the preservation of national sovereignty' and first mentioned Permanent European Structured Cooperation (2017a). The possibility of PESCO had been written into the Lisbon Treaty article 42, but had been put on the shelf in the context of numerous security crises.

The second important actor at the EU level during this critical juncture was the EEAS. It mainly played a role in drafting the European response to the increased worries over European security. The 2016 European Union Global Strategy (EUGS), formulated by the EEAS, echoed Juncker's evocation of the 'existential crisis' in which the Union found itself (High Representative of the Union for Foreign Affairs and Security Policy 2016b: 7). Both actors thus saw this crisis as an important threat to the Union: 'our Union is under threat', states the EU Global Strategy (High Representative of the Union for Foreign Affairs and Security Policy 2016b: 13). 'Our European project, which has brought unprecedented peace, prosperity and democracy, is being questioned. To the east, the European security order has been violated, while terrorism and violence plague North Africa and the Middle East, as well as Europe itself'. The HR/VP stated in the Strategy that the EU needed to become a stronger global player, 'playing its collective role in the world' (High Representative of the Union for Foreign Affairs and Security Policy 2016b: 7). Later, in an opinion piece in *Die Welt*, Mogherini highlighted the EU's need for a defence union, because 'security can only be created in the European Union if we act together' (Mogherini and Katainen 2017).

The European Commission and the EEAS both stressed that the way to a more secure Union is by tying closer together the notions of internal and external security. At a speech in Barcelona in 2015, Mogherini stated that the EU must 'find the right way between these two poles' through consistency in terms of guiding values: internal action and policies must be guided by the same interests and values as the EU's foreign policies. Information and intelligence are concrete priorities. Further, the EU needed more responsible multilateral engagement with the world (Mogherini 2015).

At the member state level, this critical juncture likewise spurred a range of proposals for policy change. France and Germany were key actors in this critical juncture. According to Sperling and Webber (2018: 230), the 'ascent of Euro-enthusiast Emmanuel Macron to the French presidency' buoyed Council support for 'strong and determined Union', including in the field of European defence.

A European security and defence union had been a process at least nominally supported by German and French foreign ministers since as early as 2002, although it gained particular momentum after the British referendum on leaving the EU in June 2016 (Bendiek 2017). The 2016 German White Paper on security policy and the future of the Bundeswehr explicitly presented the creation of a European Security and Defence Union as a long-term goal, which would mean a European defence policy which is 'harmonised, more strongly focused, and available and ready with the necessary speed' (Bundesregierung 2016: 72). The document reflects an increased willingness to take up international responsibility in this area. To underscore this, Germany pledged to significantly increase its military spending, from 1.2 per cent of GDP in 2014 to 2 per cent of GDP by 2020 (Bundesministerium der Verteidigung 2016: 32).

France was equally a key actor in this critical juncture. Early on in the crisis, Germany and France had jointly put forward a proposal on EU internal security cooperation through a 'European Security Compact' (Ayrault and Steinmeier 2016). In the autumn of 2016, the defence ministers of Germany and France drafted a non-paper in which they proposed a defence union (*Süddeutsche Zeitung* 2016; *Le Figaro* 2016). They argued that 'in the context of a deteriorating security environment … it is high time to reinforce our solidarity and European defence capabilities in order to more effectively protect the citizens and borders of Europe' (*EU Observer* 2016). The proposals included new command centres for logistics and medical assistance, that battle groups should be made operationally ready and that there should be a single budget for R&D in defence, and for joint procurement of air-lift, satellite, cyber-defence assets and surveillance drones, in a programme to be coordinated by the European Defence Agency (*Süddeutsche Zeitung* 2016). The *EU Observer* wrote that the Franco-German plan would probably win support from countries like the Czech Republic, Hungary, Poland and Slovakia, but would pose problems for other states in the Union such as the Netherlands, which were hesitant of deepening integration at a time of fierce Euroscepticism (*EU Observer* 2016).

Yet despite converging on many policy preferences, there are some differences between the policy preferences of Germany and France which impacted on the decision-making process. Some scholars argue that the French perceive the European Security and Defence Union as a project of more streamlined intergovernmental cooperation, while the Germans perceive it as a supranational project (Maulny 2016). Most importantly, the two countries disagreed on the goal of EU defence policy. For most politicians in Germany the European Security and Defence Union presented as an official goal in its White Paper means a common European Army, as the 'ultimate expression of European political unity' (Keohane 2016a). To the

French, EU defence integration was symbolically important, but it also considered EU military cooperation to be a crucial vehicle in advancing its own strategic goals and an important step towards securing the EU's emancipation from the USA as security provider (Keohane 2016b; Maulny 2016). Table 5.5 summarises the preferences for security policy reform during this critical juncture, as well as the levels at which and directions in which they were aimed.

Temporal contingency

The European security environment had changed radically in 2014. The conflict in Ukraine and the illegal annexation of the Crimea were shocks which prompted a serious reconsideration of EU relations with Russia and its wider role and responsibility in the region, especially by some European countries such as Germany.

In structural terms, scholars have identified several factors contributing to the turbulence in which the EU found itself. Among them was a changing transatlantic relationship which had been set in motion under the Obama administration. This US 'withdrawal' from Europe came into sharp focus when Donald Trump was elected as US President in 2016; he was vocal about his decreasing willingness to allow Europeans to spend less on defence because the American presence and support were continuing. His open hostility to NATO members not meeting the NATO defence investment guidelines, and his remarks about NATO being obsolete anyway, came as a shock to many European leaders. The morning after Trump's election, the German defence minister Ursula von der Leyen asked Trump to state 'clearly on which side he is. Whether he's on the side of the law, peace and democracy or whether he doesn't care about all that and instead he's looking for a best buddy (with Putin)' (Reuters 2016). Commission President Juncker had alluded to this during his Prague speech, stating 'the protection of Europe can no longer be outsourced' (2017a):

> The United States fundamentally changed its foreign policy long before the arrival of Mr Trump. Over the past decade it has become crystal clear that our American partners consider that they are shouldering too much of the burden for their wealthy European Allies. We have no other choice than to defend our own interests in the Middle East, in climate change, in our trade agreements.

At the member state level, the French Senate similarly warned (Sénat 2019) that 'the weakness of the defence effort of the European nations must be seen as a temporary interlude that eventually had to come to an end … European countries are therefore obliged to increase their defence effort'.

Table 5.5 Preferences for security policy reform

Actor	Desired level(s)	Substance	Directionality

European Commission and EEAS	Macro, meso	- Integrating internal and external security, integrating security and defence policy to other EU policies and tools
		- Promoting 'resilience' in the neighbourhood and further afield
		   ○ Stabilising neighbourhood
		   ○ Averting security risks and ability to withstand challenges
		- Creating a European Security and Defence Union by 2025
		   ○ internal and external security focus
		- creation European Defence Fund for pooled R&D investments
		- EU-wide cybersecurity policy
		- Coordinated review on military spending
			+

Germany	Macro, meso	- Creating a European Security and Defence Union in the long term through: ○ gradual and concrete refinement and strengthening of CSDP amongst others through integrating civilian and military capabilities and strengthening of the European defence industry - use of PESCO with wide membership - strengthening EU defence through a 'core group' yet open to all EU member states - 'European Security Compact' strengthening internal security	0/+

Table 5.5 Preferences for security policy reform (Continued)

Actor	Desired level(s)	Substance	Directionality

France	Macro, meso	- deeper defence cooperation
		- Creating a European Security and Defence Union through:
		  ○ Less duplication
		  ○ Stronger intergovernmental cooperation
		- 'European Security Compact' strengthening internal security
		- creation European Defence Fund for pooled R&D investments
		- use of PESCO with commitments strong enough 'to encourage ambitious, unifying projects, and above all, address the operational needs of European armed force', mandatory criteria, membership based on ambition
		- permanent EU fund for military operations, unanimous decision-making yet implemented member states
			0/+

0= no deviation from status quo, 0/+= very little deviation from status quo, += deviation from status quo, ++= significant deviation from status quo

This, according to an EU official working on European defence whom I interviewed, 'led to an understanding that the EU had to stand up to defend itself in case of real threats. The question was not whether the US would defend us in six months. But what about in thirty years?' (Interview PO55) The altered transatlantic partnership coincided with an increased sense of perceived insecurity in the European 'neighbourhood' and further afield as civil wars in Iraq and Syria persisted, whilst IS had emerged in the region. It caused the European public to agree that 'security is one of their top priorities' (Tocci 2018: 133). Brexit and the election of Trump posed subsequent shocks, as was the emerging realisation that, politically, these countries could not be relied upon.

As a final structural factor, not even those member states with the highest defence spending in the EU were able to keep up with the abilities and technological advances of the the USA and China (in particular) or the changing nature of modern warfare. Duplications in research and military equipment across the Union exacerbated this problem (A. Menon 2017). 'It became crucial for Europe to start thinking more collectively in the defence sector', states one interviewee. 'Even for the bigger states it was difficult to go it alone. They had to come with more concrete actions' (Interview PO56).

These structural trends converged with a medium-term temporal context which was unexpectedly conducive to further defence cooperation. First, the Ukraine crisis produced a strategic convergence between France and Germany, which as discussed in Chapter 3 took the lead in tackling this crisis at the head of the Weimar Triangle. Both countries had witnessed domestic changes as well. In France, the new leadership under Macron took a renewed interest in advancing security cooperation, while in Germany there was a distinct shift towards taking on greater responsibilities in this realm. At the same time, the migration crisis and *jihadi* terrorism had produced a convergence of public threat perceptions across Europe (Koenig and Walter-Franke 2017). The Brexit vote was an event both with great liminal impact and one that created a conjunctural turbulence over a longer period of time. It was a mere two days after the referendum that the HR/VP presented the EU Global Strategy (High Representative of the Union for Foreign Affairs and Security Policy 2016b), amid fears that Brexit would have a domino effect (*The Guardian* 2016).

Yet the spectre of Brexit signalled the dawn for confident steps in European defence cooperation as the prospect of a UK-less European defence emerged. 'Now that the British foot was off the brake of EU security and defence', wrote Nathalie Tocci (2018: 134), 'the rest could get on with the business.' The Implementation Plan on Security and Defence (High Representative of the Union for Foreign Affairs and Security Policy 2016a), which translated the ambitions of the EUGS into policy, was endorsed by the Council at the end of 2016. Around the same time, Juncker's Commission presented the

European Defence Action Plan (European Commission 2016b), focusing on financial steps to be taken to move towards increased defence cooperation.

The next year, 2017, was dubbed a 'watershed' year for the EU in defence (Tocci 2018), a year of 'significant activism in European security and defence'. Defence spending among NATO's European members increased by 3.6 per cent in real terms that year, with German defence spending rising by 6.6 per cent in real terms (Béraud-Sudreau and Giegerich 2018: 59). The Rome Declaration of March 2017 called on the EU to take measures in security and defence, amongst other areas. It argued the EU ought 'to take more responsibilities and to assist in creating a more competitive and integrated defence industry' and should strengthen its common security and defence (European Council 2017b).

A final conjunctural trend was the German plan to take a more proactive and assertive role in foreign policy from 2014 onwards, which necessitated the development of its military endeavours. The European context remained the preferred arena for such ambitions (Koenig and Walter-Franke 2017: 6).

Several liminal events heightened the salience of security and defence cooperation across the Union, particularly the Brexit vote and the terrorist attacks that struck Europe. In early 2015, three gunmen killed seventeen people in France, one pair attacking the headquarters of the French satirical newspaper *Charlie Hebdo* in Paris, the third taking hostages in a kosher supermarket, where he killed four people. In November of the same year, a series of terrorist attacks in Paris by IS sent shockwaves through Europe, as a total of 130 people were killed and more than 400 were injured. It was the deadliest terrorist attack in the European Union since the train bombings in Madrid eleven years earlier. As the issue of security rose higher on the European agenda, in March 2016 thirty-five people were killed in Brussels by IS terrorists, followed by an attack in Nice in July 2016 which took the lives of eighty-seven people, for which the Islamic State once more claimed responsibility. Even though counter-terrorism is perceived as primarily an issue for law enforcement, scholars have found that the annexation of the Crimea by Russia was compounded by the high number of terrorist attacks, and the 'revived spectre of conventional military conflict on the continent alongside a range of ongoing transnational threats' (Béraud-Sudreau and Giegerich 2018: 55). These attacks reverberated across Europe, and served to greatly increase the salience of European security policies during this critical juncture (Hegemann and Schneckener 2019; Græger 2016).

Policy output

In this temporal context conducive for policy change, Germany and France led attempts to persuade European member states to pool their resources in permanent structured cooperation (PESCO). This was established by Council consensus in December 2017, to enable 'willing and able member states to jointly plan, develop and invest in shared capability projects, and enhance the operational readiness and contribution of their armed force' (European Council 2017a). Twenty-five member states decided to be involved.

PESCO, of which the legal possibility had been written into the Lisbon Treaty a decade earlier, was framed by Juncker as a 'sleeping beauty' whom it was now time to wake up, to 'take European Defence to the next level' (2017a). Some tangible commitments came with PESCO, among them one to regularly increase defence budgets in real terms. Progress will be assessed annually by the Council, decreasing the likelihood that this will be another European defence project that fizzles out after a quick start. States also pledged to enter into collaborative capability projects, which will be difficult to renege on (Biscop 2018). After its launch, HR/VP Mogherini called PESCO 'something big' (*Deutsche Welle* 2017) while German Federal Defence Minister von der Leyen went as far as stating it was 'another step in the direction of a European Army' and that the signature meant the EU was 'founding the European security and defence union' (Bundesregierung 2017; Bundesministerium der Verteidigung 2017).

The policy process leading up to its establishment was not without obstacles. First, it had long been a dormant legal possibility. When it rose up the agenda, divergent policy preferences came to the fore. France had wanted PESCO to be 'as ambitious as possible in terms of the projects it takes on, while Germany wants it to include the maximum number of countries' (*Financial Times* 2017). This disagreement lasted until June 2017, when the two countries agreed on a 'pledging' framework where countries did not need to meet strict criteria to join PESCO, but had to make pledges to commit to reaching those ambitious criteria (Billon-Galland and Quencez 2017). PESCO was thus reshaped to be about capabilities and operations, a '*sui generis* capability club, a recognisable umbrella and a process preciously enshrined in the stability of EU treaties' (De France 2019: 12). PESCO has been hailed by some as a 'game changer' in European security (Euractiv 2017) and indeed it constitutes second-order policy change, as it concerns a new kind of policy instrument (although the original goals have remained unchanged). It has the potential to become a single umbrella for defence cooperation and integration, for EU member states to meet their capability targets for both NATO and the EU (Biscop 2018).

Yet despite its being a qualitative step forward, especially compared to other schemes, it is crucial that PESCO's member states sustain active leadership roles and live up to their commitments in order to achieve success, and to avoid it being diluted through rival parallel schemes. The culture of non-compliance rampant in the CSDP may repeat itself in PESCO. It would be more appropriate therefore to label PESCO a policy output, containing a seed of second-order change which, if commitments are not met, may turn out to be mere symbolic change, an accommodating gesture, not accompanied by substantive changes to settings, methods or goals. In a report by the European Defence Agency, high-ranking officials in the national capitals echo this view. The French Director-General for International Relations and Strategy warned that commitments and pledges need to be met and lived up to, so that 'PESCO must be a lever, not just a label' (European Defence Agency 2018: 10). His German counterpart echoed this: the successful implementation and development of the PESCO would be crucial to its success. The Czech Deputy Defence Policy Director, Ministry of Defence similarly described PESCO as a stepping stone, the success of which could not be guaranteed but would fully depend on the member states respecting their commitments. 'PESCO is here, and it is now the joint responsibility of all the PESCO Member States, with the support of EU institutions, to bring it to life and make it a long-term success' (European Defence Agency 2018: 15).

As Table 5.6 shows, other policy achievements have been made which deviated from the policies existing before the critical juncture, especially on the front of pursuing a European Security and Defence Union. Research and development in the field of defence received a major boost through the Preparatory Action for Defence Research in 2017 as well as the €5.5 billion European Defence Fund (EDF) exclusively for collaborative projects. PESCO aids greatly in the development of joint capabilities. French Defence Minister Florence Parly said the Fund and PESCO amount to a 'cultural revolution in Brussels' (Erlanger 2018). Finally, the EU set up a Military Planning and Conduct Capability meant to improve the crisis management structure of the EU. The MPCC is explicitly not called Headquarters and has been derided by Whitehall as 'little more than a call centre' (Samuel and Foster 2017). Nonetheless it plays an important role in streamlining command and control (Tocci 2018: 135) and has been presented as an important symbolic first step towards the medium-term goal of an Operational Head-quarters (Koenig and Walter-Franke 2017: 10).

Conclusion

This last test-drive showed that from 2014 onwards, and particularly from 2016, structural, conjunctural and liminal trends and events created a strategic convergence conducive to policy change in the area of security and defence. Obstacles to further cooperation which existed prior to the critical juncture, such as the UK's strong reluctance to further European integration in this area, temporarily lifted, an effect strongly encouraged by the illegal annexation of the Crimea by Russia, the Ukraine conflict more broadly and the election

Table 5.6 Policy output after the crisis in European security

	Policy level		
	Macro	Meso	Micro
Policy goals	Abstract policy aims - The EU as a stronger global actor, stronger defence - 'European Union and its Member States must be able to contribute decisively to collective efforts, as well as to act autonomously when and where necessary and with partners wherever possible' - Deeper European cooperation in security and defence	Policy objectives - Support strong and competitive European defence industry (0) - Support joint research and development (0/+) - Development of joint capabilities (+) - Reduce duplication, pooling resources where possible (0/+)	Policy targets - Collaborative EU-wide research and innovation in defence (+) - Initially, 17 PESCO projects (+)
Policy means	Policy implementation preferences - 'integrated approach' linking security and defence to internal security and other EU tools and policies (0/+) - Continued EU-NATO cooperation (0) - Member-state driven cooperation in this area (0)	Policy tools - European Defence Fund (+) - PESCO 25 EU states (+) - Coordinated Annual Review on Defence (CARD) done by European Defence Agency to monitor defence spending and facilitate pooling of recourses (+) - MPCC (+)	Policy tool calibrations - €5.5 billion for financing collaborative R&D initiatives (+) - MPCC 10 core and 20 support staff (0/+) - Reviewing ATHENA (0) - reaffirmed commitment to bear the 'common cost' of the battlegroups through ATHENA (+)

0= no deviation from status quo, 0/+= very little deviation from status quo, += deviation from status quo

of Donald Trump as US President and the hectoring stance he took towards European defence and the US role in it.

This decreased what the French called the culture of 'mutual suspicion' surrounding European defence cooperation across European capitals (Gouvernement Français 2013: 17). Over a series of decision-points across this longer time frame, great strides were made in European defence integration. HR/VP Mogherini even said in November of 2017 that 'we have achieved more in these last two years than we achieved in decades on security and defence in the European Union' (Euractiv 2018).

Assessing the policy changes made during this critical juncture, we can conclude that this strategic convergence has predominantly produced first- and second-order policy changes, along with policy changes we may describe as symbolic. Particularly substantive policy changes are the EDF, under which €5.5 billion has been allocated yearly to 1) defence research directly from the EU budget and 2) capability development, co-financed by the EU budget. Despite sceptics warning that ending fragmentation in defence research is complex, and that the EDF does not change the lack of synchronisation in the defence planning of member states (Drent and Zandee 2018: 8), the Fund is a qualitative step forward, particularly since it illustrates the increasing involvement of the European Commission in the realm of defence, a policy area that hitherto had been exclusively intergovernmental. Some claim it contains the seeds for potential third-order changes such as the setting-up of a DG Defence and a European Peace Facility as wholly new instruments to finance EU military operations and military support for partners (Haroche 2019).

The MPCC can be qualified as an important symbolic step towards an Operational Headquarters. Other achievements that are predominantly symbolic were the planned review of Athena (a mechanism for financing common costs relating to EU military operations), which aimed to ensure more rapid financing and deployment of EU battlegroups. Such reviews have been on the table in the past and thus cannot be dubbed significant changes (*cf.* European Council 2013). The increase in the scope of common costs of EU military operations would be small (about 5 percentage points). Moreover, as Koenig and Walter-Franke describe (2017: 11), the issue with the battlegroups extends its financing and national interests and priorities differ over when and how battlegroups should be deployed.

Opinions about what kind of change PESCO constitutes are divided amongst scholars and practitioners. On one hand, it represents a major change as its possibility had been written into the Lisbon Treaty but it had been put on the shelf in the context of numerous security crises. Both EU institutions and state leaders were quite optimistic in their early appraisals. However, there is also plentiful caution. The inclusiveness of PESCO, which includes all EU member states except for Denmark and Malta, has made it difficult to define precise commitments and objectives on defence expenditure or the harmonisation of military needs, nor is there agreement on the development of operational capabilities (Zandee 2018: 3–5). Officials I interviewed agree that the inclusiveness of PESCO may be a contradiction, as the initiative was meant to facilitate further steps in defence cooperation with those states willing and able to cooperate. One analyst warns that PESCO means 'all things to all countries'. Its real value 'lies less in itself than in the political momentum it creates and will hope to sustain' (De France 2019: 12).

The most apt description of the policy change PESCO embodied in 2017 would be that it has the potential to be second-order policy change, an 'emblematic innovation' (Blockmans 2018: 1785). Its common commitments are formally legally binding. Yet the absence of judicial enforcement of member state compliance, writes Blockmans (2018: 1819), means there is 'no legal way of keeping participating States wedded to their commitments against their will'. The push to make PESCO as exclusive as possible has watered down some of the most ambitious elements, while the same compromises have made member state opt-outs and exemptions easier. PESCO thus contains a seed of second-order change (the adoption of new instruments pursuing the same policy goals), a stepping stone towards such change, which will remain symbolic change if implementation and compliance lag behind.

Note

1 In this chapter, I refer to this multi-faceted crisis as an 'asylum crisis'. Although this term is used by a number of scholars, others, particularly politicians and media outlets, have referred to this as a 'migration crisis' or 'refugee crisis'. Particularly problematic has been the blurring of the concepts of refugees, migrants, asylum seekers and 'irregular migrants' in discussions of the issue. A *migrant* is an umbrella term which is not defined under international law, which is why I shall not use it here. It usually refers to individuals moving away from their place of usual residence, across countries or across international borders. *Asylum seekers* are individuals seeking international protection, whose claims for refugee status have not yet been legally determined. They must apply for this status on arriving at or after crossing a border. Not all asylum seekers will qualify for treatment as refugees, but all refugees are initially asylum seekers. *Refugees* are those 'unable or unwilling to return to their country of origin owing to a well-founded fear of being persecuted for reasons of race, religion, nationality, membership of a particular social group, or political opinion' (UNHCR 2020). They are protected in international law, whether or not they are in a country that is a party to

the 1951 Convention or the 1967 Protocol, or whether or not they have been recognised by their host country as a refugee (IOM 2020). Finally, in contrast to asylum seekers, immigrants are individuals moving into a country other than that of their nationality or usual residence, with the intention of settling there. In its public statements the EU often refers to *irregular migration*, meaning the 'movement of persons that takes place outside the laws, regulations, or international agreements governing the entry into or exit from the State of origin, transit or destination' (IOM 2020). The use of these terms has complicated debates. In general discourse, the term 'refugee' – which should refer to protected status under international law – has been associated with negative qualities, whereas the neutrally intended term 'migrant' has become synonymous with those seeking economic betterment of their lives. Discursive issues equally arise with the EU term 'irregular migration', which has become associated solely with crossing a border illegally, despite the fact that people arriving through irregular migration does not relieve the EU from its obligation to protect these people's rights: they can include refugees, victims of trafficking and unaccompanied migrant children.

6

Conclusion

This book raised a series of challenges confronting those aiming to explore changes to European Union foreign policy. The first challenge concerned the field of study itself. Whereas a range of studies exist dedicated to explaining stability and change in foreign policy for the US context, I explained how such a clearly delimited field of study is absent for the analysis of change in EU foreign policy. Students asking why and how particular policy areas in EU foreign policy witness change as a result of crisis were thus forced to confront the issue through a host of different lenses. These stem from the fields of public policy studies or international relations, or are based on accounts which investigate particular EU policy responses to crisis, often from an evaluative or normative point of view.

An important ambition for this book has thus been, first, to provide those wanting to study episodes of EU foreign policy change with a single, dedicated, analytical framework that serves to investigate and explain the way in which the EU adapts its foreign policy in the wake of crises. This framework can be applied to the traditional, institutional realm of EU foreign policies that fall under the CFSP and the CSDP, but also to the 'softer' areas of EU external action such as the policies in the European 'neighbourhood', and EU energy or migration policies. As the test-drives of this book have shown, this framework can be readily applied to understand past and future instances where critical junctures opened a window for foreign policy to change.

Questions that can be answered using this framework are, for example, how did political instability among the southern neighbours affect EU energy policy? Or what was the impact of the Eurozone crisis on EU trade policy towards China? How did the Ukraine conflict affect plans for a European Energy Union? Slower-burning external challenges and their effect can likewise be probed: for example, how do the recent, varying, territorial claims on the Arctic affect EU foreign policy towards the region? The framework proposed here helps us answer the questions of what the process of EU foreign policy change looks like and where it leads.

A second challenge I raised was that existing appraisals of the responsiveness, appropriateness, adaptability and especially the lack of change in the EU foreign policy would benefit from a thorough scrutiny of the decision-making process when critical junctures lead to foreign policy change at the EU level. Often these studies, which assess the actions taken or not taken by the European Union in response to crises, provide a normative appreciation of their effectiveness. They tend to focus on policy prescription and to neglect the institutional pluralism of EU foreign policymaking (Noutcheva 2015: 21). This is not to say 'change', its necessity or indeed its lack in the EU context has been absent from the canon. Indeed, there have been myriad analyses of the challenges the many crises pose to the European Union, its identity or its strategic calculations, which necessitate change (e.g. King and Le Galès 2017; Youngs 2018; Dinan, Nugent and Paterson 2017; Degner 2019). Research agendas have shifted towards systemic approaches that address the impact of the crises for the European project of cooperation and integration as a whole (Börzel and Risse 2018; Jones, Kelemen and Meunier 2015; De Wilde and Zürn 2012; Rhinard 2019). Youngs for example treats the many crises with which the EU is faced as a single 'poly-crisis' for the Union which according to him reveals 'common, structural faults in the process of European integration' (2018: 15). He asks whether the crises implore us to change the core tenets of European integration. 'Change' in these analyses does not refer to policy change in particular areas but rather to a qualitative transformation of European cooperation.

The angle in this book is different. It is not concerned with what the crises discussed imply for the process of European integration, or the European project writ large. The proposed framework is, rather, thoroughly oriented towards policy- and decision-making process. This is reflected in the case studies and test-drives investigating the specific foreign policy effects of the Arab uprisings, the Ukraine crisis, the rise in strategic disinformation across Europe, the migration crisis and the crisis in European security. This book provides a framework to unpack specific crisis episodes and how these, through the particular processes, obstacles and facilitators of foreign policy change they engender, impact on policy outputs.

My key argument has been that in order to understand EU foreign policy change in the wake of critical junctures, one needs to understand the decision-making process following those critical junctures, in order to shed light on what kinds of policy changes we did see – however minor or unsubstantiated – at what level they took place, what their actual substance was and why this particular output came out of the decision-making process. To understand the outcome, I argue, we should consider how institutions and temporal context affected this process.

Two factors explaining EU foreign policy change

Institutional plasticity

When we imagine change to EU foreign policy, I argue, we need to know two things. First, what is the institutional 'plasticity' of the policy area? Plasticity refers to the extent to which institutions give form to change, i.e. how rules and institutions constrain the key decision-makers during the process of policy change, but also the extent to which these institutions themselves were shaped by decision-makers. Institutions can give form and can take form. The more they are able to do both, the more plastic they are.

The reason institutions structure the decision-making processes of change is that their historical development, and the legacy this has created, forms the environment in which policymakers today operate, the forums in which they negotiate and the rules through which they make decisions. The reason why the country of the Netherlands has a bicameral legislature today, for example, is historical legacy. In 1815, the southern Netherlands (much of which is currently Belgium) wished the new constitution to create a Senate, so that their nobility would have a say in ruling the country. The northern Netherlanders were against this, as their nobility was few and far between. Eventually, they agreed to a bicameral legislature. With no great success: the Senate proved to be a graveyard for policies and became known as the '*ménagerie du roi*' – the King's zoo. Yet despite wide criticism – from those tasked with reforming the constitution, among others – the Senate was not abolished when Belgium seceded from the Netherlands in 1830, nor during subsequent constitutional changes in the country. Rather, it was reformed and altered on different occasions. In 2021, Dutch laws still need to be approved by the Senate, although criticism remains. Institutions thus shape the structures by which decisions are made, for better or for worse.

Conversely, institutions are not a mere intermediary between actors and political outcomes. Any process of institutional formation results in power disparities between – put simply – 'winners' and 'losers', both within institutions and between institutions. And because institutions thus instantiate power, they are also active objects of political contestation, even after they are formed (Orren and Skowronek 2004; Ikani 2020). Institutional plasticity thus refers to this mutual process of institutions both giving and taking form.

An example of plasticity in action is the United States Supreme Court: first, in the way it shows institutions as arenas of conflict even after they are created. The partisan fights over the nomination of Supreme Court Justices have shown that power struggles and battles over institutions remain. Second, it exemplifies how institutions remain malleable and changeable even after they are formed: the US Supreme Court granted *itself* the power of judicial review during a case in 1803, thereby making it the institution monitoring government actions.

Historical institutionalist scholars in the 'second wave' have taken up this concept of plasticity, although the focus remains on how institutions take form (rather than on how they both give and take form). A key task in HI scholarship, pointed out Capoccia (2016b: 1096), was to understand the conditions under which institutions are able to give form by structuring political behaviour, and the conditions under which they are likely to take form, becoming themselves the object of strategic action. When are institutions malleable and when are they constraining?

This book contributes to this research agenda by showing that plasticity is more likely under conditions where there is room for 'interpretative flexibility' – when actors are able to reinterpret an institution or to exploit its vagueness to make it more suited to their purposes. This interpretative flexibility is easier when policies have a weak legal basis, as was the case with the European Neighbourhood Policy. Another condition shown to be conducive to plasticity is institutional overlap. The ENP, again, illustrated how this works. The multitude of existing institutional arrangements means member states and other actors are more able to 'pick and choose' the way in which they develop policy approaches for a crisis. They can either focus on the existing frameworks (such as the Euro-Mediterranean Partnership), they could have focused on creating a new framework that partially overlaps with the ENP (like the Union for the Mediterranean) or they can choose to deal with the EEAS or the HR/VP rather than with the Commission or the Commission President in some issue areas, should this suit their preferences. The same was the case with migration policy, which is scattered across numerous DGs, agencies and institutions, allowing decision-makers to pick and choose which policy framework they wish to adapt/pursue to suit their preferences.

The concept of plasticity holds special value in European studies, where the conditions are conducive to the existence of plastic institutions. In many issue areas, there exist a multiplicity of institutions, often layered atop one another, especially in foreign policy. The concept complements the extant literature on institutional overlap and turf wars in EU foreign policy (Bickerton 2010; Missiroli 2001; Hofmann 2011, 2009) with an assessment of the conditions under which the institutions constrain political behaviour, and the conditions under which they themselves rather become the object of political contestation.

There are 27 EU member states with the power and possibilities to shape the European institutions by virtue of either their decision-making power or their willingness to engage in policy entrepreneurship. Actors may use the institutional setting in creative ways in order to shape and re-invent institutions, without necessarily 'breaking out of the path' these institutions are on (Strambach and Halkier 2013: 1). Many European policies are not necessarily built on formal regulative institutions in which deviation from the rules is illegal and sanctionable, but rather consist of policies that have limited legal weight and that allow room for interpretative flexibility and manoeuvre, *especially* when there is institutional overlap. An example is EU energy policy, in which there exists important overlap between different Directorates-General and in which there is room for interpretative flexibility by member states. This is where incorporating institutional plasticity in the analysis may prove useful.

Temporal contingency

In addition to institutional plasticity, an important building block of the analytical framework proposed in this book is temporal contingency. Temporal contingency in this research refers to the fact that the policy reform we saw did not *have* to be the way it turned out – this was not logically necessary – but has come out this way because of various events, not all of them foreseen or expected. Just as institutions create the institutional landscape in which the policy change process takes place, the temporal context provides the 'timescape' of the reform process. HI approaches argue that the temporal context influences the origin and transformation of political institutions (Fioretos, Falleti and Sheingate 2016: 3). This contextual causality implies that it is the interaction of institutions, actors and historical processes that defines the outcome.

Like other analyses using historical institutionalism as a theoretical approach, the analytical framework proposed in this book thus explicitly situates variables in their appropriate temporal context. Most of these analyses, however, assess institutional change taking place over periods of years or decades (Bulmer 2009; Collier and Collier 1991). The analytical framework proposed here is rather intended to serve students looking at specific and brief episodes of EU foreign policy change. To facilitate this task, I suggested dividing the temporal context into three registers which users of the framework must map in their case studies: 1) the structural context (decades, centuries); 2) the conjunctural context (a few years); and 3) the liminal context (days, weeks). The framework prioritises the policy change episode itself, preceded by an analysis of the structural and conjunctural features of the temporal context that may have impacted on the reform episode. Together, the temporal context and its structural, conjunctural and liminal features can make the policy area in question more salient, the need for reform much more urgent and render hitherto unprecedented forms of policy change possible and even desirable.

An important finding in the previous research on salience and decision-making, which the case studies in this book confirm, is that the sudden high salience of an issue area need not result in substantive policy changes. Salience is often ephemeral. Because the mobilisation that it brings about is hard to sustain over time, actors with power over the reform agenda may shelve or delay reforms.

A typology of EU foreign policy change outcomes

The final challenge this book has tried to contend with was how to conceptualise outcomes of changes to EU foreign policy, particularly changes that differ widely in scope and ambition.

Overwhelmingly dominant in public policy studies and the field of foreign policy analysis have been typologies of policy change that work on a Guttman scale. This means the levels of change are unidimensional and cumulative: each higher level of change implies that the previous levels of change have been completed. The most widely applied of these typologies is that of Hall (1993). In a seminal article he proposed three 'orders' of change: first-order change, which 'represents a change in the simplest of policy variables'; second-order change implies changes to both policy instruments and their settings; while third-order change alters all three sets of variables, radical changes which constitute a paradigm shift (1993: 293).

His typology of change has been used and refined across public policy studies (Howlett and Cashore 2009; Daugbjerg 1997; Cashore and Howlett 2007). In the realm of FPA, scholars including Hermann (1990), Holsti (2016, 1982) and Rosati (1994) offer similar incremental, cumulative typologies of foreign policy change along the Guttman scale in which third-order paradigm change always implies second- and first-order change has also taken place, while second-order change always implies first-order change. First- and second-order changes need to be completed before third-order change can occur. In the advocacy coalition framework, this graduated and cumulative approach which distinguishes minor changes from major change is equally common.

In this book I take issue with such a cumulative typology. Most importantly, the orders of change are not as obvious and straightforward when we look at outputs from processes by which European foreign policy changes. The case studies and test-drives in this book have shown that 'no change' or policy continuity does not always mean an exact repetition of past policy and practices, just as not all policy change can be categorised as ranging from minor to major change. Moreover, the various case studies exposed that policy changes contain elements of more than one order, as well as elements that fit none. How are we to conceptualise these policy changes?

I argue that the conceptualisation of three-level policy change following a cumulative scale inaccurately reflects the policy process leading towards the particular policy outputs we observed. In doing so, it risks feeding unrealistic expectations regarding how rapidly and how profoundly EU foreign policy may change. Over the past 'decade of crisis', there have been numerous assessments of the way the EU can and should change. These studies typically take a macro-approach, investigating how recent transformations in the global system affect the EU's role, influence and stability (e.g. a special issue of *International Politics* by R. Falkner 2017; or Youngs 2018). In policy circles there has been regular commentary on the necessity to 'radically rethink' the European strategy. After speaking to a wide range of scholars in EU foreign policy, the UK House of Lords for example recommended a wholly new strategy for EU foreign policy, focusing on the wider 'neighbourhood', stability, security and prosperity (House of Lords, European Union Committee 2016: 12).

The findings in this book nuance these macro-analyses, which look at the position of the EU in a global transformation, by investigating what these 'radical rethinks' of policy actually look like in more detail. This study reveals that, quite often, such about-turns in strategy rhetoric may in practice co-exist with a strong conceptual and instrumental continuity in the actual policies. This is particularly the case for the host of policies which fall under EU external action but which are not the CFSP, such as the ENP, which is essentially an umbrella framework for quite technical, on-the-ground policies; or migration policy.

This book therefore set out to improve our conceptualisation of policy change at the EU level. It did so by adopting a measurement of change from the realm of public policy studies (Cashore and Howlett, 2007; Howlett and Cashore, 2009) which disaggregates the *level* at which the change is directed from the *substance* of the policy change and third, following from this, the *directionality* of policy changes. By 'directionality' is meant the extent to which policy reflects a shift towards a new paradigm. Change that pursues the same sets of objectives as the status quo follows the same 'direction'. At the other end of the spectrum there is change that is nonlinear, representing a break with the past.

This disaggregation has proved valuable because it nuances the conclusion that there has either been 'a little' or 'a lot' of change, or that major changes (third-order changes in the traditional typology) are necessarily preceded by a wholesale revision of policy. Assessing policy change by distinguishing the level, the substance and the directionality of change is more precise in indicating what type of change we observed. This approach also renders visible policy changes that are *not* necessarily substantive in nature, for example 'major policy changes' in rhetoric that in substance deviate little from the status quo.

Based on the findings in Chapters 2 and 3 and the theoretical framework advanced in Chapter 1, the typology proposed in Chapter 4 complements the existing, three-level typology of policy change with two analytical categories: symbolic policy change and constructive ambiguity. Symbolic changes are politically useful accommodating gestures, which indicate a willingness to take immediate steps, to demonstrate that action is being taken in order to avoid future crisis. Yet despite such rhetorical gestures and statements, the main features of the policy remain intact. Temporal context is an important contributing factor to producing symbolic change. Scholars in public policy studies have found that in the wake of crisis, there is often a public pressure on decision-makers to respond, which decision-makers tend to meet with visible changes and steps. Yet despite these gestures and rhetorical commitments to profound change, the core values and policies often remain intact (Boin et al., 2009; Boin et al., 2005; Drennan and McConnell, 2007; Hart and Tindall, 2009; Rose and Davies, 1994).

Symbolic policy changes are thus almost entirely rhetorical in nature, often taking place at the macro level. The introduction of the concept 'deep democracy' in the 2011 revised ENP, discussed in Chapter 2, is a good example. It exemplifies the way in which new lexicon is drizzled over policy that is highly continuous: the six elements into which the supposedly new concept was broken down after the policy reform are essentially the same procedural take on democracy that was present in 2001 (European Commission, 2001). It rather represents another 'rhetorical variation' on themes already present in pre-2011 policy documents (Teti, Thompson and Noble 2013: 75). Indeed, in both the 2011 and the 2015 reform rounds, in the wake of the critical juncture we witnessed a clear rhetorical break with previous policy, accompanied by a declaratory commitment to radically changing course. Yet neither the rhetoric nor the declared ambition for reform in response to events was matched by a major revision of actual policy objectives or policy tools.

Although the general abstract policy aims, as well as the supposed nature of the problems stemming from the changing 'neighbourhood', were modified or reformulated in the wake of both events, this did not constitute a *paradigm change*. At times, policy changes are presented as paradigmatic changes to the way the EU approaches its neighbours, while in substance they appear to be minor adjustments or reformulations of 'first-order' and 'second-order' elements of policy.

Similarly, the second test-drive on the EU's response to the migration and asylum crisis shows the policy changes the European Commission pursued (mainly, though among others) were aimed at displaying a European solidarity, a manifest response to the salience and urgency of the crisis. Yet most measures do not address the root causes behind the crisis nor do they deviate substantially from the direction of previous policy.

The concept of symbolic change is not new. Symbolic changes are generally characterised in the literature as '*faux*-paradigmatic' changes (Cashore and Howlett 2007) which are not accompanied by substantive revisions of policy goals or tools. Even so, two important findings on symbolic change in this book stand out.

First, symbolic changes are a frequent and important outcome in EU foreign policy change. Nearly all case studies discussed in this book display some form of symbolic change. More importantly, the case studies in this book show that symbolic changes represent more than '*faux*-paradigmatic' policy changes which appear to be significant changes yet which end up being reversed soon after (Cashore and Howlett 2007). Symbolic changes, rather, have the potential to foster long-term, incremental change because they often promote knowledge- and capacity-building at the European level. The EU's CSDP missions for example, especially the independent ones which had high costs and high risks, faced fierce criticism at their launch and in the years after. Yet the operational experiences through the missions were important instances of institutional learning-by-doing, which furthered the policy area (M. E. Smith 2015). It is not always what policies do in the moment which matters for policy development, but the processes of learning and familiarisation they engender.

Perhaps even more important than knowledge- and capacity-building may be the potential of symbolic change to foster a certain 'comfort' in further integration, especially in the realm of EU foreign policy which is built on an often-fragile compromise between member states with diverging interests. Because the first steps are primarily rhetorical and made in response to intense public pressure, the key actors are more likely to agree on symbolic changes. The case of the 'military planning and conduct capability' (MPCC) established during the critical juncture in European security and defence discussed in Chapter 5 is a good example. The MPCC was agreed upon in part because of its 'embryonic' and modest nature – it was explicitly *not* called an operational headquarters. In its current form – with a staff of around thirty people – it lacks policy bandwidth and has been derided as nothing more than a 'call-centre' by the UK government. However, it acts as an important inroad into more profound change, and plays an important role in streamlining a collective command and control at the European level, and may indeed be a first step towards an actual operational headquarters. The act of creating an MPCC, cast as predominantly symbolic by many observers, thus marks acceptance of the fact that the EU can indeed build its own command and control centre, something which has long been resisted (Tardy 2017).

The reverse may equally be true: there may exist changes which we classify as first- or second-order which – if not acted upon – will turn out to be mainly symbolic. PESCO illustrates such a case, a stepping stone towards significant change, which will remain symbolic if implementation and compliance lag behind. Yet again, this potential to be mere symbolism may in part explain why member states were willing to agree on it in the first place. Symbolic change, in conclusion, thus is much more than a mere *faux*-paradigmatic accommodating gesture. It creates a placeholder which fosters knowledge-building, capacity-building and acceptance among EU member states of the desirability and capability of being active in policy areas. This may, in the long term, nurture incremental change.

The second additional conceptualisation this book offered was constructive ambiguity, to identify EU foreign policy changes which are viable because their vague formulation allows them to mean different things to different key actors, leaving significant room for interpretation and thus to garner support from diverging interests.

The notion of policy ambiguity is explored in public policy studies, though sparingly. Palier coined the term 'polysemy', which means the co-existence of multiple meanings for a word or phrase. Such polysemic changes bring together contradictory interpretations around the broadest agreement possible (Palier 2007). They are thus simultaneously ambiguous and constructive.

In the literature, this has occasionally been cast as a conspicuous form of 'incomplete contracting', in which the incomplete nature of the contracts is obscured by policymakers (Farrell and Héritier 2005; Edelman 2001). Others operationalise constructive ambiguity as a strategy which political entrepreneurs use to push for a policy initiative, whilst not offending those with the power to support or block those initiatives. Ambiguity is a strategy when clarity would face opposition (Jegen and Mérand 2014). However, authors such as Jegen and Mérand (2014) or Hoffmann (1995) argue that political entrepreneurs rarely design constructive ambiguity as a conscious strategy because it carries the risk of failure. Coalitions around vagueness and ambiguity, they say, are hard to sustain. 'There is always the moment', wrote Hoffmann (1995: 131), 'when a terrible clarifier calls for a lifting of ambiguities, at which point deadlock is more likely than resolution.'

This research has rather found that when looking at specific policy areas and change in the wake of critical junctures – in contrast to the longitudinal studies Jegen and Mérand (2014) did – constructive outcomes are a frequent outcome of EU foreign policy change processes. This is most likely attributable to the dispersed institutional basis of many areas of EU external action and the heterogeneity in member state preferences providing fertile ground for ambiguous policy changes, which carefully play into diverging policy preferences. This holds true for the ENP in particular but equally migration or defence.

In this study I argue that constructive ambiguity as the outcome of a policy change process should not be confused with the postponement of agreements or strategy, but can be a strategy in and of itself. Constructive ambiguity provides a politically viable alternative to first- and second-order changes when key actor preferences diverge. The way in which EU foreign policy is governed exacerbates the consequences of diverging member state preferences, because policy change hinges on actor agreement. Radical and substantive policy adjustments would have to be approved by all member states. Ambiguous policy changes allow decision-makers to 'muddle through' (Lindblom 1959), despite disagreement. Ambiguity, therefore, can be a politically functional outcome of policy change as it offers a way to move forward despite disagreements. Chapter 3, which investigated the 2015 ENP reform process, found a number of policy outputs that are constructively ambiguous such as the proposition in the 2015 revised ENP to make the ENP 'more political', reflecting the EU's interests better. This terminology was ambiguous because it did not mean the same thing to the key actors. To Germany and France this meant a greater role for the EEAS. France also was eager to make the ENP more adaptable to the imminent crises with which Europe was faced, through an additional budget provision for the management of crisis in the 'neighbourhood'. A 'more political ENP' to France also meant a less stringent pursuit of conditionality in a more political policy based on EU interests, focused on crisis management and security. Finally, to Poland and also to the Commission, making the ENP more political essentially meant upgrading the policy through a greater commitment by the EU: fewer bilateral policies pursued by the member states, more EU activity. Poland, finally, did not wish to see a greater role for the EEAS. There thus was a divergence in policy preferences. At the same time, the push for a more political ENP was constructive, as it aggregated the different and diverging interests of the key actors. It was a policy change the Commission and the EEAS, Germany, France and Poland had all argued in favour of.

Here we find that the use of the notion of a more 'political' ENP was ambiguous, in which divergent interpretations and a vagueness surrounding the meaning of the measure made the policy change politically viable. It indeed became one of the four major changes during the 2015 revision of the ENP.

Other examples of constructive ambiguity are the fleeting reference to the UfM in the 2015 ENP revision. In an apparent compromise to Poland and France, the revised ENP states that the EaP and the UfM are to be strengthened. The revised document argues the EU intends to 'give priority, wherever suitable, to the UfM in its regional cooperation efforts' (European Commission and High Representative for Foreign Affairs and Security Policy 2015a: 18). It is not spelled out how the UfM is supposed to fit within the new ENP and the document explicitly calls for the meetings to be ad hoc. It is precisely because of its ambiguity that it received nominal support from all actors involved. ENP changes with greater clarity would probably have failed to rally the agreement of all parties involved (e.g. to a greater role for the EEAS) or would have resulted in diluted compromises. And while arguably to give priority wherever suitable to the UfM can be called a diluted compromise, it was a compromise that made the revised ENP more palatable to actors in favour of a stronger UfM.

The East StratCom Task force discussed in Chapter 5 likewise exemplified such constructive ambiguity. The EU recognised publicly that it needed to respond to Russian disinformation. Setting up a Task Force devoted to this aim would represent a qualitative step away from previous policies. The Task Force in many respects exudes novelty, if one looks at the types of officials working there (mainly with journalistic rather than policy background) and at the modern, online, assertive approach to 'take back the narrative'. Yet the Task Force is hampered by terminological vagueness affecting both the threats to be addressed and the measures to taken to do so. This ambiguity is enshrined in its very foundation: the Task Force was a product of a compromise, a diluted form of what was initially proposed. The Task Force was not given an independent budget, had to work with 'cost-free' officials fully funded by willing member states and, perhaps most problematic of all according to interviewees, it was placed under the EEAS, meaning it was not allowed to pursue some of its original ambitious aims, such as to counter disinformation within the European Union. Yet these compromises were at the very heart of what made the Task Force politically viable.

Constructive ambiguity is thus better understood as a constructive technique of governance, used frequently in the field of EU foreign policy. Like symbolic policy changes, changes that are ambiguous in nature may act as important signposts for future policy change. They forge a place on the agenda and create a form of path dependence which can lead to the gradual expansion of the policy, fostering incremental substantive change.

I argue that seeing symbolic change and constructive ambiguity as distinct outcomes of the policy process – not as failures or as postponements of decisions – helps us to better grasp what changes were made to EU foreign policy as a response to challenges. They are 'among the options' of policy change, and they might be the outcome of a process of changing European foreign policy more often than is generally assumed, especially because the conditions for these two forms of change to occur (a highly salient temporal context and divergent member state interests) are arguably quite common in EU policymaking.

Yet their value transcends EU foreign policymaking. As mentioned in Chapter 4, most typologies of foreign policy change in FPA (Hermann 1990; Holsti 2016; Gustavsson 1999) are cumulative and do not include policy changes that do not fit the standard Guttman scale. The political functionality of constructive ambiguity, however, has already been demonstrated in international negotiations (*cf.* Dingley 2005) and the factors that make this outcome of foreign policy change more likely – divergent policy preferences and a temporal context that is not highly salient – are likely to occur in settings of foreign policy change after crisis in a non-EU setting. The same goes for the outcome symbolic change. Again, the factors that make this outcome more likely are common in international affairs – a highly salient international context combined with divergent policy preferences on what policy change should look like. Rhetorical and symbolic gestures prove to be a politically useful strategy in such contexts. As such, this book and particularly the categories it suggests speak to the wider study of foreign policy change. Further study of these forms of policy change in non-EU settings is desirable.

Future research

Research programmes should offer answers to the most pressing and relevant problems. This book aims to be of use to those studying the way the EU responds to new or future external crises which create critical junctures in particular policy areas. It develops and applies an analytical framework to a series of test-drives. Further applications of the framework, in sequences of policy change across different institutions and different areas, will hopefully follow. EU energy policy, or the EU's response to the Syrian civil war, or its issues in responding to the Libyan civil war, are all examples of critical junctures which may be tested. More historic cases may be investigated in a similar fashion, for example the window of opportunity in European security policy in the early 2000s, with Javier Solana at the helm.

Further research is equally welcome into particular stages of the analytical framework, particularly regarding how key actors perceive the critical juncture. Analysis of the process of key actor contestation around what type of crisis is at play, and what type of approach to address it is most appropriate, will benefit from theoretical approaches that use processes of framing and politicisation as explanatory factors in the critical juncture (Boin, t'Hart and McConnell 2009; Schön and Rein 1994), but also from a more sustained engagement with the IR literature on narratives. Krebs (2015: 122), for example, discusses unsettled narrative situations, critical junctures when the public demand for 'storytelling' is elevated and agency may have more room to pursue change. Decision-makers may seize these moments of rhetorical opportunity to transform the narrative landscape and thereby, policy.

In Krebs' study, these decision-makers are presidents. Future research should dive further into these unsettled narrative situations and the way decision-makers at the European level may seize these moments and how far they prove able – or not able – to transform the narrative. Again, the unique nature of the EU complicates simply transposing the existing literature to EU decision-makers, whose audience is very different from members of a national government. But the impact of narratives, their creation, reproduction and the opportunity they may present at critical times deserves further exploration.

On the output side of my analytical framework, more research is welcome into both symbolic change and constructive ambiguity. Further empirical research into instances of both will enrich our understanding of their frequency, in both an EU and a non-EU context of foreign policy change. This book shows that the outcome of policy change – whether it is change in the first, second or third order, or rather symbolic change or constructive ambiguity – depends strongly on both the institutional effects of the ENP institutions and their plasticity, and on the impact of the timing and sequencing of events in the wake of the critical juncture. We need more insight into the conditions under which symbolic change and constructive ambiguity are more likely outcomes of a change process than the traditional three orders of policy change, as well as a more nuanced understanding of how the temporal context affects policy change, and how the constellation of actor preferences may interact with this temporal context.

Second, since both appear to be a possibly common outcome of EU foreign policy change, research should investigate what the possible long-term consequences are of repeated symbolic changes or repeated ambiguous agreements in EU foreign policy making, as well as under which conditions symbolic change and constructive ambiguity are most likely. Table 4.3 in

Chapter 4 summarised how the salience of the temporal context impacts on policy change. It contrasted a salient context, i.e. a temporal context with multiple, liminal, 'triggering' events pressing upon decision-makers, with a non-salient context that is free from such contingencies. In a non-salient context, it is likely that either no change will occur when the policy preferences of the key actors diverge, or first- and second-order change will take place if the decision-makers concur regarding policy changes. In a salient context, either paradigm change or – in the absence of a convergence among the key players – symbolic change are most likely.

Furthermore, Chapter 4 shows that constructive ambiguity is a likely policy outcome when actor preferences diverge, sharing neither a common vision of the reforms nor a similar interest in the measures. Although reality is much more complex, the point is to show that the temporal context has a bearing on policy change, through increasing the salience of a policy, in this case the ENP, by increasing the urgency of reform, by bringing together actors and even by affecting their leverage during the reform window.

Under what conditions symbolic change and constructive ambiguity are more likely outcomes of a change process than the traditional three orders of policy change, which all include substantive policy changes that are progressively achieved, warrants further research. Other authors (Andersen and Eliassen 2001; Olsen 2001; Peters 1994) have described how the heterogeneity and the complexity of EU policymaking advantages ambiguous policy outcomes. 'Far from being an aberration', writes Zahariadis, 'ambiguity is an integral part of EU policymaking' (Zahariadis 2008: 527). But while a few authors have focused on the role of ambiguity in European defence and energy policy (Jegen and Mérand 2014), it is under-studied in analyses of EU foreign policy, despite having the potential to provide a similar, politically functional, outcome to the policy process.

No single framework or approach can purport to conclusively explain an issue as complex as foreign policy change. For a full picture of the process of policy change and all its constitutive aspects, a combination of rationalist approaches which argue that fundamental policy change may be attributed to learning (Dunn 1994), or constructivist perspectives that focus on the ideational sphere of decision-making, how narratives, symbolism and language affect the policy change, may be helpful (Scholten 2017). As our understanding of the European policy process becomes more sophisticated, argued Sandholtz (1993: 39), scholars increasingly find our 'goals are best served by specifying the analytic strengths – and limitations – of approaches that work better in combination than alone'. This definitely applies to the problem of EU foreign policy change after crisis.

Nonetheless, the framework put forward in this book has been able to provide a comprehensive account of different change episodes, which explains not just the decision-making process leading to the output of policy change, but also the variation in change outcomes. By including both institutional explanations and temporal contingencies as important explanatory factors, this analytical framework aims to produce more accurate explanations of why change did or did not occur, and why these particular changes emerged from the policymaking process.

Bibliography

Achilli, Luigi. 2018. 'Why are we not reforming the Dublin Regulation yet?', *Euractiv*, 25 October 2018.

Alink, Fleur, Arjen Boin and Paul t'Hart. 2001. 'Institutional crises and reforms in policy sectors: the case of asylum policy in Europe', *Journal of European Public Policy*, 8: 286–306.

Alliot-Marie, Michèle, Dimitris Droutsas, Markos Kyprianou, Trinidad Jiménez, Tonio Borg, and Samuel Zbogar. 2011. 'Non-papier. Action de l'Union européenne en direction du voisinage Sud', accessed 11 May 2021. www.diplomatie.gouv.fr/IMG/pdf/11-02-17_Non-papier_Action_de_l_Union_europeenne_en_direction_du_voisinage_Sud.pdf.

Allison, G. T., and P. Zelikow. 1999. *Essence of decision: explaining the Cuban missile crisis* (Longman: New York).

Allison, Roy. 2014. 'Russian "deniable" intervention in Ukraine: how and why Russia broke the rules', *International Affairs*, 90: 1255–97.

Andersen, Svein S., and Kjell A. Eliassen. 2001. *Making policy in Europe* (SAGE: London).

Ashbee, Edward, and Steven Hurst. 2020. 'The Trump foreign policy record and the concept of transformational change', *Global Affairs*, 6: 5–19.

Ashton, Catherine. 2011a. 'Address to the European Parliament on the United Nations General Assembly, the Middle East peace process and the Arab Spring', *SPEECH/11/608*, 2011/09/27, accessed 22 March 2021. https://ec.europa.eu/commission/presscorner/detail/en/SPEECH_11_608.

———. 2011b. 'EU declaration by HR Ashton on events in Libya', *6795/1/11*.

———. 2011c. 'The EU wants "deep democracy" to take root in Egypt and Tunisia', *The Guardian*, 4 February, section 'Comment is free'.

———. 2011d. 'Remarks at the senior officials' meeting on Egypt and Tunisia', *SPEECH/11/122*.

———. 2012. 'Speech by EU High Representative Catherine Ashton at the EU Conference "Egyptian women: the way forward", Cairo, Egypt', *A 338/12*.

———. 2014. 'Statement by EU High Representative Catherine Ashton on the developments in Ukraine's Crimea'. https://eeas.europa.eu/archives/ashton/media/statements/docs/2014/140301_01_en.pdf.

Aspinwall, Mark D., and Gerald Schneider. 2000. 'Same menu, separate tables: the institutionalist turn in political science and the study of European integration', *European Journal of Political Research*, 38: 1–36.

Assemblée Nationale, Commission des Affaires Étrangères. 2015. 'Proposition de résolution Européenne: sur la révision de la Politique européenne de voisinage – 2881'. www.assemblee-nationale.fr/14/europe/resolutions/ppe2772.asp.

Association of Accredited Public Policy Advocates to the European Union. 2016. 'EEAS staff facts & figures', accessed 23 September 2020. www.aalep.eu/eeas-staff-facts-figures#:~:text=At%20the%20end%20of%202015%2C%20there%20were%20in%20total%20434,in%20the%20crisis%20management%20structures.

Auer, Stefan. 2015. 'Carl Schmitt in the Kremlin: the Ukraine crisis and the return of geopolitics', *International Affairs*, 91: 953–68.

Auswärtiges Amt. 2014a. 'An agreement on the settlement of the crisis in Ukraine is signed', *Auswärtiges Amt*, 21 February, accessed 19 May 2017. www.auswaertiges-amt.de/EN/Aussenpolitik/Laender/Aktuelle_Artikel/Ukraine/140221_Ukraine-Vereinbarung.html.

———. 2014b. 'Weimar triangle: Foreign Minister Steinmeier to meet his French and Polish counterparts in Weimar', German Federal Foreign Office, *Auswärtiges Amt*, 26 March.

———. 2015. 'Europäische Nachbarschaftspolitik', German Federal Foreign Office, *Auswärtiges Amt*.

Ayrault, Jean-Marc, and Frank-Walter Steinmeier. 2016. 'A strong Europe in a world of uncertainties', accessed 19 August 2020. www.auswaertiges-amt.de/en/aussenpolitik/europa/160624-bm-am-fra-st/281702.

Baezner, Marie. 2018. 'Cyber and information warfare in the Ukrainian conflict', Center for Security Studies (CSS), ETH Zürich.

Baldwin, Richard, and Francesco Giavazzi. 2015. *The Eurozone crisis: a consensus view of the causes and a few possible remedies* (Centre for Economic Policy Research: London).

Balfour, Rosa. 2007. 'Italy's policies in the Mediterranean' in Haizam Amirah Fernández and Richard Youngs (eds), *The Euro-Mediterranean partnership: assessing the first decade* (FRIDE/Real Instituto Elcano: Madrid).

———. 2012. 'EU conditionality after the Arab Spring', *PapersIEMed*: 1–33.

Barbé, Esther. 1996. 'The Barcelona conference: launching pad of a process', *Mediterranean Politics*, 1: 25–42.

Barbulescu, Roxana. 2016. 'Still a beacon of human rights? Considerations on the EU response to the refugee crisis in the Mediterranean', *Mediterranean Politics*, 22: 301–8.

Barroso, José Manuel. 2011a. 'José Manuel Durão Barroso President of the European Commission Statement by President Barroso on the situation in North Africa', *SPEECH/11/137*.

———. 2011b. 'Partners in freedom: the EU response to the Arab Spring', *SPEECH/11/523*.

———. 2013. 'Statement of President Barroso on the current situation in Ukraine'. https://ec.europa.eu/commission/presscorner/detail/en/MEMO_13_1116.

———. 2014. 'Remarks by President Barroso following the extraordinary meeting of EU Heads of State and Government on Ukraine'. https://ec.europa.eu/commission/presscorner/detail/en/SPEECH_14_190.

Bauer, Michael W., and Christoph Knill. 2014. 'A conceptual framework for the comparative analysis of policy change: measurement, explanation and strategies of policy dismantling', *Journal of Comparative Policy Analysis: Research and Practice*, 16: 28–44.

Baumgartner, Frank R. 2013. 'Ideas and policy change', *Governance*, 26: 239–58.

Baumgartner, Frank R., Christian Breunig, Christoffer Green-Pedersen, Bryan D. Jones, Peter B. Mortensen, Michiel Nuytemans, and Stefaan Walgrave. 2009.

'Punctuated equilibrium in comparative perspective', *American Journal of Political Science*, 53: 603–20.

Baumgartner, Frank R., and Bryan D. Jones. 1993. *Agendas and instability in American politics* (University of Chicago Press: Chicago).

———. 2002. *Policy dynamics* (University of Chicago Press: Chicago).

Baumgartner, Frank R., Bryan D. Jones and Peter B. Mortensen. 2017. 'Punctuated equilibrium theory: explaining stability and change in public policymaking' in Christopher M. Weible and Paul A. Sabatier (eds), *Theories of the policy process* (Westview Press: New York).

BBC News. 2013. 'Huge Ukraine rally over EU agreement delay', 24 November, section Europe. www.bbc.co.uk/news/world-europe-25078952.

———. 2015a. 'Greece debt crisis: has Grexit been avoided?', accessed 22 March 2021. www.bbc.com/news/world-europe-32332221.

———. 2015b. 'Migrant crisis: Merkel warns of EU "failure"', accessed 22 March 2021. www.bbc.com/news/world-europe-34108224.

———. 2016. 'Greece's Tsipras condemns sanctions against Russia', accessed 22 March 2021. www.bbc.com/news/world-europe-36403129.

Beach, Derek, and Rasmus Brun Pedersen. 2012. "Case selection techniques in process-tracing and the implications of taking the study of causal mechanisms seriously" in APSA 2012 Annual Meeting, New Orleans.

———. 2013. *Process-tracing methods: foundations and guidelines* (University of Michigan: Ann Arbor, MI).

Behr, Timo. 2012a. 'After the revolution: the EU and the Arab transition', *Notre Europe Policy Paper*, 54: 26.

———. 2012b. 'The EU's Mediterranean policies after the Arab Spring: can the leopard change its spots?', *Amsterdam Law Forum*, 4: 76–88.

———. 2012c. 'Germany and the Arab Spring', *Actuelles de l'Ifri*.

———. 2015. 'Power politics in the making of Euro-Mediterranean policies: exploring the role of the north–south split' in Timo Behr and Teija Tiilikainen (eds), *Northern Europe and the making of the EU's Mediterranean and Middle East policies: normative leaders or passive bystanders?* (Ashgate: Farnham).

Bendiek, Annegret. 2008. 'EU foreign policy perspectives. A call for the revival of the Weimar triangle', *SWP Comments*: 1–8.

———. 2017. 'A paradigm shift in the EU's Common Foreign and Security Policy: from transformation to resilience', accessed 11 May 2021. www.swp-berlin.org/fileadmin/contents/products/research_papers/2017RP11_bdk.pdf.

Bennett, Andrew, and Jeffrey T. Checkel. 2015. *Process tracing: from metaphor to analytic tool* (Cambridge University Press: Cambridge).

Bentzen, Naja. 2015. 'Understanding propaganda and disinformation PE 571.332', European Parliamentary Research Service, accessed 22 March 2021. www.europarl.europa.eu/RegData/etudes/ATAG/2015/571332/EPRS_ATA%282015%29571332_EN.pdf.

Bentzen, Naja, and Martin Russell. 2015. 'European Parliament briefing: Russia's manipulation of information on Ukraine and the EU's response'. www.europarl.europa.eu/RegData/etudes/BRIE/2015/559471/EPRS_BRI(2015)559471_EN.pdf.

Béraud-Sudreau, Lucie, and Bastian Giegerich. 2018. 'NATO defence spending and European threat perceptions', *Survival*, 60: 53–74.

Berridge, Geoff, and Alan James. 2003. 'Constructive ambiguity' in Geoff Berridge and Alan James (eds), *A dictionary of diplomacy* (Palgrave Macmillan: Basingstoke).

Best, Jacqueline. 2008. 'Ambiguity, uncertainty, and risk: rethinking indeterminacy', *International Political Sociology*, 2: 355–74.

Bicchi, Federica. 2002. 'Actors and factors in European foreign policy making: insights from the Mediterranean case', European University Institute Working Paper: 1–33.

———. 2011. 'The Union for the Mediterranean, or the changing context of Euro-Mediterranean relations', *Mediterranean Politics*, 16: 3–19.

Bicchi, Federica, and Richard Gillespie. 2014. *The Union for the Mediterranean* (Routledge: London).

Bickerton, Christopher J. 2010. 'Functionality in EU foreign policy: towards a new research agenda?', *Journal of European Integration*, 32: 213–27.

Biermann, Felix, Nina Guérin, Stefan Jagdhuber, Berthold Rittberger and Moritz Weiss. 2017. 'Political (non-)reform in the euro crisis and the refugee crisis: a liberal intergovernmentalist explanation', *Journal of European Public Policy*, 26: 246–66.

Bigo, Didier, Sergio Carrera, Elspeth Guild and Valsamis Mitsilegas. 2016. 'The EU and the 2016 terrorist attacks in Brussels: better instead of more information sharing' in *CEPS Commentary*. Centre for European Policy Studies (CEPS).

Billon-Galland, Alice, and Martin Quencez. 2017. 'Can France and Germany make PESCO work as a process toward EU defense?', German Marshall Fund of the United States, accessed 25 August 2020. www.jstor.org/stable/resrep18774.

Birkland, Thomas A. 2006. *Lessons of disaster: policy change after catastrophic events* (Georgetown University Press: Washington, DC).

Biscop, Sven. 2018. 'European defence: give PESCO a chance', *Survival*, 60: 161–80.

Blauberger, Michael, and Dorte Sindbjerg Martinsen. 2020. 'The Court of Justice in times of politicisation: "law as a mask and shield" revisited', *Journal of European Public Policy*, 27: 382–99.

Blockmans, Steven. 2018. 'The EU's modular approach to defence integration: an inclusive, ambitious and legally binding PESCO?', *Common Market Law Review*: 1785–826.

Bloomberg. 2014. 'US fighters circle Baltics as Putin fans fear of Russia', 3 July.

Bloomberg Business Week. 2013. 'Ukraine cuts a deal it could soon regret', 17 December, section 'Europe'.

Boin, Arjen, Allan McConnell, and Paul t'Hart (eds). 2008. *Governing after crisis* (Cambridge University Press: Cambridge).

Boin, Arjen, Paul t'Hart and Allan McConnell. 2009. 'Crisis exploitation: political and policy impacts of framing contests', *Journal of European Public Policy*, 16: 81–106.

Boin, Arjen, Paul t'Hart, Eric K. Stern and Bengt Sundelius. 2005. *The politics of crisis management: public leadership under pressure* (Cambridge University Press: Cambridge).

Börzel, Tanja, and Bidzina Lebanidze. 2015. 'European Neighbourhood Policy at the crossroads', Maxcap Working Paper, accessed 17 March 2020. http://userpage.fu-berlin.de/kfgeu/maxcap/system/files/maxcap_wp_12_0.pdf.

Börzel, Tanja, and Thomas Risse. 2018. 'From the euro to the Schengen crises: European integration theories, politicization, and identity politics', *Journal of European Public Policy*, 25: 83–108.

Börzel, Tanja, Thomas Risse and Assem Dandashly. 2015. 'The EU, external actors, and the Arabellions: much ado about (almost) nothing', *Journal of European Integration*, 37: 135–53.

Böttger, Katrin. 2008. 'The development of the European Neighbourhood Policy (ENP): the EU as a regional power for peace and order?" paper presented at 4th Pan-European Conference on EU Politics, University of Latvia.

Brockmeier, Sarah. 2013. 'Germany and the intervention in Libya', *Survival*, 55: 63–90.

Bulmer, Simon. 2009. 'Politics in time meets the politics of time: historical institutionalism and the EU timescape', *Journal of European Public Policy*, 16: 307–24.

Bundesministerium der Verteidigung. 2016. 'Bericht des Bundesministeriums der Verteidigung zu Rüstungsangelegenheiten' (Bundesministerium der Verteidigung: Berlin).

———. 2017. 'Permanent structured cooperation: Ein Meilenstein auf dem Weg zur Verteidigungsunion', accessed 22 March 2021. www.bmvg.de/de/aktuelles/pesco-ein-meilenstein-auf-dem-weg-zur-verteidigungsunion-19806.

Bundesregierung. 2014. 'Regierungserklärung von Bundeskanzlerin Merkel'. www.bundeskanzlerin.de/bkin-de/aktuelles/regierungserklaerung-von-bundeskanzlerin-merkel-443682.

———. 2015. '"The Eastern Partnership is more important than ever" – government statement in the German Bundestag'. www.bundesregierung.de/breg-en/news/-the-eastern-partnership-is-more-important-than-ever–442500.

———. 2016. 'White Paper on German security policy and the future of the Bundeswehr'. www.gmfus.org/file/8970/download.

———. 2017. 'Stronger together thanks to PESCO', accessed 22 March 2021. www.bundesregierung.de/breg-en/news/stronger-together-thanks-to-pesco-440036.

Buras, Piotr. 2015a. 'Can Poland remain a leader of EU foreign policy?', European Council on Foreign Relations.

———. 2015b. 'Poland and the Eastern Partnership: the view from Warsaw', 19 May, accessed 11 May 2021. www.ecfr.eu/article/commentary_poland_and_the_eastern_partnership_the_view_from_warsaw3038.

Buzan, Barry, and R. J. Barry Jones. 1981. *Change and the study of international relations: the evaded dimension* (St Martin's Press: New York).

Cadier, David. 2014. 'Eastern Partnership vs Eurasian Union? The EU–Russia competition in the shared neighbourhood and the Ukraine crisis', *Global Policy*, 5: 76–85.

Cafruny, Alan W. 2015. 'Europe's twin crises: the logic and tragedy of contemporary German power', *Valdai Papers*: 1–14.

Capoccia, Giovanni. 2016a. 'Critical junctures' in Karl Orfeo Fioretos, Tulia Gabriela Falleti and Adam D. Sheingate (eds), *The Oxford handbook of historical institutionalism* (Oxford University Press: Oxford).

———. 2016b. 'When do institutions "bite"? Historical institutionalism and the politics of institutional change', *Comparative Political Studies*, 49: 1095–127.

Capoccia, Giovanni, and R. Daniel Kelemen. 2007. 'The study of critical junctures: theory, narrative, and counterfactuals in historical institutionalism', *World Politics*, 59: 341–69.

Capoccia, Giovanni, and Daniel Ziblatt. 2010. 'The historical turn in democratization studies: a new research agenda for Europe and beyond', *Comparative Political Studies*, 43: 931–68.

Cardwell, Paul James. 2011. 'EuroMed, European Neighbourhood Policy and the Union for the Mediterranean: overlapping policy frames in the EU's governance of the Mediterranean', *JCMS: Journal of Common Market Studies*, 49: 219–41.

Carlsnaes, Walter. 1993. 'On analysing the dynamics of foreign policy change: a critique and reconceptualization', *Cooperation and Conflict*, 28: 5–30.

————. 2004. 'Where is the analysis of European foreign policy going?', *European Union Politics*, 5: 495–508.

Carp, Suzana, and Tobias Schumacher. 2015. 'From survival to revival: the Riga Summit 2015 and the revised ENP', Egmont Institute Security Policy Brief.

Carrera, Sergio, Steven Blockmans, Daniel Gros and Elspeth Guild. 2015. 'The EU's response to the refugee crisis taking stock and setting policy priorities', CEPS Essay.

Cashore, Benjamin, and Michael Howlett. 2007. 'Punctuating which equilibrium? Understanding thermostatic policy dynamics in Pacific Northwest forestry', *American Journal of Political Science*, 51: 532–51.

Casier, Tom. 2013. 'The EU–Russia Strategic Partnership: challenging the normative argument', *Europe–Asia Studies*, 65: 1377–95.

Casier, Tom, Elena Korosteleva and Richard G. Whitman. 2014. 'Building a stronger Eastern Partnership: towards an EaP 2.0', Global Europe Centre Policy Paper: 1–13.

Charap, Samuel, and Jeremy Shapiro. 2015. 'The looming New Cold War and its consequence', *Politics and Strategy. The Survival Editors' Blog*, 2 May.

Chassany, Anne-Sylvaine. 2015. 'France's National Front taps into rising anti-immigrant mood', *Financial Times*, 6 September.

Chonghaile, Clár Ní. 2015. 'UN official decries toxic backdrop as EU debates new migration policies', *The Guardian*, 31 March.

Chrisafis, Angelique. 2011. 'Sarkozy admits France made mistakes over Tunisia', *The Guardian*, 24 January.

Cianciara, Agnieszka K. 2020. 'The politics of the European Neighbourhood Policy' in Richard Whitman and Richard Youngs (eds), *Routledge studies in European foreign policy*, 1 online resource (Routledge: Abingdon, New York).

Collett, Elizabeth. 2015. 'The development of EU policy on immigration and asylum: rethinking coordination and leadership', Migration Policy Institute.

Collett, Elizabeth, and Aliyyah Ahad. 2017. 'EU migration partnerships, a work in progress', Migration Policy Institute.

Collier, David. 2011. 'Understanding process tracing', *Political Science and Politics*, 44: 823–30.

Collier, Ruth Berins, and David Collier. 1991. *Shaping the political arena: critical junctures, the labor movement, and regime dynamics in Latin America* (Princeton University Press: Princeton, NJ).

Commisione I. I. I. Affari Esteri e Comunitari. 2012. 'Resoconto stenografico indagine conoscitiva' (Camera dei Deputati XVI Legislatura: Rome).

Copsey, Nathaniel. 2008. 'Member state policy preferences on the integration of Ukraine and the other Eastern neighbours', 26 August, accessed 11 May 2021. http://wider-europe.org/files/The%20Member%20States%20and%20the%20ENP.pdf.

Copsey, Nathaniel, and Karolina Pomorska. 2014. 'The influence of newer member states in the European Union: the case of Poland and the Eastern Partnership', *Europe–Asia Studies*, 66: 421–43.

Cornish, Paul, Julian Lindley-French and Claire Yorke. 2011. 'Strategic communications and national strategy', Chatham House Report.

Council of the European Union. 2016. 'Joint statement of EU Ministers for Justice and Home Affairs and representatives of EU institutions on the terrorist attacks in Brussels on 22 March 2016'. www.consilium.europa.eu/en/press/press-releases/2016/03/24/statement-on-terrorist-attacks-in-brussels-on-22-march/?utm_source=dsms-auto&utm_medium=email&utm_campaign=Joint+statement+of+EU+Ministers+for+Justice+and+Home+Affairs+and+representatives+of+EU+institutions+on+the+terrorist+attacks+in+Brussels+on+22+March+2016.

Cristina Paciello, Maria. 2010. 'The impact of the economic crisis on Euro-Mediterranean relations', *The International Spectator*, 45: 51–69.

Daugbjerg, Carsten. 1997. 'Policy networks and agricultural policy reforms: explaining deregulation in Sweden and re-regulation in the European Community', *Governance*, 10: 123–41.

Daviter, Falk. 2011. *Policy framing in the European Union* (Palgrave Macmillan: Basingstoke, New York).

De France, Olivier. 2019. 'PESCO: the French perspective', Ares Policy Paper.

De Hoop Scheffer, Alexandra, and Martin Quencez. 2015. 'France's perspectives and priorities for the European Neighborhood Policy', The German Marshall Fund of the United States.

De Maizière, Thomas, and Bernard Cazeneuve. 2015. 'Joint declaration of Federal Minister de Maizière and Minister Cazeneuve on the relocation mechanism regarding asylum seekers in clear need of protection'. www.bmi.bund.de/SharedDocs/downloads/EN/news/g6-moritzburg-joint-declaration-fra-und-ger.pdf?__blob=publicationFile&v=1.

De Wilde, Pieter, and Michael Zürn. 2012. 'Can the politicization of European integration be reversed?' *JCMS: Journal of Common Market Studies*, 50: 137–53.

Debomy, Daniel. 2016. 'The EU, despite everything? European public opinion in the face of crisis (2005–2015)' In: Notre Europe – Jacques Delors Institute, accessed 11 May 2021. https://institutdelors.eu/wp-content/uploads/2020/08/eupublicopinionandcrisis-debomy-jdi-june16.pdf.

Degner, Hanno. 2019. 'Public attention, governmental bargaining, and supranational activism: explaining European integration in response to crises', *JCMS: Journal of Common Market Studies*, 57: 242–59.

Delegation of the European Union to Ukraine. 2014. 'Statements of Ukrainian officials on EU integration course of Ukraine (03/02/2014)', accessed 11 May 2021. https://web.archive.org/web/20160628053009/http://eeas.europa.eu/delegations/ukraine/press_corner/all_news/news/2014/2014_02_03_2_en.htm.

Delgado, Mireia. 2011. 'France and the Union for the Mediterranean: individualism versus co-operation', *Mediterranean Politics*, 16: 39–57.

Dempsey, Judy. 2015. 'Alexis Tsipras and Greece's miserable foreign policy', Carnegie Europe, accessed 13 August 2020. https://carnegieeurope.eu/strategiceurope/?fa=58864.

Dennison, Susi. 2013. 'The EU and North Africa after the revolutions: a new start or *plus ça change?*', *Mediterranean Politics*, 18: 119–24.

Dennison, Susi, Ulrike Esther Franke and Paweł Zerka. 2018. 'The nightmare of the dark: the security fears that keep Europeans awake at night', European Council on Foreign Relations.

Dernbach, Andrea. 2015. 'Germany suspends Dublin agreement for Syrian refugees', *Euractiv*, 26 August.

Deutsche Welle. 2014. 'EU Parliament President Schulz weighs in on crisis in Crimea', accessed 11 May 2021. www.dw.com/en/eu-parliament-president-schulz-weighs-in-on-crisis-in-crimea/a-17484180.

———. 2017. 'Can PESCO provide a new European identity?' www.dw.com/en/can-pesco-provide-a-new-european-identity/a-41362789.

'Deutschlands Zukunft Gestalten. Koalitionsvertrag zwischen CDU, CSU und SPD 18. Legislaturperiode'. 2013, accessed 11 May 2021. http://isl-ev.de/attachments/article/1048/koalitionsvertrag-FINAL.pdf.

DG Migration and Home Affairs. 2016. 'Global approach to migration and mobility', accessed 17 August 2020. https://ec.europa.eu/home-affairs/what-we-do/policies/international-affairs/global-approach-to-migration_en.

———. 2020. 'Temporary reintroduction of border control', accessed 17 August 2020. https://ec.europa.eu/home-affairs/what-we-do/policies/borders-and-visas/schengen/reintroduction-border-control_en.

Dinan, Desmond, Neill Nugent and William E. Paterson (eds). 2017. *The European Union in crisis* (Red Globe Press: London).

Dingley, James. 2005. 'Constructive ambiguity and the peace process in Northern Ireland', *Low Intensity Conflict & Law Enforcement*, 13: 1–23.

Diuk, Nadia. 2014. 'Euromaidan: Ukraine's self-organizing revolution', *World Affairs*, 176: 9–16.

Dougherty, Jill. 2014. 'Everyone lies: the Ukraine conflict and Russia's media transformation', Discussion Paper Series, Shorenstein Center on Media, Politics, and Public Policy 2–29.

Dragneva, Rilka, and Kataryna Wolczuk. 2013. *Eurasian economic integration: law, policy and politics* (Edward Elgar: Cheltenham).

Drennan, Lynn T., and Allan McConnell. 2007. *Risk and crisis management in the public sector* (Routledge: London, New York).

Drent, Margriet, and Dick Zandee. 2018. 'More European defence cooperation the road to a European defence industry?' Clingendael Institute.

Duke, Simon. 2017. 'The return of geopolitics and relations to the East' in Simon Duke (ed.), *Europe as a stronger global actor: challenges and strategic responses* (Palgrave Macmillan: London).

Dunn, William N. 1994. *Public policy analysis: an introduction* (Prentice Hall: Englewood Cliffs, NJ).

Echagüe, Ana. 2011. 'Time for Spain to lead the EU's Mediterranean policy', FRIDE Policy Brief.

Echagüe, Ana, Hélène Michou and Barah Mikail. 2011. 'Europe and the Arab uprisings: EU vision versus member state action', *Mediterranean Politics*, 16: 329–35.

Economist, The. 2015. 'Aux armes, journalistes!' 19 March, accessed 24 March 2021. www.economist.com/europe/2015/03/19/aux-armes-journalistes.

Edelman, Murray. 2001. *The politics of misinformation* (Cambridge University Press: Cambridge).

Elgindy, Khaled. 2001. 'When ambiguity is destructive', Brookings Institution.

Emerson, Michael, Gergana Noutcheva and Nicu Popescu. 2007. 'European Neighbourhood Policy two years on: time indeed for an "ENP plus"', CEPS Policy Brief.

Erlanger, Steven. 2018. 'US revives concerns about European defense plans, rattling NATO allies', *New York Times*, 18 February.

Estonian Center of Eastern Partnership. 2015. 'EU-related communication in Eastern Partnership countries', *The Eastern Partnership Review*: 1–36.

EU Observer. 2007. 'Merkel criticises Sarkozy's Mediterranean Union plans', accessed 17 February 2017. https://euobserver.com/news/25284.

———. 2011. 'Mediterranean EU states block stronger action on Tunisia', accessed 29 September 2020. https://euobserver.com/foreign/31644.

———. 2015. 'Mogherini: EU at risk of committing "suicide"', accessed 29 September 2020. https://euobserver.com/tickers/131677.

———. 2016. 'France and Germany propose EU "defence union"', accessed 29 September 2020. https://euobserver.com/foreign/135022.

Euractiv. 2013. 'Ukraine stuns EU by putting association deal on ice', 21 November.
———. 2014. 'Sikorski: if Poland is a hawk, Russia is what?' 12 September.
———. 2015a. 'European Parliament adopts tough resolution on Russia', 11 June.
———. 2015b. 'Latvia proposes "alternative" to Russian TV propaganda', 8 January.
———. 2015c. 'Many EU countries say "no" to immigration quotas', 8 June. www.euractiv.com/section/justice-home-affairs/news/many-eu-countries-say-no-to-immigration-quotas/.
———. 2015d. 'Mogherini's timid *mea culpa* on EU Neighbourhood Policy', *EURACTIV.com*, 4 March.
———. 2015e. 'Tiny EU task force set up to counter Russian propaganda', 28 August.
———. 2017. 'The brief: sowing the seed of the PESCO tree', 11 December. www.euractiv.com/section/all/news/the-brief-sowing-the-seed-of-the-pesco-tree/.
———. 2018. '2019 lookahead: Europe's security and defence coming of age', 27 December, accessed 28 September 2020. www.euractiv.com/section/defence-and-security/news/2019-lookahead-europes-security-and-defence-coming-of-age/.
European Commission. 1995. 'Barcelona Declaration adopted at the Euro-Mediterranean conference'. https://ec.europa.eu/commission/presscorner/detail/en/DOC_95_7.
———. 2001. 'Communication from the Commission to The Council and the European Parliament – the European Union's role in promoting human rights and democratisation in third countries COM(2001) 252 final'. www.europarl.europa.eu/meetdocs/committees/afet/20020218/com(2001)252en_acte_f.pdf.
———. 2003. 'Wider Europe – neighbourhood: a new framework for relations with our Eastern and Southern neighbours', *COM(2003) 104 final*.
———. 2014. 'Communication from the Commission to the Council and the European Parliament on EU return policy', *COM(2014) 199 final*.
———. 2015a. 'A European agenda on migration', *COM(2015) 240 final*.
———. 2015b. 'The European agenda on security', *COM(2015) 185 final*.
———. 2015c. 'European Commission makes progress on agenda on migration'. https://ec.europa.eu/commission/presscorner/detail/en/IP_15_5039.
———. 2015d. 'Joint press conference by High Representative/Vice-President Federica Mogherini and Commissioner Johannes Hahn on European Neighbourhood Policy review'. http://europa.eu/rapid/press-release_SPEECH-15-4553_en.htm.
———. 2015e. 'Review of the European Neighbourhood Policy (ENP) – list of contributions received'. File no longer available; accessed 4 July 2015.
———. 2016a. 'Communication from the European Commission to the European Parliament, the European Council and the Council. Delivering on the European agenda on security to fight against terrorism and pave the way towards an effective and genuine security union', *COM(2016) 230 final*. https://eur-lex.europa.eu/resource.html?uri=cellar:9aeae420–0797–11e6-b713–01aa75ed71a1.0022.02/DOC_1&format=PDF.
———. 2016b. 'European defence action plan: towards a European defence fund'. https://ec.europa.eu/commission/presscorner/detail/en/IP_16_4088.
———. 2016c. 'Overview – instrument for pre-accession assistance'. https://ec.europa.eu/neighbourhood-enlargement/instruments/overview_en#:~:text=The%20Instrument%20for%20Pre%2Daccession,positive%20developments%20in%20the%20region.
———. 2017. 'Reflection paper on the future of European defence', *COM(2017) 315*. https://ec.europa.eu/commission/sites/beta-political/files/reflection-paper-defence_en.pdf.

———. 2019. 'A Europe that protects: continued efforts needed on security priorities'. https://ec.europa.eu/commission/presscorner/detail/en/IP_19_4413.

———. 2020a. 'Euro-Mediterranean partnership'. https://ec.europa.eu/trade/policy/countries-and-regions/regions/euro-mediterranean-partnership/#:~:text=The%20key%20objective%20of%20the,the%20Southern%20Mediterranean%20countries%20themselves.

———. 2020b. 'New pact on migration and asylum', accessed 12 May 2021. https://ec.europa.eu/info/strategy/priorities-2019-2024/promoting-our-european-way-life/new-pact-migration-and-asylum_en.

European Commission and High Representative for Foreign Affairs and Security Policy. 2011a. 'A new response to a changing neighbourhood', *COM(2011) 303 final*.

———. 2011b. 'A partnership for democracy and shared prosperity with the Southern Mediterranean', *COM(2011) 200 final*.

———. 2015a. 'Review of the European Neighbourhood Policy', *JOIN (2015) 50 final*.

———. 2015b. 'Towards a new European Neighbourhood Policy: the EU launches a consultation on the future of its relations with neighbouring countries', *Enlargement and Neighbourhood*. https://ec.europa.eu/commission/presscorner/detail/en/IP_15_4548.

European Council. 2010. 'Press release 3028th Council meeting, General Affairs, Brussels'. https://data.consilium.europa.eu/doc/document/ST-12550–2010-INIT/en/pdf.

———. 2011a. 'Council Decision appointing a European Union Special Representative for the Southern Mediterranean region'. https://eur-lex.europa.eu/legal-content/EN/TXT/PDF/?uri=CELEX:32011D0424&from=EN.

———. 2011b. 'Declaration on Egypt and the Region'. www.consilium.europa.eu/uedocs/cms_Data/docs/pressdata/en/ec/119143.pdf.

———. 2013. 'Council Conclusions 19–20 December 2013'. www.consilium.europa.eu/uedocs/cms_data/docs/pressdata/en/ec/140214.pdf.

———. 2014a. 'Council Conclusions 26/27 June 2014'. www.consilium.europa.eu/uedocs/cms_Data/docs/pressdata/en/ec/143478.pdf.

———. 2014b. 'Council Conclusions 20 February 2014'. www.consilium.europa.eu/uedocs/cms_data/docs/pressdata/EN/foraff/141110.pdf.

———. 2015a. 'Council Conclusions 19/20 March 2015'. www.consilium.europa.eu/media/21888/european-council-conclusions-19-20-march-2015-en.pdf.

———. 2015b. 'Council conclusions on the Review of the European Neighbourhood Policy'. www.consilium.europa.eu/en/press/press-releases/2015/04/20/council-conclusions-review-european-neighbourhood-policy/.

———. 2017a. 'Council Decision (CFSP) 2017/2315 of 11 December 2017 establishing permanent structured cooperation (PESCO) and determining the list of participating Member States'. https://eur-lex.europa.eu/legal-content/EN/TXT/?uri=CELEX%3A32017D2315.

———. 2017b. 'Declaration of the leaders of 27 member states and of the European Council, the European Parliament and the European Commission'. www.consilium.europa.eu/en/press/press-releases/2017/03/25/rome-declaration/.

———. 2019. 'EU asylum reform'. www.consilium.europa.eu/en/policies/migratory-pressures/ceas-reform/.

European Council on Foreign Relations (ECFR). 2014. 'ECFR's scorecard 2014: France'. https://ecfr.eu/scorecard/2014/countries/france.

European Defence Agency. 2018. 'Quantum leap: how PESCO could shape European defence'. www.eda.europa.eu/docs/default-source/eda-magazine/edm-issue-15_web.

European External Action Service. 2015. 'Action plan on strategic communication', accessed 7 March 2019. https://web.archive.org/web/20200722120612/http://archive.eap-csf.eu/assets/files/Action%20PLan.pdf.

European Parliament. 2014. 'European Parliament resolution of 13 March 2014 on the invasion of Ukraine by Russia'. www.europarl.europa.eu/sides/getDoc.do?pubRef=-//EP//TEXT+TA+P7-TA-2014-0248+0+DOC+XML+V0//EN.

———. 2015a. 'European Parliament resolution of 10 June 2015 on the state of EU-Russia relations', *P8_TA(2015)0225*. www.europarl.europa.eu/doceo/document/TA-8–2015–0225_EN.html?redirect.

———. 2015b. 'European Parliament resolution of 15 January 2015 on the situation in Ukraine', *P8_TA(2015)0011*. www.europarl.europa.eu/doceo/document/TA-8–2015–0011_EN.html?redirect.

European Parliament and European Council. 2014. 'Regulation EU No232/2014 of the European Parliament and of the Council', *Official Journal of the European Union*, L 77.

European Union Institute for Security Studies. 2016a. 'EU strategic communications with a view to counteracting propaganda'. www.europarl.europa.eu/RegData/etudes/IDAN/2016/578008/EXPO_IDA%282016%29578008_EN.pdf.

———. 2016b. 'Towards an EU global strategy – consulting the experts.'. www.iss.europa.eu/sites/default/files/EUISSFiles/EUGS_Expert_Opinions.pdf.

Eurostat. 2016. 'Record number of over 1.2 million first time asylum seekers registered in 2015', accessed 17 August 2020. https://ec.europa.eu/eurostat/web/products-press-releases/-/3-04032016-AP.

Falkner, Gerda. 2016. 'The EU's current crisis and its policy effects: research design and comparative findings', *Journal of European Integration*, 38: 219–35.

Falkner, Robert. 2017. 'Rethinking Europe's external relations in an age of global turmoil: an introduction', *International Politics*, 54: 389–404.

Farrell, Henry, and Adrienne Héritier. 2005. 'A rationalist-institutionalist explanation of endogenous regional integration 1', *Journal of European Public Policy*, 12: 273–90.

Fetzer, James H. 2004. 'Disinformation: the use of false information', *Minds and Machines*, 14: 231–40.

Figaro, Le. 2016. 'La feuille de route franco-allemande pour relancer l'Europe de la défense', 11 November, accessed 11 May 2021. www.lefigaro.fr/international/2016/09/11/01003-20160911ARTFIG00140-la-feuille-de-route-franco-allemande-pour-relancer-l-europe-de-la-defense.php.

Financial Times. 2013. 'Ukraine refuses to sign up to Europe deal', 29 November.

———. 2014. 'Poland calls for NATO troop deployment', 1 April.

———. 2017. 'EU states poised to agree joint defence pact', accessed 11 May 2021. www.ft.com/content/29f6fe76-c2eb-11e7-a1d2-6786f39ef675.

Fioretos, Karl Orfeo, Tulia Gabriela Falleti and Adam D. Sheingate. 2016. 'Historical institutionalism in political science' in Karl Orfeo Fioretos, Tulia Gabriela Falleti and Adam D. Sheingate (eds), *The Oxford handbook of historical institutionalism* (Oxford University Press: Oxford).

Fiott, Daniel (ed.). 2020. *The CSDP in 2020: the EU's legacy and ambition in security and defence* (European Union Institute for Security Studies: Paris).

Fix, Liana, and Anna-Lena Kirch. 2016. 'Germany and the Eastern Partnership after the Ukraine crisis', *Ifri – Note du Cerfa*: 1–24.

Fleurant, Aude, Sam Perlo-Freedman, Pieter D. Wezeman and Siemon T. Wezeman. 2016. 'Trends in world military expenditure, 2015', Stockholm International Peace Research Institute.

Foreign ministers of Denmark, Estonia, Finland, Iceland, Latvia, Lithuania, Norway and Sweden. 2015. 'Statement from Nordic-Baltic Foreign Minister's meeting 6 May 2015.' https://um.dk/en/news/newsdisplaypage/?newsid=4b527908-4e71-4c0d-af55-2c7b2dbf8c2b.

Foreign ministers of the Weimar Triangle. 2014. 'Building a stronger compact with our neighbours: a new momentum for the European Neighbourhood Policy – Statement by the Foreign Ministers of the Weimar Triangle', 1 April. www.auswaertiges-amt.de/en/newsroom/news/140401-erkl-weimar/261278.

Frattini, Franco. 2011. 'A pact for Euro-Mediterranean stability', *Financial Times*, 17 February 2011.

Freedman, Lawrence. 2014. 'Ukraine and the art of crisis management', *Survival*, 56: 7–42.

Frontex. 2011. 'Request for help over migratory pressure in Lampedusa', accessed 6 June 2016. http://frontex.europa.eu/news/request-for-help-over-migratory-pressure-in-lampedusa-0H2ukS.

———. 2016. 'Frontex annual risk analysis 2016'. https://data.europa.eu/euodp/en/data/dataset/ara-2016.

Füle, Štefan. 2011. 'Speech on the recent events in North Africa', *SPEECH/11/130*.

———. 2013. 'Association agreements with Eastern partners: opening new doors to investment and trade', *SPEECH/13/988*.

———. 2014. 'EU response to events in Ukraine', accessed 19 May 2017. http://europa.eu/rapid/press-release_SPEECH-14-162_en.htm.

García, Bernabé López, and Miguel Hernando de Larramendi. 2002. 'Spain and North Africa: towards a "dynamic stability"', *Democratization*, 9: 170–91.

Gebhard, Carmen. 2010. 'The ENP's strategic conception and design overstretching the enlargement template?' in Richard G. Whitman and Stefan Wolff (eds), *The European Neighbourhood Policy in perspective: context, implementation and impact* (Palgrave Macmillan: New York).

George, Alexander, and Timothy J. McKeown. 1985. 'Case studies and theories of organizational decision making' in Robert F. Coulam and Richard A. Smith (eds), *Advances in information processing in organizations* (JAI Press: Greenwich, CN).

Gillespie, Richard. 2000. *Spain and the Mediterranean* (Palgrave Macmillan: Basingstoke).

Gilpin, Robert. 1981. *War and change in world politics* (Cambridge University Press: New York).

Goldmann, Kjell. 1988. *Change and stability in foreign policy: the problems and possibilities of détente* (Princeton University Press: Princeton, NJ).

Goodwin, Jeff. 2011. 'Why we were surprised (again) by the Arab Spring', *Swiss Political Science Review*, 17: 452–56.

Gourevitch, Peter. 1996. 'Squaring the circle: the domestic sources of international cooperation', *International Organization*, 50: 349.

Gouvernement Français. 2013. 'French White Paper on defence and national security'. https://otan.delegfrance.org/White-Paper-on-Defence-and-National-Security.

———. 2015. 'La France à l'action face à la crise migratoire'. www.gouvernement.fr/la-france-a-l-action-face-a-la-crise-migratoire-2817.

Government, HM. 2015. 'National security strategy and strategic defence and security review 2015: a secure and prosperous United Kingdom' (Stationery Office: Norwich).

Government Offices of Sweden. 2015. 'Swedish Foreign Service action plan for feminist foreign policy 2015–2018 including focus areas for 2016', accessed 17 July 2017.

www.government.se/4ad6e7/contentassets/b799e89a0e06493f86c63a561e869e91/
action-plan-feminist-foreign-policy-2015-2018.

Græger, Nina. 2016. 'European security as practice: EU–NATO communities of
practice in the making?', *European Security*, 25: 478–501.

Guardian, The. 2013a. 'Ukraine aligns with Moscow as EU summit fails', 29
November.

———. 2013b. 'Ukraine's EU trade deal will be catastrophic, says Russia', 22
September.

———. 2014a. 'Ukraine's bloodiest day: dozens dead as Kiev protesters regain
territory from police', 21 February, section 'Global'.

———. 2014b. 'Ukrainian president approves strict anti-protest laws', 17 January,
section 'World news'.

———. 2015. 'UN says 800 migrants dead in boat disaster as Italy launches rescue
of two more vessels', 20 April.

———. 2016. 'Would Brexit trigger a domino effect in Europe?' 10 June.

Guiraudon, Virginie. 2003. 'The constitution of a European immigration policy
domain: a political sociology approach', *Journal of European Public Policy*, 10:
263–82.

Gustavsson, Jakob. 1998. *The politics of foreign policy change: explaining the
Swedish reorientation on EC membership* (Lund University Press: Lund, Sweden).

———. 1999. 'How should we study foreign policy change?', *Cooperation and
Conflict*, 34: 73–95.

Hahn, Johannes. 2014. 'Answers to the European Parliament questionnaire to
the Commissioner-Designate Johannes Hahn: European Neighbourhood Policy
and enlargement negotiations', accessed 14 January 2017. https://ec.europa.eu/
commission/sites/cwt/files/commissioner_ep_hearings/hahn-reply_en.pdf.

———. 2015. 'Theorizing the European Neighbourhood Policy', paper presented to
conference 'Theorizing the European Neighbourhood Policy', Bruges.

Hall, Peter. 1993. 'Policy paradigms, social learning, and the state: the case of
economic policymaking in Britain', *Comparative Politics*, 25: 275.

———. 2003. 'Aligning ontology and methodology in comparative research' in James
Mahoney and Dietrich Rueschemeyer (eds), *Comparative historical analysis in
the social sciences* (Cambridge University Press: Cambridge, New York).

———. 2010. 'Historical institutionalism in rationalist and sociological perspective' in James Mahoney and Kathleen Thelen (eds), *Explaining institutional
change: ambiguity, agency, and power* (Cambridge University Press: Cambridge,
New York).

———. 2016. 'Politics as a process structured in space and time' in Karl Orfeo
Fioretos, Tulia Gabriela Falleti and Adam D. Sheingate (eds), *The Oxford handbook
of historical institutionalism* (Oxford University Press: Oxford).

Hall, Peter, and Rosemary C. R. Taylor. 1996. 'Political science and the three new
institutionalisms', *Political Studies*, 44: 936–57.

Hallahan, Kirk, Derina Holtzhausen, Betteke van Ruler, Dejan Verčič and Krishna-
murthy Sriramesh. 2007. 'Defining strategic communication', *International Journal
of Strategic Communication*, 1: 3–35.

Haroche, Pierre. 2019. 'Supranationalism strikes back: a neofunctionalist account
of the European Defence Fund', *Journal of European Public Policy*, 27: 853–72.

Haukkala, Hiski. 2015. 'From cooperative to contested Europe? The conflict in
Ukraine as a culmination of a long-term crisis in EU–Russia relations', *Journal
of Contemporary European Studies*, 23: 25–40.

Hay, Colin. 2011. 'Political ontology' in Robert E. Goodin (ed.), *The Oxford handbook of political science* (Oxford University Press: Oxford).

Hegemann, Hendrik, and Ulrich Schneckener. 2019. 'Politicising European security: from technocratic to contentious politics?' *European Security*, 28: 133–52.

Hermann, Charles F. 1990. 'Changing course: when governments choose to redirect foreign policy', *International Studies Quarterly*, 34: 3–22.

Herweg, Nicole, Nikolaos Zahariadis and Reimut Zohlnhöfer. 2017. 'The multiple streams framework: foundations, refinements, and empirical applications' in Christopher M. Weible and Paul A. Sabatier (eds), *Theories of the policy process* (Westview Press: New York).

High Representative of the Union for Foreign Affairs and Security Policy. 2016a. 'Implementation plan on security and defence.' https://eeas.europa.eu/sites/default/files/implementation_plan_on_security_and_defence_02-03-2018.pdf.

———. 2016b. 'Shared vision, common action: a stronger Europe. A global strategy for the European Union's foreign and security policy.' https://op.europa.eu/en/publication-detail/-/publication/3eaae2cf-9ac5-11e6-868c-01aa75ed71a1.

Hillion, Christophe. 2013. 'The EU neighbourhood competence under Article 8 TEU', Notre Europe Policy Paper.

Hoffmann, Stanley. 1995. *The European Sisyphus: essays on Europe, 1964–1994* (Westview Press: Boulder, CO).

Hofmann, Stephanie C. 2009. 'Overlapping institutions in the realm of international security: the case of NATO and ESDP', *Perspectives on Politics*, 7: 45–52.

———. 2011. 'Why institutional overlap matters: CSDP in the European security architecture', *JCMS: Journal of Common Market Studies*, 49: 101–20.

Hogan, John. 2006. 'Remoulding the critical junctures approach', *Canadian Journal of Political Science*, 39: 657–79.

Holsti, Kalevi J. 1982. *Why nations realign: foreign policy restructuring in the postwar world* (Allen & Unwin: London).

———. 2016. 'The problem of change in international relations theory' in Kalevi Holsti (ed.), *Kalevi Holsti: A Pioneer in International Relations Theory, Foreign Policy Analysis, History of International Order, and Security Studies* (Springer International Publishing: Cham, Switzerland).

Hom, Andrew, and Ryan Keith Beasley. 2020. 'Constructing time in foreign policymaking: Brexit's timing entrepreneurs, malcontents, and apparatchiks', *International Affairs*: 267–85.

Hooghe, Liesbet, and Gary Marks. 2002. 'The making of a polity: the struggle over European integration', *SSRN Electronic Journal*: 1–26.

House of Lords, European Union Committee. 2015. 'The EU and Russia: before and beyond the crisis in Ukraine.' London: House of Lords. https://publications.parliament.uk/pa/ld201415/ldselect/ldeucom/115/115.pdf.

———. 2016. 'Europe in the world: towards a more effective EU foreign and security strategy.' London: House of Lords. https://publications.parliament.uk/pa/ld201516/ldselect/ldeucom/97/9706.htm.

Howlett, Michael. 2009. 'Process sequencing policy dynamics: beyond homeostasis and path dependency', *Journal of Public Policy*, 29: 241–62.

Howlett, Michael, and Benjamin Cashore. 2009. 'The dependent variable problem in the study of policy change: understanding policy change as a methodological problem', *Journal of Comparative Policy Analysis: Research and Practice*, 11: 33–46.

Howorth, Jolyon. 2014. *Security and defence policy in the European Union* (Red Globe Press: London).

Hudson, Valerie M. 2005. 'Foreign policy analysis: actor-specific theory and the ground of international relations: foreign policy analysis', *Foreign Policy Analysis*, 1: 1–30.

Hudson, Valerie M., and Christopher S. Vore. 1995. 'Foreign policy analysis yesterday, today, and tomorrow', *Mershon International Studies Review*, 39: 209.

I. X. Legislatura – Comisión Mixta para la Unión Europea. 2011a. 'Diario de Sesiones de las Cortes Generales', Cortes Generales, Madrid.

I. X. Legislatura – Congreso de los Diputados. 2011b. 'Boletín Oficial de las Cortes Generales', Cortes Generales, Madrid.

Ikani, Nikki. 2019. 'Change and continuity in the European Neighbourhood Policy: the Ukraine crisis as a critical juncture', *Geopolitics*, 24: 20–50.

———. 2020. 'European foreign policy in times of crisis: a political development lens', *Journal of European Integration*, 42: 767–82.

Ikenberry, G. John. 2001. *After victory: institutions, strategic restraint, and the rebuilding of order after major wars* (Princeton University Press: Princeton, NJ).

Immergut, Ellen M. 2006. 'Historical-institutionalism in political science and the problem of change' in Andreas Wimmer and Reinhart Kössler (eds), *Understanding change: models, methodologies and metaphors* (Palgrave Macmillan: Basingstoke).

Interfax. 2015. 'Shoigu: information becomes another armed forces component'. www.interfax.com/newsinf.asp?id=581851.

International Organization for Migration (IOM). 2020. 'Key migration terms', accessed 22 March 2021. www.iom.int/key-migration-terms.

———. 2016. 'Dangerous journeys – international migration increasingly unsafe in 2016', IOM Global Migration Data Analysis Centre. https://publications.iom.int/system/files/gmdac_data_briefing_series_issue4.pdf.

Jacobs, Alan M., and R. Kent Weaver. 2015. 'When policies undo themselves: self-undermining feedback as a source of policy change: self-undermining feedback', *Governance*, 28: 441–57.

Janda, Jakub, Veronika Víchová, Monika Richter, Ilyas Sharibzhanov and Jakub Fišer. 2017. 'Overview of countermeasures by the EU28 to the Kremlin's subversion operations', European Values.

Jegen, Maya, and Frédéric Mérand. 2014. 'Constructive ambiguity: comparing the EU's energy and defence policies', *West European Politics*, 37: 182–203.

Jenkins-Smith, Hank C., Daniel Nohrstedt, Christopher M. Weible and Paul A. Sabatier. 2014. 'The advocacy coalition framework: foundations, evolution, and ongoing research' in Paul A. Sabatier and Christopher M. Weible (eds), *Theories of the policy process* (Westview Press: Boulder, CO).

Jones, Erik, R. Daniel Kelemen and Sophie Meunier. 2015. 'Failing forward? The euro crisis and the incomplete nature of European integration', *Comparative Political Studies*, 49: 1010–34.

Juncker, Jean-Claude. 2014a. 'Mission letter from the President of the Commission to the Commissioner for European Neighbourhood Policy and enlargement negotiations', accessed 21 January 2017. https://ec.europa.eu/commission/sites/cwt/files/commissioner_mission_letters/hahn_en.pdf.

———. 2014b. 'A new start for Europe. Opening statement in the European Parliament plenary session.' https://ec.europa.eu/commission/presscorner/detail/en/SPEECH_14_567.

———. 2015. 'State of the Union 2015'. https://ec.europa.eu/commission/sites/beta-political/files/state_of_the_union_2015_en.pdf.

———. 2016. 'State of the Union 2016'. https://op.europa.eu/en/publication-detail/-/publication/c9ff4ff6–9a81–11e6–9bca-01aa75ed71a1/language-en/format-PDF/source-30945725.

———. 2017a. 'Speech by President Jean-Claude Juncker at the Defence and Security Conference Prague: In defence of Europe', accessed 24 October 2019. https://europa.eu/rapid/press-release_SPEECH-17-1581_en.htm.

———. 2017b. 'State of the Union 2017', accessed 21 August 2020. https://ec.europa.eu/commission/presscorner/detail/en/SPEECH_17_3165.

Jünemann, Annette. 2007. 'German policies in the Mediterranean' in Haizam Amirah Fernández and Richard Youngs (eds), *The Euro-Mediterranean Partnership: assessing the first decade* (Madrid: FRIDE/Real Instituto Elcano), 111–120.

Juppé, Alain. 2011a. 'Closing speech by Alain Juppé, Ministre d'État, Minister of Foreign Affairs, to the Arab World Institute', accessed 11 May 2021. https://web.archive.org/web/20191108113942/https://uk.ambafrance.org/Arab-spring-symposium-Closing.

———. 2011b. 'Éditorial', *Mondes*, 8: 3–4, accessed 22 March 2021. www.diplomatie.gouv.fr/IMG/pdf/INT_MONDES_N8-FR-EDITO_A_JUPPE.pdf.

———. 2011c. 'La France et l'évolution de la situation politique dans le monde arabe – 13e législature', *Journal Officiel du Sénat*: 3248.

Kaarbo, Juliet. 2003. 'Foreign policy analysis in the twenty-first century: back to comparison, forward to identity and ideas', *International Studies Review*, 5: 155–202.

Kandil, Hazem. 2012. *Soldiers, spies, and statesmen: Egypt's road to revolt* (Verso: London, New York).

Katznelson, Ira. 2003. *Comparative historical analysis in the social sciences* (Cambridge University Press: Cambridge, New York).

Katznelson, Ira, and Barry R. Weingast. 2005. *Preferences and situations: points of intersection between historical and rational choice* (Russell Sage Foundation: New York).

Kausch, Kristina, and Richard Youngs. 2009. 'The end of the "Euro-Mediterranean vision"', *International Affairs*, 85: 963–75.

Kelemen, R. Daniel, and Susanne K. Schmidt. 2012. 'Introduction – the European Court of Justice and legal integration: perpetual momentum?', *Journal of European Public Policy*, 19: 1–7.

Kelley, Judith. 2006. '"New wine in old wineskins": promoting political reforms through the new European Neighbourhood Policy', *Journal of Common Market Studies*, 44: 29–55.

Kempe, Iris. 2015. 'A new *Ostpolitik*? Priorities and realities of Germany's EU council presidency', Sozialwissenschaftliche Fakultät, Centrum für angewandte Politikforschung (CAP) (Bertelsmann Forschungsgruppe Politik: Munich).

Keohane, Daniel. 2016a. 'A greater military role for Germany?' Carnegie Europe. https://carnegieeurope.eu/strategiceurope/?fa=63741.

———. 2016b. 'Policy or project? France, Germany, and EU defense', Carnegie Europe. https://carnegieeurope.eu/strategiceurope/64222.

Khalifa Isaac, Sally. 2012. 'Europe and the Arab revolutions. From a weak to a proactive response to a changing neighborhood', Working paper, KFG The Transformative Power of Europe.

King, Desmond S., and Patrick Le Galès. 2017. *Reconfiguring European states in crisis* (Oxford University Press: Oxford).

Kingdon, John W. 1984. *Agendas, alternatives and public policies* (Little Brown: Boston).

———. 1995. *Agendas, alternatives, and public policies*, 2nd edn (Longman: New York).

Kingsley, Patrick. 2015. 'Record number of migrants expected to drown in Mediterranean this year', Euractiv, accessed 18 August 2020. www.euractiv.com/section/justice-home-affairs/news/record-number-of-migrants-expected-to-drown-in-mediterranean-this-year/.

Kleistra, Yvonne, and Igor Mayer. 2001. 'Stability and flux in foreign affairs', *Cooperation and Conflict*, 36: 381–414.

Koenig, Nicole. 2016. 'Taking the ENP beyond the conception–performance gap', Jacques Delors Institut Berlin Policy Paper.

Koenig, Nicole, and Marie Walter-Franke. 2017. 'France and Germany: spearheading a European security and defence union?', Jacques Delors Institut Berlin Policy Paper.

Koenig-Archibugi, Mathias. 2004. 'Explaining government preferences for institutional change in EU foreign and security policy', *International Organization*, 58: 137–74.

Koopmann, Martin. 2016. 'Europe needs Weimar: perspectives on the Weimar triangle in times of crisis', *Genshagener Papiere*: 1–22.

Korosteleva, Elena. 2011. 'Change or continuity: is the Eastern partnership an adequate tool for the European neighbourhood?', *International Relations*, 25: 243–62.

———. 2012. *The European Union and its eastern neighbours: towards a more ambitious partnership?* (Routledge: London).

Krasner, Stephen D. 1984. 'Approaches to the state: alternative conceptions and historical dynamics', *Comparative Politics*, 16: 223.

Kratochwil, Friedrich. 1993. 'Norms versus numbers: multilateralism and the rationalist and reflexivist approaches to institutions – a unilateral plea for communicative rationality', in John Gerard Ruggie (ed.), *Multilateralism matters: the theory and praxis of an institutional form* (Columbia University Press: New York).

Krebs, Ronald R. 2015. *Narrative and the making of US national security* (Cambridge University Press: New York).

Kurowska, Xymena, and Anatoly Reshetnikov. 2018. 'Russia's trolling complex at home and abroad' in Nicu Popescu and Stanislav Secrieru (eds), *Hacks, leaks and disruptions: Russian cyber strategies*, European Union Institute for Security Studies, Chaillot Paper No. 148: 25–32.

Larsen, Henrik. 2005. *Analysing the foreign policy of small states in the EU: the case of Denmark* (Palgrave Macmillan: Basingstoke, New York).

Lavenex, Sandra. 2015. 'Multilevelling EU external governance: the role of international organizations in the diffusion of EU migration policies', *Journal of Ethnic and Migration Studies*, 42: 554–70.

———. 2016. 'On the fringes of the European peace project: the neighbourhood policy's functionalist hubris and political myopia', *The British Journal of Politics and International Relations*, 19: 63–76.

Lebow, Richard Ned. 2000. 'Contingency, catalysts, and international system change', *Political Science Quarterly*, 115: 591–616.

Lenta.ru. 2014. 'Шойгу назвал паранойей обвинения киевских властей', 17 April. https://lenta.ru/news/2014/04/17/shoygu/.

Levgold, Robert. 2014. 'Managing the New Cold War', *Foreign Affairs*, 8 July.

Lidegaard, Martin, Keit Pentus-Rosimannus, Linas Linkevičius and Philip Hammon. 2015. 'EU strategic communication responding to propaganda: non-paper', accessed 24 March 2021. http://club.bruxelles2.eu/wp-content/uploads/2015/02/Let-StratCommRussie-DkEstLitUk@UK150108.pdf.

Lieberman, Robert C., Suzanne Mettler, Thomas B. Pepinsky, Kenneth M. Roberts and Richard Valelly. 2019. 'The Trump Presidency and American democracy: a historical and comparative analysis', *Perspectives on Politics*, 17: 470–79.

Lieģis, Imants. 2015. 'Latvia's foreign policy 2014/2015: players, events and challenges' in Andris Sprūds and Diāna Potjomkina (eds), *Latvian Foreign and Security Policy 2015* (Latvian Institute of International Affairs: Riga).

Lindblom, Charles E. 1959. 'The science of "muddling through"', *Public Administration Review*, 19: 79.

Lohmann, Susanne. 2003. 'Why do institutions matter? An audience-cost theory of institutional commitment', *Governance*, 16: 95–110.

Lookingglass Cyber Threat Intelligence Group. 2015. 'Operation Armageddon: cyber espionage as a strategic component of Russian modern warfare', accessed 24 March 2021. www.lookingglasscyber.com/wp-content/uploads/2015/08/Operation_Armageddon_Final.pdf.

Luhmann, Niklas. 1998. *Observations on modernity* (Stanford University Press: Stanford, CA).

Lynch, Marc. 2013. *The Arab uprising: the unfinished revolutions of the new Middle East* (PublicAffairs: Washington, DC).

Maccanico, Yasha. 2011. 'The EU's self-interested response to unrest in north Africa: the meaning of treaties and readmission agreements between Italy and north African states', *Statewatch Journal*, 21: online, accessed 30 November 2011. http://database.statewatch.org/article.asp?aid=31737.

MacFarlane, Neil, and Anand Menon. 2014. 'The EU and Ukraine', *Survival*, 56: 95–101.

Macnamara, Jim, and Anne Gregory. 2018. 'Expanding evaluation to progress strategic communication: beyond message tracking to open listening', *International Journal of Strategic Communication*, 12: 469–86.

Mahoney, James. 2000. 'Path dependence in historical sociology', *Theory and Society*, 29: 507–48.

Malmström, Cecilia. 2011. 'A better management of migration to the EU', accessed 4 July 2016. http://europa.eu/rapid/press-release_SPEECH-11-310_en.htm.

March, James G., and Johan P. Olsen. 1984. 'The new institutionalism: organizational factors in political life', *The American Political Science Review*, 78: 734–49.

Marcinkowska, Paula. 2016. 'European Neighbourhood Policy, a Polish perspective', *Revista UNISCI*, 40: 27–42.

Maulny, Jean-Pierre. 2016. 'La France, l'Allemagne et l'Europe de la défense', Friedrich Ebert Stiftung.

Mckeown, Timothy J. 1986. 'The limitations of "structural" theories of commercial policy', *International Organization*, 40: 43–64.

Mead, Walter Russell. 2014. 'The return of geopolitics: the revenge of the revisionist powers', *Foreign Affairs*, 93: 69–79.

Mearsheimer, John. 2014. 'Why the Ukraine crisis is the West's fault', *Foreign Affairs*, 93: 77–884.

Menon, Anand. 2011. 'European defence policy from Lisbon to Libya', *Survival*, 53: 75–90.

———. 2017. 'Defence policy and the European state: insights from American experience' in Desmond S. King and Patrick Le Galès (eds), *Reconfiguring European states in crisis* (Oxford University Press: Oxford).

Menon, Rajan, and Eugene B. Rumer. 2015. *Conflict in Ukraine: the unwinding of the post-Cold War order* (The MIT Press: Cambridge, MA).

Mérand, Frédéric, Martial Foucault and Bastien Irondelle. 2011. *European security since the fall of the Berlin Wall* (University of Toronto Press: Toronto).

Merkel, Angela. 2007. 'Die Mittelmeerregion ist unser aller Aufgabe in Europa.' Die Bundeskanzlerin. www.bundeskanzlerin.de/bkin-de/aktuelles/-die-mittelmeerregion-ist-unser-aller-aufgabe-in-europa–609392.

———. 2011. 'Hilfe für Nordafrika ist historische Verpflichtung.' https://archiv.bundesregierung.de/archiv-de/hilfe-fuer-nordafrika-ist-historische-verpflichtung-387350.

———. 2013. 'The door is still open for Ukraine.' www.bundeskanzlerin.de/bkin-en/news/the-door-is-still-open-for-ukraine-388438.

———. 2014. 'Rede von Bundeskanzlerin Merkel am Lowy Institut für Internationale Politik am 17. November 2014'. www.bundeskanzlerin.de/bkin-de/aktuelles/rede-von-bundeskanzlerin-merkel-am-lowy-institut-fuer-internationale-politik-am-17-november-2014-425572.

Ministry of Foreign Affairs of the Russian Federation. 2014a. 'Основные внешнеполитические события 2014 года (Main foreign policy events of 2014)', accessed 11 March 2015. www.mid.ru/brp_4.nsf/newsline/76C4E9FF55433787C3257DBB003BCE46.

———. 2014b. 'Доклад о результатах и основных направлениях деятельности Министерства иностранных дел Российской Федерации в 2013 году и задачах на среднесрочную перспективу (Report on the results and main activities of the Ministry of Foreign Affairs of the Russian Federation in 2013 and objectives for the medium term)', accessed 2 October 2015. http://mid.ru/bdomp/activity.nsf/0/4A9EF395E87DBF7844257CC900411999.

Ministry of Foreign Affairs, Poland. 2014. 'Oświadczenie MSZ o eskalacji sytuacji na Ukrainie wschodniej', accessed 22 May 2017. www.msz.gov.pl/pl/aktualnosci/wiadomosci/oswiadczenie_msz_o_eskalacji_sytuacji_na_ukrainie_wschodniej.

Miskimmon, Alister. 2012. 'German foreign policy and the Libya crisis', *German Politics*, 21: 392–410.

Missiroli, Antonio. 2001. 'European security policy: the challenge of coherence', *European Foreign Affairs Review*, 6: 177–96.

Mogherini, Federica. 2014. 'Remarks by High Representative Federica Mogherini following her meeting with NATO Secretary General Jens Stoltenberg', European Union External Action Service. https://eeas.europa.eu/headquarters/headquarters-Homepage/354/node/354_ka.

———. 2015. 'Speech of the HR/VP Federica Mogherini. The EU internal–external security nexus: terrorism as an example of the necessary link between different dimensions of action', European Union External Action Service. http://eeas.europa.eu/archives/docs/statements-eeas/2015/151126barcelona_strategy_en.pdf.

Mogherini, Federica, and Jyrki Katainen. 2017. 'Wir sollten die EU zu echter Verteidigungsunion entwickeln', *Die Welt*, 27 January, accessed 24 March 2021. www.welt.de/debatte/kommentare/article161587224/Wir-sollten-die-EU-zu-echter-Verteidigungsunion-entwickeln.html.

Monde, Le. 2011. 'Tunisie: les propos "effrayants" d'Alliot-Marie suscitent la polémique', 13 January.

Mourlon-Druol, Emmanuel. 2020. 'Adjusting an institutional framework to a globalising world: the creation of new institutions in the EEC, 1957–1992', *Journal of Economic Policy Reform*: 1–17.

Moynihan, Donald P. 2006. 'Ambiguity in policy lessons: the agentification experience', *Public Administration*, 84: 1029–50.

Mundo, El. 2011. 'Jiménez viajará a Egipto dentro de dos semanas para respaldar la transición España', accessed 21 February 2017. www.elmundo.es/elmundo/2011/03/01/espana/1298976229.html.

NATO Center of Excellence on Strategic Communications. 2014. 'Analysis of Russia's information campaign against Ukraine'. www.act.nato.int/images/stories/events/2015/sfpdpe/sfpdpe15_rr03.pdf.

Natorski, Michał, and Karolina Pomorska. 2017. 'Trust and decision-making in times of crisis: the EU's response to the events in Ukraine', *JCMS: Journal of Common Market Studies*, 55: 54–70.

Nisbet, Robert A. 1972. *Social change and history: aspects of the Western theory of development* (Oxford University Press: New York).

Nitoiu, Cristian. 2016. 'Towards conflict or cooperation? The Ukraine crisis and EU–Russia relations', *Southeast European and Black Sea Studies*, 16: 375–90.

Nitoiu, Cristian, and Monika Sus. 2017. 'The European Parliament's diplomacy – a tool for projecting EU power in times of crisis? The case of the Cox-Kwasniewski mission: Europe's hybrid foreign policy', *JCMS: Journal of Common Market Studies*, 55: 71–86.

North, Douglass C. 1990. *Institutions, institutional change, and economic performance* (Cambridge University Press: Cambridge, New York).

Notteboom, Theo, Peter De Langen and Wouter Jacobs. 2013. 'Institutional plasticity and path dependence in seaports: interactions between institutions, port governance reforms and port authority routines', *Journal of Transport Geography*, 27: 26–35.

Nougayrède, Natalie. 2015. 'France and the Eastern Partnership: the view from Paris', 19 May, accessed 2 November 2016. www.ecfr.eu/article/commentary_france_and_the_eastern_partnership_the_view_from_paris3033.

Noutcheva, Gergana. 2015. 'Institutional governance of European Neighbourhood Policy in the wake of the Arab Spring', *Journal of European Integration*, 37: 19–36.

Oliver, Michael J., and Hugh Pemberton. 2004. 'Learning and change in 20th-century British economic policy', *Governance*, 17: 415–41.

Olsen, Johan P. 2001. 'Garbage cans, new institutionalism, and the study of politics', *The American Political Science Review*, 95: 191–8.

Orren, Karen, and Stephen Skowronek. 2004. *The search for American political development* (Cambridge University Press: Cambridge).

Pace, Michelle. 2005. *The politics of regional identity: meddling with the Mediterranean* (Routledge: London).

Palier, Bruno. 2005. 'Ambiguous agreement, cumulative change: French social policy in the 1990s' in Wolfgang Streeck and Kathleen Thelen (eds), *Beyond continuity: institutional change in advanced political economies* (Oxford University Press: Oxford).

———. 2007. 'Tracking the evolution of a single instrument can reveal profound changes: the case of funded pensions in France', *Governance*, 20: 85–107.

Pamment, James. 2020. 'The EU's role in fighting disinformation: taking back the initiative' in *Future Threats, Future Solutions*, Carnegie Endowment for International Peace.

Paul, Amanda. 2015. 'Crimea one year after Russian annexation', EPC Foreign Policy Brief, 24 March.

Peters, B. Guy. 1994. 'Agenda-setting in the European community', *Journal of European Public Policy*, 1: 9–26.

Peterson, John, and Niklas Helwig. 2017. 'Common foreign and security policy: institutionalizing Europe's global role' in Dermot Hodson and John Peterson (eds), *The institutions of the European Union* (Oxford University Press: Oxford).

Peterson, John, and Helene Sjursen. 1998. *A common foreign policy for Europe?: competing visions of the CFSP* (Routledge: London).

Pew Research Center. 2016. 'Number of refugees to Europe surges to record 1.3 million in 2015.', accessed 11 May 2021. www.pewresearch.org/global/2016/08/02/number-of-refugees-to-europe-surges-to-record-1-3-million-in-2015/.

Pierson, Paul. 1996. 'The path to European integration: a historical institutionalist analysis', *Comparative Political Studies*, 29: 123–63.

———. 2000a. 'Increasing returns, path dependence, and the study of politics', *The American Political Science Review*, 94: 251–67.

———. 2000b. 'The limits of design: explaining institutional origins and change', *Governance*, 13: 475–99.

———. 2000c. 'Not just what, but when: timing and sequence in political processes', *Studies in American Political Development*, 14: 72–92.

———. 2004. *Politics in time: history, institutions, and social analysis* (Princeton University Press: Princeton, NJ).

Pinfari, Marco. 2013. 'The EU, Egypt and Morsi's rise and fall: "strategic patience" and its discontents', *Mediterranean Politics*, 18: 460–66.

Planet, Ana I., and Miguel Hernando de Larramendi. 2013. 'Spain and Islamist movements: from the victory of the FIS to the Arab Spring' in Lorenzo Vidino (ed.), *The West and the Muslim Brotherhood after the Arab Spring* (Foreign Policy Research Institute/Al Mesbar Studies & Research Centre: Philadelphia, PA, Dubai).

Politico. 2014. 'Juncker's ten priorities', 17 November, accessed 11 May 2021. www.politico.eu/article/junckers-ten-priorities/.

———. 2015a. 'EU forces through refugee deal', 21 September, accessed 24 March 2021. www.politico.eu/article/eu-tries-to-unblock-refugee-migrants-relocation-deal-crisis/.

———. 2015b. 'Tusk's summit task: "European unity"', 17 September, accessed 24 March 2021. www.politico.eu/article/the-eu-nuclear-option-on-migration/.

Pond, Elizabeth, and Hans Kundmani. 2015. 'Germany's real role in the Ukraine crisis: caught between East and West', *Foreign Affairs*, 94: 173.

Pralle, Sarah B. 2003. 'Venue shopping, political strategy, and policy change: the internationalization of Canadian forest advocacy', *Journal of Public Policy*, 23: 233–60.

President of the Council of Ministers, Italy. 2011. '2011 Report on Security Intelligence Policy.', accessed 11 May 2021. https://cryptome.wikileaks.org/2012/08/it-sec-spy-2011.pdf.

Prodi, Romano. 2002. 'A wider Europe – a proximity policy as the key to stability', paper presented to 'Peace, security and stability – international dialogue and the role of the EU' Sixth ECSA–World Conference. Jean Monnet Project.

Putin, Vladimir. 2014. 'Direct line with Vladimir Putin'. http://en.kremlin.ru/events/president/news/20796.

Pynnöniemi, Katri. 2019. 'Information – psychological warfare in Russian security strategy' in Roger E. Kanet (ed.), *Routledge handbook of Russian security* (Routledge: London).

Rasmussen, Morten. 2014. 'Revolutionizing European law: a history of the *Van Gend en Loos* judgment', *International Journal of Constitutional Law*, 12: 136–63.

Ratka, Edmund. 2012. 'Germany and the Arab Spring: foreign policy between new activism and old habits', *German Politics and Society*, 30.

Regelsberger, Elfriede, Philippe de Schoutheete and Wolfgang Wessels. 1997. *Foreign policy of the European Union: from EPC to CFSP and beyond* (Lynne Rienner Publishers: Boulder, CO).

Reinprecht, Michael, and Henrietta Levin. 2015. *Democratization through public diplomacy: an analysis of the European Parliament's reaction to the Arab Spring* (Figueroa Press: Los Angeles, CA).

Reuters. 2011. 'Berlusconi calls Mubarak wise man, urges continuity', accessed 11 May 2021. www.reuters.com/article/us-egypt-italy-berlusconi/berlusconi-calls-mubarak-wise-man-urges-continuity-idUSTRE71334Q20110204.

———. 2013. 'Russia starts delivering $1 billion arms package to Azerbaijan', accessed 24 February 2015. www.reuters.com/article/2013/06/18/us-russia-azerbaijan-arms-idUSBRE95H0KM20130618.

———. 2015. 'Juncker calls for EU army, says would deter Russia', 8 March, accessed 24 March 2021. www.reuters.com/article/us-eu-defence-juncker/juncker-calls-for-eu-army-says-would-deter-russia-idUSKBN0M40KL20150308.

———. 2016. 'German defence minister says Trump can't treat NATO like a business', 10 November, accessed 24 March 2021. https://uk.reuters.com/article/uk-trump-germany-nato-idUKKBN1352SV.

Rhinard, Mark. 2019. 'The crisisification of policy-making in the European Union', *JCMS: Journal of Common Market Studies*, 57: 616–33.

Riols, Yves-Michel. 2013. 'La France observe la crise à Kiev avec prudence et discrétion', *Le Monde*, 12 December, section 'International'.

Ripoll Servent, Ariadna. 2019. 'Failing under the "shadow of hierarchy": explaining the role of the European Parliament in the EU's "asylum crisis"', *Journal of European Integration*, 41: 293–310.

Ripoll Servent, Ariadna, and Florian Trauner. 2014. 'Do supranational EU institutions make a difference? EU asylum law before and after "communitarization"', *Journal of European Public Policy*, 21: 1142–62.

Rosati, Jerel A. 1994. 'Cycles in foreign policy restructuring: the politics of continuity and change in US foreign policy' in Jerel A. Rosati, Joe D. Hagan and Martin W. Sampson (eds), *Foreign policy restructuring: how governments respond to global change* (University of South Carolina Press: Columbia, SC).

Rose, Richard, and Phillip L. Davies. 1994. *Inheritance in public policy: change without choice in Britain* (Yale University Press: New Haven, CT).

Roth, Andrew. 2014. 'Putin tells European official that he could "take Kiev in two weeks"', *New York Times*, 2 September.

Rutherford, Bruce. 2012. 'Egypt: the origins and concepts of the January 25th uprising' in Mark L. Haas and David W. Lesch (eds), *The Arab Spring: change and resistance in the Middle East* (Westview Press: Boulder, CO).

Sabatier, Paul A. 1988. 'An advocacy coalition framework of policy change and the role of policy-oriented learning therein', *Policy Sciences*, 21: 129–68.

Sabatier, Paul A., and Hank C. Jenkins-Smith. 1993. *Policy change and learning: an advocacy coalition approach* (Westview Press: Boulder, CO).

Sabatier, Paul A., and Christopher M. Weible. 2007. *The advocacy coalition framework: innovations and clarifications* (Westview Press: Boulder, CO).

Sakwa, Richard. 2007. 'Vladimir Putin and Russian foreign policy towards the West: towards a new realism' in Jackie Gower and Graham Timmins (eds), *Russia and Europe in the twenty-first century: an uneasy partnership* (Anthem: London).

———. 2014. *Frontline Ukraine: crisis in the borderlands* (I. B. Tauris: London).

———. 2017. 'The Ukraine syndrome and Europe: between norms and space', *The Soviet and Post-Soviet Review*, 44: 9–31.

Samuel, Henry, and Peter Foster. 2017. 'New EU army headquarters branded little more than a "call centre"', *Daily Telegraph*, 20 May.

Sanders, Elizabeth. 2009. 'Historical institutionalism' in A. Binder Sarah, R. A. W. Rhodes, Bert A. Rockman and Elizabeth Sanders (eds), *The Oxford handbook of political institutions* (Oxford University Press: Oxford).

Sandholtz, Wayne. 1993. 'Choosing union: monetary politics and Maastricht', *International Organization*, 47: 1–39.

Sarkozy, Nicolas. 2011. 'XIXe Conférence des Ambassadeurs – Discours du Président'. https://hr.ambafrance.org/Conference-des-Ambassadeurs-M,1786.

Saunders, Elizabeth N. 2011. *Leaders at war. How presidents shape military interventions* (Cornell University Press: Ithaca, NY).

Schäfer, Isabel. 2011. 'Les politiques euro-méditerranéennes à la lumière du printemps arabe', *Mouvements*, 66: 117.

Schetyna, Grzegorz. 2015. 'Minister Grzegorz Schetyna addresses priorities of Polish diplomacy – chief of Polish diplomacy delivers address on the goals of Polish foreign policy in 2015 to the Sejm', accessed 18 January 2017. http://msz.gov.pl/en/news/minister_grzegorz_schetyna_addresses_priorities_of_polish_diplomacy.

Schimmelfennig, Frank. 2018. 'European integration (theory) in times of crisis. A comparison of the euro and Schengen crises', *Journal of European Public Policy*, 25: 969–89.

Schmidt, Vivien A. 2014. 'Institutionalism' in M.T. Gibbons (ed.), *The encyclopedia of political thought* (Wiley Blackwell: Chichester).

Schmidt-Felzmann, Anke. 2015. 'Taking the neighbours seriously – the view from Stockholm', European Council on Foreign Relations.

Schneider, Gerald, and Mark Aspinwall. 2001. *The rules of integration: the institutionalist approach to European studies* (Manchester University Press: Manchester).

Scholten, Peter. 2017. 'The limitations of policy learning: a constructivist perspective on expertise and policy dynamics in Dutch migrant integration policies', *Policy and Society*, 36: 345–63.

Schön, Donald A, and Martin Rein. 1994. *Frame reflection: toward the resolution of intractable policy controversies* (Basic Books: New York).

Schumacher, Tobias. 2011. 'The EU and the Arab Spring: between spectatorship and actorness', *Insight Turkey*, 13: 107–19.

———. 2015a. 'Uncertainty at the EU's borders: narratives of EU external relations in the revised European Neighbourhood Policy towards the southern borderlands', *European Security*, 24: 381–401.

———. 2015b. 'The European Union and democracy promotion. Readjusting to the Arab Spring' in Larbi Sadiki (ed.), *Routledge handbook of the Arab Spring: rethinking democratization* (London: Routledge), 559–73.

Schumacher, Tobias, and Dimitris Bouris. 2017. 'The 2011 revised European Neighbourhood Policy: continuity and change in EU foreign policy' in Dimitris Bouris and Tobias Schumacher (eds), *The revised European Neighbourhood Policy: continuity and change in EU foreign policy* (Palgrave Macmillan: London).

Scipioni, Marco. 2017. 'Failing forward in EU migration policy? EU integration after the 2015 asylum and migration crisis', *Journal of European Public Policy*, 25: 1357–75.

Seibel, Wolfgang. 2017. 'The European Union, Ukraine, and the unstable East' in Desmond Dinan, Neill Nugent and William E. Patersen (eds), *The European Union in crisis* (Palgrave Macmillan: London).

Sénat. 2015. 'Les relations avec la Russie: comment sortir de l'impasse?' www.senat.fr/rap/r15-021/r15-0212.html.

———. 2019. 'European defence: the challenge of strategic autonomy – rapport d'information n° 626 (2018–2019) au nom de la Commission des affaires étrangères, de la défense et des forces armées'. www.senat.fr/notice-rapport/2018/r18-626-2-notice.html.

Shepherd, Alistair J. K. 2009. '"A milestone in the history of the EU": Kosovo and the EU's international role', *International Affairs (Royal Institute of International Affairs 1944–)*, 85: 513–30.

Sikorski, Radoslaw, Frank-Walter Steinmeier, Laurent Fabius and Vladimir Lukin. 2014. 'Agreement on the settlement of crisis in Ukraine', accessed 21 March 2016. www.auswaertiges-amt.de/cae/servlet/contentblob/671350/publicationFile/190051/140221-UKR_Erklaerung.pdf.

Silver, Nate. 2017. 'The Comey letter probably cost Clinton the election', *FiveThirtyEight*, accessed 3 May 2017. https://fivethirtyeight.com/features/the-comey-letter-probably-cost-clinton-the-election/.

Simms, Brendan. 2012. 'Towards a mighty Union: how to create a democratic European superpower', *International Affairs*, 88: 49–62.

Skidmore, David. 1994. 'Explaining state responses to international change: the structural sources of foreign policy rigidity and change' in Jerel A. Rosati, Joe D. Hagan and Martin W. Sampson (eds), *Foreign policy restructuring: how governments respond to global change* (University of South Carolina Press: Columbia, SC).

Skocpol, Theda. 1979. *States and social revolutions: a comparative analysis of France, Russia and China* (Cambridge University Press: Cambridge).

———. 1995. 'Why I am an historical institutionalist', *Polity*, 28: 103–6.

Smith, Karen E. 2014. *European Union foreign policy in a changing world* (Polity: Cambridge).

Smith, Michael E. 2004. *Europe's foreign and security policy: the institutionalization of cooperation* (Cambridge University Press: Cambridge).

———. 2015. 'The new intergovernmentalism and experiential learning in the CSDP' in Christopher J. Bickerton, Dermot Hodson and Uwe Puetter (eds), *The new intergovernmentalism: states and supranational actors in the post-Maastricht era* (Oxford University Press: Oxford).

Soifer, H. D. 2012. 'The causal logic of critical junctures', *Comparative Political Studies*, 45: 1572–97.

Soler i Lecha, Eduard. 2012. 'Cuando las crisis se superponen: Europa y España ante la primavera árabe', Barcelona Centre for International Affairs.

Sorensen, Andre. 2015. 'Taking path dependence seriously: an historical institutionalist research agenda in planning history', *Planning Perspectives*, 30: 17–38.

Sperling, James, and Mark Webber. 2018. 'The European Union: security governance and collective securitisation', *West European Politics*, 42: 228–60.

Spiegel, Der. 2011. 'Libyan crisis: Italy warns of a new wave of immigrants to Europe', 24 February.

———. 2013a. '*Bonjour tristesse*: the economic and political decline of France', 5 June.

———. 2013b. 'Putin's gambit: how the EU lost Ukraine', 25 November. www.spiegel.de/international/europe/how-the-eu-lost-to-russia-in-negotiations-over-ukraine-trade-deal-a-935476.html.

Stefano, Mark Di. 2020. 'NBC sells stake in Euronews as focus shifts to new global TV channel', *Financial Times*, 20 April.

Steinmo, Sven. 2008. 'Historical institutionalism' in Donatella Della Porta and Michael Keating (eds), *Approaches and methodologies in the social sciences: a pluralist perspective* (Cambridge University Press: Cambridge).

Stewart, Susan. 2014. 'Ukraine' in David Cadier (ed.), *The geopolitics of Eurasian economic integration*, LSE Ideas Special Report, London School of Economics.

Stiftung Wissenschaft und Politik and The German Marshall Fund of the United States. 2014. 'New power, new responsibility: elements of a German foreign and security policy for a changing world.'

Stone Sweet, Alec. 2004. *The judicial construction of Europe* (Oxford University Press: Oxford).

Strambach, Simone, and Henrik Halkier. 2013. 'Reconceptualising change. Path dependency, path plasticity and knowledge combination', *Zeitschrift für Wirtschaftsgeographie*, 57: 1–14.

Streeck, Wolfgang, and Kathleen Thelen. 2005. *Beyond continuity: institutional change in advanced political economies* (Oxford University Press: Oxford).

Sus, Monika. 2017. 'Institutional innovation of EU's foreign and security policy: big leap for EU's strategic actorness or much ADO about nothing?', *International Politics*, 56: 411–25.

Szeptycki, Andrzej. 2020. 'Poland versus Russia: competition in Ukraine', *East European Politics and Societies: and Cultures*, accessed 24 March 2021. https://doi.org/10.1177/0888325420950803.

Tardy, Thierry. 2017. 'MPCC: towards an EU military command?' European Union Institute for Security Studies.

Teti, Andrea. 2012. 'The EU's first response to the "Arab Spring": a critical discourse analysis of the partnership for democracy and shared prosperity', *Mediterranean Politics*, 17: 266–84.

Teti, Andrea, Darcy Thompson and Christopher Noble. 2013. 'EU democracy assistance discourse in its "New response to a changing neighbourhood"', *Democracy and Security*, 9: 61–79.

't Hart, Paul, and Karen Tindall. 2009. 'Understanding crisis exploitation: leadership, rhetoric and framing contests in response to the economic meltdown' in Paul t'Hart, Karen Tindall and R. A. W. Rhodes (eds), *Framing the global economic downturn: crisis rhetoric and the politics of recessions* (ANU E Press: Canberra).

Thelen, Kathleen. 1999. 'Historical institutionalism in comparative politics', *Annual Review of Political Science*, 2: 369–404.

Thelen, Kathleen, and James Conran. 2016. 'Institutional change' in Karl Orfeo Fioretos, Tulia Gabriela Falleti and Adam D. Sheingate (eds), *The Oxford handbook of historical institutionalism* (Oxford University Press: Oxford).

Thelen, Kathleen, and Sven Steinmo. 1992. 'Historical institutionalism in comparative polities' in Sven Steinmo, Kathleen Thelen and Frank Longstreth (eds), *Structuring politics: historical institutionalism in comparative analysis* (Cambridge University Press: Cambridge).

Thomas, Timothy. 2004. 'Russia's reflexive control theory and the military', *The Journal of Slavic Military Studies*, 17: 237–56.

Time. 2015. 'Europe mulls a Russian language tv channel to counter Moscow propaganda', 19 January.

Toal, Gerard, and John O'Loughlin. 2017. '"Why did MH17 crash?": blame attribution, television news and public opinion in southeastern Ukraine, Crimea and the *de facto* states of Abkhazia, South Ossetia and Transnistria', *Geopolitics*: 1–35.

Tocci, Nathalie. 2018. 'Towards a European security and defence union: was 2017 a watershed?', *JCMS: Journal of Common Market Studies*, 56: 131–41.

Tocci, Nathalie, and Jean-Pierre Cassarino. 2011. 'Rethinking the EU's Mediterranean policies post-1/11', Istituto Affari Internazionali Working Paper.

Tömmel, Ingeborg. 2013. 'The new neighborhood policy of the EU: an appropriate response to the Arab Spring?', *Democracy and Security*, 9: 19–39.

Trauner, Florian. 2016. 'Asylum policy: the EU's "crises" and the looming policy regime failure', *Journal of European Integration*, 38: 311–25.

United Nations High Commissioner for Refugees (UNHCR). 2012. 'Mediterranean takes record as most deadly stretch of water for refugees and migrants in 2011'. www.unhcr.org/4f27e01f9.html.

———. 2015. 'Over one million sea arrivals reach Europe in 2015'. www.unhcr.org/news/latest/2015/12/5683d0b56/million-sea-arrivals-reach-europe-2015.html.

———. 2020. 'What is a refugee?'. www.unhcr.org/what-is-a-refugee.html.

United Nations Security Council. 2014. 'Ukraine, in emergency meeting, calls on Security Council to stop military intervention by Russian Federation. Security Council 7124th Meeting', accessed 11 May 2016. www.un.org/press/en/2014/sc11302.doc.htm.

Unwala, Azhar, and Shaheen Gori. 2015. 'Brandishing the cybered bear: information war and the Russia–Ukraine conflict', *Military Cyber Affairs*, 1.

Van der Pijl, Kees. 2018. *Flight MH17, Ukraine and the new cold war: prism of disaster* (Manchester University Press: Manchester).

van Ham, Peter. 2010. 'The power of war: why Europe needs it', *International Politics*, 47.

Van Rompuy, Herman. 2011a. 'Herman Van Rompuy, President of the European Council, convenes an extraordinary European Council'. www.consilium.europa.eu/uedocs/cms_data/docs/pressdata/en/ec/119538.pdf.

———. 2011b. 'We want to turn this Arab Spring into a true new beginning.' *PCE 062/11*.

Vanhoonacker, Sophie, and Karolina Pomorska. 2013. 'The European External Action Service and agenda-setting in European foreign policy', *Journal of European Public Policy*, 20: 1316–31.

Verdun, Amy. 2015. 'A historical institutionalist explanation of the EU's responses to the euro area financial crisis', *Journal of European Public Policy*, 22: 219–37.

Viegas, Miguel. 2015. 'Question for written answer E-008611–15 to the Commission Rule 130 Miguel Viegas (GUE/NGL)'. www.europarl.europa.eu/doceo/document//E-8–2015–008611_EN.html.

Visegrad Group. 2014. 'Statement of the prime ministers of the Visegrad Group countries on Ukraine'. www.visegradgroup.eu/statement-of-the-prime.

———. 2015. 'Joint statement of the Heads of Government of the Visegrad Group countries'. www.visegradgroup.eu/calendar/2015/joint-statement-of-the-150904.

Warkotsch, Alexander. 2006. 'The European Union and democracy promotion in bad neighbourhoods: the case of central Asia', *European Foreign Affairs Review*, 11: 509–25.

Weiler, Joseph H. H. 1991. 'The transformation of Europe', *The Yale Law Journal*, 100: 2403–83.

Welch, David. 2005. *Painful choices: a theory of foreign policy change* (Princeton University Press: Princeton, NJ).

Westerwelle, Guido. 2011a. 'Regierungserklärung durch Bundesaußenminister Westerwelle vor dem Deutschen Bundestag zum Umbruch in der arabischen Welt'. www.auswaertiges-amt.de/de/newsroom/110316-bm-bt-arab-welt/242700.

———. 2011b. 'Zusagen für Nordafrika an Reformen knüpfen', *Frankfurter Allgemeine Zeitung*, 18 February.

White, Brian. 1999. 'The European challenge to foreign policy analysis', *European Journal of International Relations*, 5: 37–66.

———. 2001. *Understanding European foreign policy* (Palgrave: Basingstoke).

Whitehead, Laurence. 2015. 'On the "Arab Spring": democratization and related political seasons' in Larbi Sadiki (ed.), *Routledge handbook of the Arab Spring: rethinking democratization* (Routledge: London).

White House, The – Office of the Press Secretary. 1999. 'Statement by the President to the nation – the Oval Office'. https://clintonwhitehouse2.archives.gov/WH/New/html/19990324-2872.html.

Whitman, Richard G., and Ana E. Juncos. 2009. 'The Lisbon Treaty and the foreign, security and defence policy: reforms, implementation and the consequences of (non-)ratification', *European Foreign Affairs Review*, 14: 25–46.

———. 2012. 'The Arab Spring, the Eurozone crisis and the neighbourhood: a region in flux', *Journal of Common Market Studies*, 50: 147–61.

Wolff, Sarah. 2012. *The Mediterranean dimension of the European Union's internal security* (Palgrave Macmillan: Basingstoke, New York).

Wright, Nicholas. 2018. 'No longer the elephant outside the room: why the Ukraine crisis reflects a deeper shift towards German leadership of European foreign policy', *German Politics*, 27: 479–97.

Yaffa, Johsua. 2014. 'Dmitry Kiselev is redefining the art of Russian propaganda', *The New Republic*, 2 July.

Youngs, Richard. 2010. *Europe's decline and fall: the struggle against global irrelevance* (Profile: London).

———. 2015. '20 years of the Euro-Mediterranean Partnership', Carnegie Europe.

———. 2018. *Europe reset: new directions for the EU* (I. B. Tauris: London).

Yousfi, Hèla. 2015. 'The Tunisian revolution: narratives of the UGTT' in Larbi Sadiki (ed.), *Routledge handbook of the Arab Spring: rethinking democratization* (Routledge: London).

Zahariadis, Nikolaos. 2008. 'Ambiguity and choice in European public policy', *Journal of European Public Policy*, 15: 514–30.

———. 2017. *Frameworks of the European Union's policy process* (John Wiley: Chichester).

Zandee, Dirk. 2018. 'PESCO implementation: the next challenge.' Clingendael Policy Report, Clingendael Institute.

Zeitung, Süddeutsche. 2016. 'Deutschland und Frankreich wollen Verteidigungspolitik der EU reformieren', 9 September, accessed 24 March 2021. www.sueddeutsche.de/politik/vor-gipfeltreffen-deutschland-und-frankreich-wollen-verteidigungspolitik-der-eu-reformieren-1.3155310.

Zetter, Kim. 2014. 'Russian "Sandworm" hack has been spying on foreign governments for years', Wired.com, 14 October. www.wired.com/2014/10/russian-sandworm-hack-isight/.

List of interviews

Institution	Transcript code	Date of interview	Location of interview
EEAS, Brussels	PO1	20/08/2019	Brussels
EEAS, EU Delegation	PO2	20/08/2019	Phone interview
EEAS, Brussels	PO3	04/09/2019	Brussels
EEAS, Brussels	PO4	05/09/2019	Brussels
EEAS, Brussels	PO5	09/09/2019	Brussels
EEAS, Brussels	PO6	09/09/2019	Brussels
EEAS, Brussels	PO7	11/09/2019	Brussels
EEAS, Brussels	PO8	11/09/2019	Brussels
EEAS, Brussels	PO9	11/09/2019	Brussels
EEAS, Brussels	PO10	11/09/2019	Brussels
EEAS, Brussels	PO11	11/09/2019	Brussels
EEAS, Brussels	PO12	19/09/2019	Brussels
EEAS, Brussels	PO13	19/09/2019	Brussels
EEAS, Brussels	PO14	23/09/2019	Phone interview
EEAS, Brussels	PO15	03/10/2019	Phone interview
EEAS, Brussels	PO16	09/10/2019	Brussels
EEAS, Brussels	PO17	11/10/2019	Brussels
EEAS, Brussels	PO18	04/12/2019	Phone interview
EEAS, Brussels	PO19	05/11/2019	London
EEAS, Brussels	PO20	05/06/2020	Phone interview
Expert interview	PO21	26/03/2015	London
Expert interview	PO22	02/07/2015	Oxford
EEAS, EU Delegation	PO23	29/04/2015	Phone interview
EEAS, EU Delegation	PO24	12/05/2015	Phone interview
EEAS, EU Delegation	PO25	15/05/2015	Phone Interview
European Commission, DG NEAR	PO26	19/05/2015	Brussels
EEAS, EU Delegation	PO27	27/05/2015	Phone interview
EEAS, EU Delegation	PO28	27/05/2015	Phone interview
EEAS, Brussels	PO29	29/05/2015	Phone interview

Institution	Transcript code	Date of interview	Location of interview
EEAS, EU Delegation	PO30	03/06/2015	Phone interview
European Council	PO31	03/06/2015	Phone interview
EEAS, OSCE	PO32	18/06/2015	Phone interview
Kati Piri, Member of the European Parliament	PO33	23/06/2015	Brussels
European Commission, DG NEAR	PO34	24/06/2015	Brussels
EEAS, Brussels	PO35	10/07/2015	Phone interview
EEAS, Brussels	PO36	28/07/2015	Brussels
EEAS, EU Delegation	PO37	17/11/2015	Phone interview
Seconded official	PO38	17/11/2015	Phone interview
EEAS, Brussels	PO39	01/12/2015	Brussels
EEAS, Brussels	PO40	01/12/2015	Brussels
EEAS, Brussels	PO41	26/11/2015	Phone interview
EEAS, Brussels	PO42	01/02/2016	Phone interview
Russian Mission to the European Union	PO43	23/06/2016	Brussels
EEAS	PO44	07/03/2016	Phone interview
East StratCom Task Force	PO45	18/05/2016	Phone interview
East StratCom Task Force	PO46	20/05/2016	Phone interview
Seconded official	PO47	01/12/2015	Brussels
EEAS, Brussels	PO48	22/06/2017	Phone interview
EEAS, Brussels	PO49	23/06/2017	Phone Interview
European Commission	PO50	29/06/2017	Phone interview
EEAS, Brussels	PO51	03/07/2017	Phone interview
European Commission	PO52	04/07/2017	Phone interview
EEAS, Brussels	PO53	11/07/2017	Phone interview
East StratCom	PO54	10/07/2020	Phone interview
European Defence Agency	PO55	13/07/2020	Phone interview
European Defence Agency	PO56	20/07/2020	Phone interview
EEAS, Brussels	PO57	20/07/2020	Phone interview
DG Home	PO58	13/08/2020	Video interview
East StratCom Task Force	PO59	14/08/2020	Phone interview
DG Home	PO60	20/08/2020	Video interview
East StratCom Task Force	PO61	24/08/2020	Video interview
DG Home	PO62	27/08/2020	Video interview
EEAS, Brussels	PO63	27/08/2020	Video interview
DG Home	PO64	04/09/2020	Phone interview

Index

EU authorised representative for GPSR:
Easy Access System Europe, Mustamäe tee 50,
10621 Tallinn, Estonia
gpsr.requests@easproject.com